Knowledge
and Power
in Higher Education

A READER

Edited by

RICHARD HARVEY BROWN
and

J. DANIEL SCHUBERT

TEACHERS
COLLEGE
PRESS

Teachers College, Columbia University
New York and London

Published by Teachers College Press, 1234 Amsterdam Avenue, New York, NY
10027

Library of Congress Cataloging-in-Publication Data
Knowledge and power in higher education : a reader / edited by Richard
  Harvey Brown and J. Daniel Schubert.
    p. cm.
  Includes bibliographical references and index.
    ISBN 0-8077-3906-5 (alk. paper). — ISBN 0-8077-3905-7 (pbk. :
alk. paper)
    1. Education, Higher—Political aspects.   2. Knowledge, Sociology
of.   3. Scientism—Political aspects.   4. Higher education and
state.   I. Brown, Richard Harvey.   II. Schubert, J. Daniel.
  LC171.K62   2000
  378—dc21   99-44312

ISBN 0-8077-3905-7 (paper)
ISBN 0-8077-3906-5 (cloth)

Printed on acid-free paper
Manufactured in the United States of America

07 06 05 04 03 02 01 00   8 7 6 5 4 3 2 1

CONTENTS

PART I

Introduction

ONE

ACADEMIC KNOWLEDGE AND POLITICAL POWER IN LATE CAPITALIST SOCIETIES

RICHARD HARVEY BROWN AND J. DANIEL SCHUBERT

THE ACADEMY is contested terrain in contemporary western societies. Budget crunches, departmental closings, and calls for increased accountability among professors are the news of the day, especially in state-sponsored colleges and universities. The public, it seems, wants to know just what it is that academics do with their time, what the value is of what they do, and if what they do is worthy of taxpayers' dollars. Efforts at diversity and affirmative action are under siege, as the U.S. Congress and state legislators move to reduce federal and state monies for student loans and financial assistance based on minority status. At the same time, both private and public institutions of higher learning are becoming corporatized, as private industry moves into the academy by sponsoring specific research projects and whole academic programs and centers (Aronowitz, 1998; Dickson, 1988). Such political, economic, and administrative pressures have been matched by confusion among scholars about their production of academic knowledge and its uses by others. Scholars in a number of fields have gone so far as to argue that their disciplines are in crisis.[1]

In the midst of these changes within the academy, academic knowledge and its technical extensions have become a central force in the polity, economy, and culture. Scientific research increasingly is funded by corporations and government in the stated interest of national security and economic competitiveness. Moreover, science and technology are so useful for so many purposes that they easily come to dominate in ethics and politics, where they may not be appropriate guides for practice. As this occurs, the value-neutral manipulation of things becomes an amoral manipulation of persons. In this technicist discourse and practice, all things (including nature, animals, machines, humans, traditions, ethics, and institutions) are conceived as fields for the application of scientific rationality, which is understood as instrumental calculation—that is, as theory supporting technique. In this view, science is focused on prediction and control, ends are reduced to means, values become utilities, people become objects, and scientists become specialists. This is the cultural and moral threat that technicism poses to citizenship, democracy, and dignity. By making experts superior to and more competent than citizens, technicist discourse undermines the cultural bases of freedom and dignity.

The essays in this book are authored primarily by social scientists who are concerned with relationships between academic knowledge and political power. These authors seek to inform the public more fully about the place of the academy in contemporary society as well as about the actual practices of academic researchers, particularly scientists. Most accounts of science view politics as both exterior to the production of knowledge and a distortion of the workings of reason. Indeed, to the extent that scientific activities are influenced by politics, they are thought to be automatically derationalized. Given this assumption, scientific rationality is viewed as a fortress to be defended against rhetorical persuasion, bureaucratic politics, or personal ambition.

While the early critiques of science focused on contributions to weapons research, environmental degradation, and gender and racial discrimination, more recent and more systematic challenges of the very content and method of science have been made by scholars in such fields as history and philosophy of science, rhetoric, and social studies of science. These scholars assert not only that the production of knowledge is political through and through, but also that politics in academic communities has a special character and can be a creative and not merely distorting force in the production of knowledge. Scientists had largely ignored this mounting body of scholarship until 1992, when "two prominent works of science popularization, Wolpert (1993) and Weinberg (1992), devoted entire chapters to describing the threat posed by academic left critiques of science, conveying the general impression that it constituted a frontal assault on 'civilization as we know it'" (Fuller, 1995, p. 115). Then, in 1994, Paul Gross and Norman Levitt published *The Higher Superstition,* the first book devoted entirely to explicating and responding to the academic left critique. The general reaction of scientists to social and rhetorical critiques has been hostile. Similarly, the politically liberal but epistemologically conservative *New York*

Review of Books often publishes attacks on authors who write with less than positivistic enthusiasm for science (e.g., Peretz, 1995).

What is new here is not the insularity and privilege of scientists, but that these are now under attack by informed scholars who also criticize the ideology of scientism itself. On the one hand, as Nelkin (1987, p. 155) notes, research scientists have long been suspicious of *any* nontechnical reporting of their work. On the other hand, when scientists themselves try to explain their work to the lay public, they are dismissed by their colleagues as vulgar. It would appear that while scientists favor publicity about science that would stir public support, they also fear that an informed public might limit the autonomy of scientists by extending their accountability beyond the scientific community and the interests it serves. In this sense, a high level of public understanding of science may not be in the immediate interest of scientists. Instead, from the viewpoint of scientists, "public understanding of science" should consist of an acceptance of the ideology of science as impartial, heroic, and useful, and of a benign ignorance of how science actually works.

The authors in the present volume cannot be characterized as "anti-science." Indeed, our efforts at cogency and precision of argument certainly are within the realm of the scientific, broadly understood. Moreover, without some use of science's technical rationality we will not be able to address such complex threats as the imbalance of food and population, ecological breakdown, or global economic crises. Yet, as Jürgen Habermas (1975) and others have argued, the very instrumentalism of the techniques that can be brought to bear on these issues tends to undermine the autonomy and dignity of persons who are its objects. Moreover, the technical, commercial, and military applications of scientific innovation may cause ecological or social damage that annuls whatever good they achieve.

As technical control comes to predominate, power shifts from citizens to experts, and democratic consensus becomes just another problem of social engineering for the techno-administrators or the corporate and statist elites whom they serve. Rather than a balance of what C. P. Snow (1969) called the "two cultures," a scientific-technical orientation becomes dominant in civic life. This means that politics as well as aspects of the life-world are redefined as technical or economic or scientific problems, whereas formerly they were not so considered. Because technicism gives privileges and authority to persons with specialized knowledge, technicist discourse encourages us to replace self-direction by citizens with efficient control by experts. In contrast, to be a citizen means to act as a whole moral agent in the public sphere. In Western cultures, moral agency was institutionalized above all in civic and political life, where the person was seen to act with reason and freedom. Thus, at the extreme, the increasing privilege of experts displaces reasoned ethical judgment by citizens in directing their lives.

Scientific knowledge helps create policy expertise by providing a theoretical legitimation for rational planning and management. This is because knowledge of the laws of nature, including the supposed laws of social and human nature, are held to be applicable to the redesign of society and humans. Such projects easily become scientism or technicism, the extension of scientific technique to inappropriate domains such as ethics or politics. A focus on efficient means replaces reflection on appropriate ends—as, for example, in the deployment of scientifically advanced military technologies to serve politically unclear and morally dubious ends.

Scientism is difficult to avoid because science itself has become so integral to the operation of modern political economies. Earlier liberal democracies had a market conception of politics that matched their market conception of economics. In advanced capitalist societies, however, centralized coordination is necessary to rationalize the market and guide the welfare state. With this, planning and administration come to be viewed as necessary to rationalize society in general (Habermas, 1975). In such a society, citizens are felt to be acting rationally only when they are conforming to the dictates of scientific, economic, or technical necessity. Public action by citizens, when it is not simply conformity to the requirements of the cybernetic state, is possible only as a nonrational, even a noncognitive, expression of wishes, desires, and interests.

In this model of societal guidance, whether only a possibility or already upon us, the public sphere is equated with mass behavior that can be aggregated into statistical facts (such as "public opinion") that in turn are ideally manipulable by cost-efficient techniques of communication and control. At the same time, the ever-shrinking personal realm is seen as that sphere into which one can withdraw from the corporate state. Indeed, today this realm is narrowing toward the point where it will contain only that which is irrelevant to administrative interests and market calculation. With the reduction of reason to scientific or technical calculation, morally and politically affirmative definitions of freedom and the self come to seem either irrational or obsolete, and democratic participation is restricted to either irrational moralism or to those roles deemed functionally necessary by social scientists and systems engineers. It is as though technical rationality as public discourse has rendered the public either irrational or nonexistent. For example, to the extent that public policy on the environment is captured by biologists, climatologists, oceanographers, and other scientists or technical policy analysts, ordinary citizens are excluded from this "public" policy.

THE POSTMODERN VIEW OF SCIENCE
AS RHETORICAL CONSTRUCTION

Amidst this surplus of challenges, there are efforts to define and decide the future of the academy on both the political right and the political left. It is within this arena that the authors of the present collection offer a voice. These authors tend to view scientific knowledge as a form of social narration of the world, and to believe that politics cannot be divorced from scientific practice. Science is political, even if science and politics are not the same institution. One advantage of this approach is that it renders scientific thought more accessible to ordinary citizens insofar as we all know how to narrate—that is, to tell and understand and evaluate stories. Science and its technical extensions thereby become, in principle, stories that are subsumable within larger narrations of our common civic life.

Science is practices infused with power, and so we can properly understand science only by shifting from epistemological critique to social analysis. Both science and politics can be viewed as discursive practices, though each is conducted within a distinct institutional domain or field. Given that science, like politics, depends centrally on persuasion, a rhetorical conception of scientific discourse and scientific progress is useful (Brown, 1998; Simons, 1990). Postmodernists recognize that science is a rhetorical—that is, a political and aesthetic—construction. Such a recognition has encouraged an imminent critique of the ways in which scientific findings and discoveries are made, but it also suggests how these ways may be improved. In studying the discourses of scientific communities, we find that they employ multiple rhetorics as often as they employ strict, singular logics (Brown, 1998; Nelson, Megill, & McCloskey, 1987; Stockton, 1995). Scientists do not exclusively depend upon, nor even follow, the official methods of logic of their fields. Instead, they often convince themselves and others of the truth of their theories by means of persuasion that are not provided for, nor sanctioned by, their accepted methodologies. Though these strategies of communication are often outside the formal rules of method of particular disciplines, they do in fact persuade, and can be explained by, rhetorical theory (Nelson, 1990). Logic of method is also used in this way. It functions not only as a logic of discovery, but mainly as a rhetoric through which scientific practices and their results are constituted publicly *as* a discovery. Thus, postmodernists reverse the modernist conception of "mere rhetoric" and place rhetoric at the heart of the production of knowledge. "Rhetoric" now describes our intellectual activity as scientists, and rhetorical theory seeks to explain that activity.

The concerns outlined above transcend—and to some extent provide

the basis for a critique of—the boundaries of the established social sciences
and humanities. The essays gathered here are directed toward an interdisciplinary audience, but one that has as its main concern the place of the
academy and its practitioners in contemporary society. The authors of
the essays in this collection address the very place and *raison d'être* of the
academy in contemporary society. In the light of the dramatic changes that
have taken place both inside and outside of the academy in recent years,
the point of departure for these authors is whether or not the academy
itself should continue to exist. This question is crucial because many of the
activities of universities could well be done by other institutions—applied
research by the very corporations that already fund it, sports by clubs or
professional teams, training by various job preparation programs. Given ris-
ing costs of tuition and of much research, what, then, if any, are the indis-
pensable functions of today's universities?

   The authors in the next section of this book address the institutional
politics of knowledge production. Academic practice includes, by definition, activity that takes place within academic institutions. Thus, the effects
of institutional dynamics must be considered when attempting to understand the relationships between academic knowledge and political power.
The image of isolated scholars, teachers, and students heroically engaged
in an unfettered quest for "truth" has been exploded, and the authors of the
chapters in Part II describe some of the institutional influences on academic
practices.

   Richard Harvey Brown and Remi Clignet, in Chapter 2, "Democracy
and Capitalism in the Academy," explain how the university itself, particularly in the United States, is facing various changes that threaten its existence as a relatively autonomous democratic institution. Using the idea of
reproduction as an orienting concept, the authors explore long-term contradictions in American higher education. These include corporatist versus
populist ideologies, differing rates of change of economic and educational
institutions, different criteria of assessment and systems of stratification between these two spheres, and the role of decentralization. The authors then
examine how shorter-term contradictions inherent in demographic, economic, and ideological changes have pushed American colleges and universities toward further commercialization at the expense of intellectual autonomy and civic education. Brown and Clignet elaborate these contentions by
examining more closely the commodifications of learning, the ambiguities
inherent in the notion of "relevance," the quantification of the curriculum,
the bureaucratization of teaching, and the commercialization of scholarship.

   The politics of academic practice in late capitalist society also is central
to Steven Fuller in Chapter 3, "Science as a Vocation: Circa 2000." Fuller
frames his discussion by invoking the spirit of Max Weber.[2] Yet he argues

that circa 2000 science is less a vocation than an industrial mode of production and consumption. The science industry, says Fuller, controls knowledge through "epistemic cartels" and invisible colleges and the career trajectories of its producers. Thus Fuller argues that the vocation of science at the end of the century differs from that identified by Weber at its beginning. No longer can scientists assume that their work will be read, even by others in their field. Indeed, for those few scientists who gain access to the major journals within a field, changes in writing and reading methods are such that if their work is acknowledged at all, it is much more likely to be cited than it is to be read and discussed. The social sciences and humanities might contribute to the production of scientific knowledge production through humanistic studies of science and technology. In light of the political economy of science that Fuller offers in this essay, however, the likelihood of success for such a program is admittedly slim.

Karl-Michael Brunner, Johanna Hofbauer, and Gerald Prabitz examine the changing character of academic discourse in light of Zygmunt Bauman's (1992) thesis that contemporary intellectuals have moved from the role of "legislator" to that of "interpreter." In Chapter 4, "Intellectual Discourse in the Academy and Society," they argue that battles over the interpretation and legitimation of academic knowledge have resulted in the rise of "management talk" and of the intellectual as manager. This view of academic practice challenges Bauman's assertion that intellectuals today are less legitimators of existing interests and power relations and instead are becoming interpreters within and between different communities. Brunner, Hofbauer, and Prabitz argue that such a shift is occurring, but in a somewhat different direction than Bauman suggests. Borrowing from Pierre Bourdieu (1988), they suggest that intellectuals today are the dominated segment of the dominant class, whose language they speak and refine. Thus, the *lingua franca* of contemporary discourse in general, and academic discourse in particular, is not critical, synthetic analysis or interpretation, but management talk.

Hans Mommaas, in Chapter 5, "Leisure and the Intellectuals: The End of the Legislator?" also examines Bauman's thesis that modern intellectuals have served in modernity as an authoritative scientific voice for powerful groups in society; and that, in contrast, postmodern intellectuals are and will continue to be interpreters of textuality both in and across communities of discourse (including scientific communities). Mommaas's unique insight into Bauman's thesis comes when he examines how Bauman's notions of the intellectual as "legislator" or as "interpreter" might apply to Dutch scholars engaged in the study of leisure. The notion of free time, which is a creation of the modern era, is at the heart of leisure studies. Mommaas examines the status of free time, and those who study it, in both modern and postmodern settings. Mommaas's reflexive examination of the history of leisure studies suggests that Bauman's thesis may not hold in this type of social research.

In the last chapter of this section, John P. Radford considers the legitimation of knowledge and the ideological aspect of scientific investigation in "Academy and Asylum: Power, Knowledge, and Mental Disability." The ideology of "mental defectiveness" encourages segregation and justifies marginalization of the "mentally deficient." The academic disciplines and related professions that depend in part on the existence of the "mentally deficient," such as law, education, medicine, and psychology, serve to legitimate the establishment of asylums for those very people constituted by their discourses. Thus, argues Radford, the relation of academic knowledge and political power in contemporary society is not one of thorough integration. By establishing the basic categories as public discourse—categories such as idiot, moron, or mental defective—academic discourses foster a world of meaning and action. In the case of studies of intellectually disabled persons, this discourse was embedded in racial "science" and eugenic policies, traces of which continue within the academy today.

In Chapter 7, "The Ivory Commonwealth," the essay that opens the third section of the book, Manfred Stanley asks whether the university in late capitalism can retain any purpose that is morally unique to itself. He begins with a brief allusion to the most longstanding moral significance of the university: its claim to be a venue in which a whole civilization can confront the question of how it can best balance the constraints of reason with the vertigo of freedom (however these two concepts are defined at any given historical moment). He then proceeds to an account of what is sometimes called late capitalism, an era characterized by economic globalization, by an extreme utopian view of market logic as the morally best and empirically most efficient institution for transacting social relations in everyday life, and by the cultural condition currently called postmodernism. Various institutional implications of these trends for the university as a critically autonomous institution are set forth, resulting in a rather pessimistic conclusion regarding the university's future ability to serve as a school for democracy. Then Stanley explores why, given the difficulties, anyone would want to envision such a role for the university. Stanley argues that whether one likes it or not, the university already performs a number of civil religious functions simply in conducting its commonly accepted duties. These include, among others, the articulation of moral order, the integration of private psyches into the societal division of labor, and the institutionalization of civic education. Once one understands these functions of civil religion, it is difficult to imagine any other institution able to provide them.

In Chapter 8, "Toward a Relegitimation of Higher Education: Reinvigorating the Humanities and Social Sciences," Grahame Thompson, an economist, suggests that we must change metaphors when considering the plight of the academy in society. We have, in economic terms, traditionally considered the output of universities to be a *production good*. "Thus, higher education is seen . . . as an element in the inputs that go to make a viable and productive economic structure." Thompson claims that academics must begin to see higher education as members of the general population see it—that is, as a *consumption good*. In the final section of his chapter, Thompson suggests that if presented as a consumption good, the university becomes something to be demanded in its own right, rather than as an instrument in the "production" of something else.

David R. Shumway then argues in Chapter 9, "Objectivity, Relativism, and the Public Authority of the Scholar," that recent attacks on the humanities in academia came just when academics began moving beyond their roles as legitimators of dominant interests. Although these attacks have taken two fundamentally inconsistent forms, their success has thrown the authority of the scholar into question. On the one hand, scholars in the humanities have been accused of placing the notion of truth in disrepute by espousing the relativism of all knowledge. On the other, these same scholars have been charged with threatening democracy by instituting standards of political correctness on college campuses.

Shumway suggests that these attacks are ultimately intended to threaten intellectuals and limit their autonomy. Thus, for Shumway, what is at issue is precisely the relationship between academic knowledge and political power. He is somewhat critical of academicians who have succumbed to these assaults because they take deconstructionism to absolute limits, and thereby subvert their own authority in public discourse. He therefore asks scholars to affirm the kinds of knowledge that speak credibly to and for broader democratic publics.

In our final chapter, "The Erotics of Academic Conversation: Love, Ethics, and Reason in Scholarly and Civic Discourse," Richard Harvey Brown offers an alternative and more hopeful vision of academic practice. Brown argues that a basis for democratic civic action is implicit in the act of conversation. His vision differs significantly from the well-known communicative ethics advocated by Habermas and others (see, for example, the descriptions of communicative ethics in Benhabib & Dallmayr, 1990). Instead, Brown grounds his ethics in an erotics of conversation. He offers not the self-interested *eros* that toppled Marcuse's emancipatory project in *Eros and Civilization* (1955), however, but rather an *eros* that has reconciled its differences with *agape*. Possession and submission are not aspects of Brown's conception. His erotics, like his conversation, are rooted in *philos* and *caritas*. By creating space for the other to reveal her- or himself, love and conversation are mutually creative practices that respect and nurture their participants while co-creating their object.[3] Extending Aristotle's concept of civic friendship, Brown then shows how *erotic conversation*—not only rational-critical, but also sensual and spiritual—can provide a more democratic and nurturing academic and public discourse.

NOTES

1. The classic statement of crisis in sociology, for example, is Gouldner (1970), but see also Brown (1989a, 1989b), among others. Sociology is certainly not alone it its concern.

2. For the essay that provides the title for Fuller's piece, see "Science as a Vocation" in Gerth & Mills (1946).

3. For a complete account of the relationship between *eros, agape,* and *caritas,* especially as they pertain to a critical theory employing a Kleinian metapsychology, see Alford (1989).

REFERENCES

Alford, C. F. (1989). *Melanie Klein and critical social theory: An account of politics, art, and reason based on her psychoanalytic theory.* New Haven, CT: Yale University Press.

Aronowitz, S. (1998). The corporate university: Higher education becomes higher training. *Dollars and Cents, 216,* 32–35.

Bauman, Z. (1992). *Intimations of postmodernity.* New York: Routledge.

Benhabib, S., & Dallmayr, F. (1990). *The communicative ethics controversy.* Cambridge: MIT Press.

Bourdieu, P. (1988). *Homo academicus* (P. Collier, Trans.). Cambridge, UK: Polity.

Brown, R. H. (1989a). *A poetic for sociology: Toward a logic of discovery for the human sciences.* Chicago: University of Chicago Press.

Brown, R. H. (1989b). *Social science as civic discourse: Essays on the invention, uses, and legitimation of social theory.* Chicago: University of Chicago Press.

Brown, R. H. (1998). *Toward a democratic science: Scientific narration and civic communication.* New Haven, CT: Yale University Press.

Dickson, D. (1988). *The new politics of science.* Chicago: University of Chicago Press.

Fuller, S. (1995). A tale of two cultures and other higher superstitions. *History of Human Sciences, 8*(1), 115–125.

Gerth, H., & Mills, C. W. (Eds.). (1946). *From Max Weber.* New York: Oxford University Press.

Gouldner, A. (1970). *The coming crisis of western sociology.* New York: Basic Books.

Gross, P., & Levitt, N. (1994). *The higher superstition: The academic left and its quarrels with science.* Baltimore: Johns Hopkins University Press.

Habermas, J. (1975). *Legitimation crisis.* Boston: Beacon Press.

Marcuse, H. (1955). *Eros and civilization.* Boston: Beacon Press.

Nelkin, D. (1987). *Selling science.* New York: W. H. Freeman.

Nelson, J. (1990). Political foundations of the rhetoric of inquiry. In H. W. Simons (Ed.), *The rhetorical turn: Invention and persuasion in the conduct of inquiry* (pp. 258–292). Chicago: University of Chicago Press.

Nelson, J. S., Megill, A., & McCloskey, D. N. (Eds.). (1987). *The rhetoric of the human sciences: Language and argument in scholarship and public affairs.* Madison: University of Wisconsin Press.

Peretz, M. F. (1995, December 21). The private science of Louis Pasteur. *New York Review of Books, 42*(20), 54.

Simons, H. W. (Ed.). (1990). *The rhetorical turn: Invention and persuasion in the conduct of inquiry.* Chicago: University of Chicago Press.

Snow, C. P. (1969). *Two cultures.* New York: Cambridge University Press.

Stockton, S. (1995). Writing in history: Narrating the subject of time. *Written Communication, 12*(1), 47–73.

Weinberg, S. (1992). *Dreams of a final theory.* New York: Pantheon.

Wolpert, L. (1993). *The unnatural history of science.* Cambridge, MA: Harvard University Press.

PART II

The Institutional Politics of Knowledge Production

Two

DEMOCRACY AND CAPITALISM IN THE ACADEMY
The Commercialization of American Higher Education

RICHARD HARVEY BROWN AND REMI CLIGNET

AMERICAN COLLEGES and universities are still considered showcases of modernity, but the U.S. education system as a whole has ceased to be a model for less fortunate nations, and American higher education is itself under threat. There are several major signs of the diminished prestige of American education. First, the academic achievement of American undergraduates has fallen behind that of students of other countries, even some developing nations. The decline in average scores on college scholastic aptitude tests is matched by a corresponding decrease in the proportion of individuals with top performances. This impression of low performance is reinforced by comparatively low rates of graduation (Rubin, 1994).

Second, course contents, teaching styles, and research agendas are subjected to conflicting criticisms and a plethora of incompatible proposals. Some assert that the knowledge offered by institutions of higher learning is much too general for students who need specific skills and disciplines for a postindustrial economy. Others lament that colleges and universities have become narrow trade schools that do not foster the skills of citizenship. Similarly, whereas some complain of the decline of core disciplines and of intellectual life, others deride the presumed purity of the disciplines and encourage multicultural activities that valorize alternative forms of knowledge.

In effect, the ivory tower has become a cultural battleground over apparent dichotomies and their respective political constituencies—diversity versus the canon, affirmative action versus meritocracy, access versus excellence, free speech versus political correctness, teaching versus research, and applied versus basic research. On these issues and others, universities are now infested by the sorts of lawsuits that plague other American institutions. They are accused of mismanaging public funds, of overcharging both government and students, and of malpractice, price fixing, student loan defaults, and discrimination in the way they select students and hire or promote faculty (Beverly, 1978).

Although the vast majority of these proposals for reform suggest that universities should better serve the needs of the information economy, their number and variety indicate a crisis without consensus on its solution. Moreover, there often is a lack of fit between the proposed reforms, the needs of the labor market, the amounts of monies allocated, and the values that universities are supposed to represent, all of which gives an air of implausibility to all the proposals. This gives rise to a cynicism that the more that educators need money, the more they will say what they think potential patrons wish to hear.

Against this backdrop, we show in historical perspective how the difficulties and successes of American colleges reflect the conjunction of demographic, economic, and ideological forces. Some of these forces are aspects of advanced societies and not specific to the United States. Yet their impact is dramatized by both the decentralization and the laissez-faire ideology typical of American education. As a result, American educational relations have become disheartened and corrupt, more a subset of the labor market and commercial values than an autonomous creative force in the society.

Our analysis rests upon a critical reading of the concept of reproduction, a term elaborated by the French sociologists Pierre Bourdieu and Jean-Claude Passeron (1990). Analysts of education often argue that schools *reproduce* the contradictions and inequalities of society. But what is it that universities actually reproduce and how do they reproduce it? To what extent does reproduction also involve struggle and resistance (Apple, 1993; Giroux, 1983; Weiss, 1988)? Do existing elites perpetuate the current system of social stratification? Accordingly, do these elites control policies and practices of educational institutions? If so, is their influence indirect only? That is, do educators anticipate successfully the demands of their "masters" and thence respond to seemingly impersonal forces? Or have university administrators and professors squandered their own autonomy, making excessive compromises with commercial and governmental patrons instead of advancing the values and interests of higher learning itself? Or could it be that the contradictory behaviors of educators reproduce the contradictions that plague all segments of society, including elites themselves?

In short, the concept of reproduction raises other theoretical and political questions. First, the notions of conscious, unconscious, or voluntary and involuntary replication must be distinguished. Schools may deliberately imitate a specific educational model, as when Americans were inspired by the German or British universities. But American educational patterns also may reflect modes of dominance prevailing in American society, even if the main actors are not aware of it. For instance, though official ideology stresses the mobility that is supposed to be facilitated by schooling, various obstacles still prevent lower-income and minority students from acceding proportionately to the higher rungs of educational or career ladders. Moreover, unless expansion of higher education is matched by a corresponding increase of positions in the upper part of the occupational structure, increased access to higher education leads *not* to overall increases in social mobility but, instead, to increased competition and frustration.

In addition, processes of reproduction reflect both *short-* and *long-*term pressures. Educational patterns reproduce current social class patterns, but they also reproduce archaic practices and past patterns of domination that have selectively survived. As an example, the contemporary organization of schooling in Latin America reflects a historical succession of Jesuit, Napoleonic, and North American conceptions of education and general culture.

Still other phenomena are subsumed under the label *reproduction*. While reproduction refers mainly to structural factors, it also is mediated by cultural interpretations—students and teachers reinterpret their experiences at school according to their respective ethnic, religious, gender, or class perspectives. Further, through their personal beliefs and actions, individuals keep modifying the form and the extent of processes of reproduction.

Thus, the seeming ubiquity of America's educational crisis often masks real differences in its sources and dimensions. Analysis of the American system of higher education therefore requires us to identify its long- and short-term dynamics and the diverging perceptions and values of the persons centrally involved. Overall, we believe that these dynamics have brought about a reduction of autonomy of the universities and an increase in their commercialization.

LONG-TERM CONTRADICTIONS OF
AMERICAN HIGHER EDUCATION

A historical review suggests that laments about the dire state of American education follow cyclical patterns. Versions of "Johnny can't read" are rediscovered periodically. The recurrence of such criticisms may be due to the

ambiguities of the links between universities and popular social movements, on the one hand, and elite political and economic organizations, on
the other. These ambiguities reflect four contradictory forces:

- Ideological and conceptual contradictions in public discussions about
  higher education.
- Differing rates and directions of change of economic and educational
  organizations.
- The differing criteria of assessment and systems of stratification between universities and other institutions.
- The uneven character of these developments across regions and economic sectors.

First, views on the legitimate mission of public education have always
been in conflict in the United States. In addition to the difficulties that we
have just mentioned, ideological and conceptual confusion about higher
education also is due to the ideological barriers to value consensus posed
by a liberal-democratic market society. A society so conceived is not, in
principle, an explicit moral community. It is, rather, an association of individuals and communities whose primary mode of social interaction is economic exchange in pursuit of the satisfaction of privately defined wants.
Much of education, however, has evolved into a public enterprise (Stanley,
1986). As such, it requires a public legitimation in other than individualistic
utilitarian terms (e.g., as instruction in job skills). Indeed, liberal individualistic or utilitarian justifications do not even acknowledge the *collective* value
consensus, which could ratify moral and political socialization, that is a
central component of education as an explicitly *public* mission.

A related issue in American debates on education has been the tendency to think of moral education as an activity largely of the churches,
leaving the so-called secular schools to identify themselves with utilitarian
ends, plus some seemingly noncontroversial themes such as "good citizenship" and the "Protestant work ethic." The constitutional separation of
church and state helped Americans avoid the *conceptual* task of separating
moral and secular education. Again, the public schools were left to specialize in secular, mostly utilitarian tasks (Stanley, 1986).

A further ideological and conceptual confusion has been the confound-
ing of education and training. The "outputs" or "products" of education
have usually been assessed in utilitarian terms. These include literacy skills,
habits appropriate to business-oriented social intercourse, and motives and
information useful for vocational advancement. These outputs can be met
through training, and indeed, when education is discussed as a *means,* it

remains less controversial. But when one discusses the broader *ends* of education (or of education *as* an end), then controversy flares. Nonetheless, the reduction of education to training reduces the overall legitimacy of the university as an autonomous institution.

Second, changes in economic and educational institutions are often out of sync. The increase in scale and complexity of the American economy and its increasing globalization have been accompanied by a parallel specialization both of occupational roles and of the knowledge that is transmitted by schools. Yet the greater the specialization in both education and the economy, the greater also is the need for multi- and transdisciplinary generalists to span this fragmentation. In the heyday of post–World War II expansion, the major function of colleges and universities was to prepare students with the general knowledge required of the managers and professionals of the expanded tertiary or service sector of the economy, which today is about 75% of America's GNP. Even greater post–World War II expansion occurred in junior and community colleges, which sought to prepare less qualified and generally working-class and minority students with skills as techno-artisans or paraprofessionals.

After this period of rapid growth, however, changes in the occupational structure and the declining growth rate of the economy had contradictory implications for education. On the one hand, the assembly line was extended to the service sector, and repetitive, narrow, and simple tasks moved higher up the occupational ladder. These tasks are no longer performed exclusively by blue-collar workers of the industrial factories alone, but now mostly by service workers such as insurance clerks, fast-food servers, bank tellers, or supermarket cashiers, who are aided by computers. At the same time, many U.S. manufacturing assembly lines have been automated or closed in favor of production in foreign lower-wage economies. This restructuring of the American economy, done with vengeance in the 1980s under the rubric of "competitiveness," also was accompanied by the computerization of much office work, thereby eliminating the need for most supervisory personnel. These changes resulted in the massive firings of medium-skilled factory and office workers, as well as middle managers, and the creation of many new low-level positions, and some new jobs for highly skilled techno-literate persons.

This narrowing of the cognitive requirements of many white-collar occupations has encouraged the simplification of training programs in their respective "feeder institutions," including colleges and universities. As noted, vocationally oriented community colleges expanded greatly in the postwar period, and universities themselves have become more like vocational schools that prepare people to perform repetitive tasks. For example, the rote learning necessary to score well on the ubiquitous multiple-choice exams probably prepares students for their future occupations more than whatever unremembered "content" such exams are supposed to reflect.

At the same time, however, labor guilds in various specialized professions seek to protect their privileges by raising the educational credentials demanded of job-seekers, even for relatively modest and low-skilled positions (Collins, 1979). There also has been a change in the functions of top executives, who are expected to display greater social and verbal skills than ever before. Thus, colleges and universities are exposed to conflicting forces that induce them to simultaneously require both less and more from their students—greater technical specialization *and* greater communicative generalization.

Further, American educational institutions have not experienced the same flexible centralization as American firms. Corporate enterprises have grown in functional and geographic scope even while maintaining highly coordinated flexibility in their managerial control. By contrast, American educational institutions have remained radically decentralized, geographically local, and inflexible and hierarchic in their management practices. Thus, colleges and universities remain dwarfs in relation to the giant major corporations, and there is a growing asymmetry between economic and educational institutions in their relative tactical agility, financial resources, and political powers. For example, whereas the scale and flexibility of American businesses allows them to either standardize *or* redesign tasks both within and across occupational categories, the segmentation of educational worlds causes rigid specializations or universalizations in admission policies, curricula, teaching styles, and the evaluation of students. Indeed, the combination of a segmented structure and a universalistic ideology operates to mask educational status markets that are based more on the ascriptive social class or ethnic origin of students than on students' achievements.

Moreover, since there is virtually no standardization of colleges and universities by a national educational authority, particularistic criteria (such as reputation of schools, family traditions, tuition charged, or composition of the student body) determine the value imputed to schools and their graduates. In effect, tracking is practiced more *among* schools than within them. This accentuates the vulnerability of colleges to both short-term vagaries of the market and the opportunistic strategies of the consumers of schooling, students and their parents.

Third, because the rank ordering of colleges and universities does not follow the same logic as the patterns of stratification in the society at large, the interaction of these status systems is unstable. To be sure, the ideology of equal opportunity for social advancement has long dominated American discourse on education. Moreover, given the Enlightenment ideals and radical individualism of most Americans, both politicians and citizens have long asserted that schooling corrects most human woes. This stance has enabled the official discourse to attribute differences in incomes or life chances among races or classes either to the educational failings of subordinate groups or to the inadequacy of the schools. Yet today as yesterday, social mobility from educational investments is plausible only to the extent that the economy grows more rapidly than formal schooling, particularly in its upper occupational sectors. Conversely, the benefits of schooling become doubtful or selective whenever economic expansion is limited or declining. Institutions of higher learning act mainly as agencies of socialization for new positions during periods of economic expansion, and mainly as an expensive alternative to unemployment during periods of economic contraction.

Moreover, the professional privileges and personal calling of academics involve participation in "the life of the mind," that is, intellectual cultivation beyond lay knowledge. This contrasts to the utilitarian, pragmatic, and anti-intellectual orientation of American culture generally. Thus both structurally and culturally the status system of most universities is at least partly disharmonious with that of the other social sectors that support them. These disjunctions between educational and economic criteria adversely affect social evaluations of educational quality.

In economic terms, insofar as there is little standardization in higher education and, hence, of the human capital that graduates into the labor market, one could expect public authorities to streamline the national educational market and to limit the fluctuations in the value of educational currency. Yet, because of America's decentralized and laissez-faire educational system, and because of Americans' liberal conception of the utilitarian state, the federal government cannot easily set national quality standards for students, in order to identify the best ways to assess such qualities or to coordinate admission policies on a national or regional basis. Indeed, President Clinton's efforts to do this in 1997 were quickly thwarted by conservative, localist, and libertarian forces both within and outside of Congress. Instead, the value of educational currency, whether one talks about schools or students, is based mainly on informal reputation.

Fourth, these contradictory expectations of higher education also vary by region and economic sector. Some regions and sectors wish to turn universities into trade schools that provide students with saleable skills; others claim that high rates of technological change make literate generalists more productive in the long term than narrowly specialized workers. In short, differentiation of regions and firms generates parallel divergences in the national, regional, and sectorial pressures on schools. This segmentation of American educational markets leads to diminished solidarity among colleges and universities. Their purposes are now more divergent; they have more difficulty in speaking with a common voice; and, hence, they are less politically effective in defense of their autonomy.

There also is variability in the kinds of schooling to which various categories of students and parents aspire. For some groups, colleges serve as finishing schools and status markers of general culture; for others, they offer educational investments and avenues of upward mobility; for still others, they are places of self-discovery and intellectual growth. This distribution of resources and aspirations also is effected by broader economic and labor market conditions, as well as the differential quality of the schooling that different classes can afford. For example, even in a declining market, schools may transform the lives of some young people even while serving as holding pens to keep others out of trouble and off the unemployment rolls.

The long-term tensions of American education result both from the localism and relative autonomy enjoyed by each school in relation to the increased scale and flexible standardization of the American economy, and from the diverging ideological legitimations of education as serving both democracy and capitalism. Given the ambiguities that flow from this structural disparity and ideological contradiction, the challenges to the future of higher education cannot be exclusively imputed to financial or cultural hegemony of corporate capitalists or governmental elites. These challenges are also structurally generated by the decentralized nature of school systems, the emerging postindustrial character of capitalist enterprises, the pressures of the business cycle on competition between individuals and between institutions, and the longstanding ideological ambiguity of the American educational project.

SHORT-TERM CONTRADICTIONS IN AMERICAN HIGHER EDUCATION

Since about 1970, American colleges and universities have faced severe short-term demographic, economic, and ideological dilemmas. These dilemmas have generated both cultural malaise and institutional change, and have opened the universities to greater influence by corporate interests and commercial values.

Short-Term Demographic Pressures

Urbanization and industrialization generate declines in rates of marriage and fertility and, therefore, in the number of eligible students. But these declines are not necessarily continuous or cumulative, and they can be made up by immigration or by changing the standards of admission to enlarge the pool of potential students. Demographers have debated whether the baby boom after World War II and the consequent increased demand for schooling some years later were cyclical or accidental. These debates had practical implications, since the college-age population kept declining from the late 1970s until the 1990s, to around 2.5 million persons, drastically affecting the size of schools' clienteles, budgets, and staffs. Hence, the tasks have been to ascertain whether the demographic declines would reverse or not, and then to project the sizes of birth cohorts, to estimate what their impact would be on scarcities or gluts in educational facilities, and thence to determine what resources should be put aside for education.

American colleges and universities expanded enormously in the postwar period in order to prepare workers for the postindustrial Cold War economy, and also in response to later status demands by minorities and women. In 1940 there were 1,700 institutions of higher education enrolling 1.5 million students and employing 147,929 faculty in all ranks, including non–tenure track appointments. In 1994 there were 3,600 such institutions, 14.7 million students, and over 750,000 faculty members (Altbach, 1995). The student population increased tenfold, and the numbers of advanced education programs and their faculties increased by a factor of five. The proportional increases are similar for the number of Ph.D.s awarded during this period—about five times as many as are needed to fill new openings in institutions of higher learning.

These short-term demographic changes have led to several shifts in American higher education since the end of the 1960s. A two-tiered academic labor market emerged, with a "labor aristocracy" at the top and a "permanent underprivileged stratum of untouchables at the bottom" (Wilke, 1979, p. xii) consisting of untenured professors, graduate student instructors and laboratory workers, and semi-employed possessors of Ph.D.s who roam the country from each one-year appointment to the next (Tuckman, Caldwell, & Fogler, 1978).

Further, although the social class origins of faculty and students has not broadened since the late 1960s, American universities have "democratized" to some extent through greater inclusion of women, minorities, and older persons (Bochow, 1985). As competition for students among institutions increases with demographic downswings, universities and colleges, whose populations are less "captive" than those of primary and secondary schools, tend to "create" additional students in order to cover their fixed costs, often by lowering the criteria for admission or retention. Thus the demographic and educational expansion that followed the postwar baby boom, and the later decline in the "normal" student population, were probably significant factors in the new openness of colleges and universities to women, minorities, the elderly, the poor, the newly immigrated, and part-time and foreign students. Although the relative value of a college degree has declined because of these changes, expansion of enrollments and faculty cutback have become necessary for the survival of mass institutions and nonelite private colleges.

The extreme decentralization of American higher education accentuates the difficulties of coping with demographic upswings and downswings and their consequences. For example, the lack of coordination between federal, state, and local agencies that collect data and set policies makes it difficult for each school to anticipate changes in educational demand and the adequacy of their particular response to it. Further, insofar as laissez-faire decentralization encourages a market orientation on the part of both schools and students, most people feel only a limited and instrumental commitment toward specific schools. The competitive libertarian conception of education enables them to move elsewhere when they are dissatisfied with the services of any given provider in the educational marketplace. Thus, decentralization accentuates uncertainties in educational markets due to demographic downswings as well as the competition between schools to attract or retain students.

Short-Term Economic Forces

The consequences of the demographic shifts have been accentuated by several economic factors. First, deficit spending was pushed by the escalation of the Vietnam War during the 1960s, the energy crisis during the 1970s, and deficit military spending in the 1980s, and this inflation increased the operating costs of schools. These costs also increased due to greater administrative overhead and support for new student populations. Second, there was a slowdown in the growth of the American economy between about 1970 and 1990 that limited the resources that families and communities could allocate to institutions of higher learning. Third, the occupational and class structures of the United States have become increasingly skewed since the 1980s, with a small number of excellent positions at the top, stagnation in the middle, and a push toward poverty on the working class. Thus individuals and families investing in education have become more cautious in response to soaring educational costs and greater occupational risk even for those who have a college degree. At the same time, a college degree becomes even more necessary given the highly competitive labor market for executive and professional positions, partly because many students can no longer afford to attend college or university, especially the elite institutions. The result has been "an overeducated, overqualified labor force with a decreasing supply of suitable jobs, increasing job dissatisfaction, defeated expectations, alienation and contradiction producing discrepancies between the American dream and reality" (Mayes, 1977, p. 18; see O'Toole, 1975).

Fourth, since college presidents and major donors are tempted to measure their success in terms of construction that adds physical evidence of institutional growth, universities found themselves with excessive plant capacity and fixed operating costs when the period of demographic downswing arrived. Not only did the likelihood of declining enrollments jeopardize the usefulness of these buildings, but their upkeep put additional pressure on academic budgets. Past achievements became current liabilities.

Finally, the wages paid to professors tend to increase at least enough to competitively attract competent persons to the professoriate, but there is no corresponding increase in productive output per professor. Consequently, the cost of higher education per student inevitably rises. Inflation exacerbates this increased per-student cost. Universities try to escape this cycle of potentially astronomically increasing costs by several tactics: They raise tuition fees and expand the population of eligible students; they increase the number of students per class; they seek technological solutions that substitute capital for labor, such as computerized teaching programs or "distance learning"; and they pursue additional funds through donations, contract research, and other nontuition sources. Further, to decrease costs of instructional personnel, universities have exploited the large pool of Ph.D. degree holders relative to the academic job market. In effect, the overproduction of Ph.D.s has created a lumpenproletariat of specialized claimants for nonexistent jobs whom universities then use as nonsalaried visiting part-time staff who do piecework on commission. Thus financial constraints have led universities "to emulate the employment practices of business corporations" (Vidich, 1994, p. 665).

Marxists have correctly argued that the rhetorics of educational equality and the expansion of the universities and their clienteles served the needs of corporate capitalism in two ways: first, and earlier, by expanding the pool of more literate workers for the expanding high end of the service economy; second, and later, by offering new opportunities for status inclusion to dissident groups of the 1960s without having to alter the occupational structure or relations of production. Our point here, however, is that the ethos of democratization, the practice of greater access to higher learning, and the greater corporatist style of universities also are self-interested responses to demographic forces. Institutions have tried to survive the contraction of their market—a dwindling population of adolescents.

The Short-Term Ideological Crisis

The demographic and economic downturns beginning around 1965 and 1970 are associated with the blossoming of diverse ideological movements. First, civil rights workers sought to complete the struggle for democracy begun in World War II by ending racial segregation in the United States.

Other activists were keen to stop the war in Vietnam, which they perceived as imperialism abroad that encouraged inequality at home. In short, there was a growing awareness that commitments toward domestic and international equity were not inseparable. Other cultural leaders preferred to promote liberty rather than equality, sometimes equating free drugs and free sex with free speech (Lasch, 1979).

Although the cultural rebellion of the 1960s opened up space for new groups and ideas within institutions of higher learning, it also made their operations more complex. Many champions of a hedonistic or unrestricted liberty had no theory of authority and indeed rejected hierarchical or even organized relations as a matter of principle. Thus, their groups and movements were often plagued by anarchic disorder or were captured by autocratic caesars. Movement leaders also failed to explore the contradictions between liberty and equality. For example, the social equality to be gained by blacks was treated as identical to the sexual liberty demanded by gays. Later the critical spirit of the 1960s issued into political and intellectual movements such as feminism, Afro-centricism, multiculturalism, and postmodernism, all of which tended to relativize absolutist claims to knowledge and to inspire attacks on "political correctness" from right-wing ideologues and even liberal academics both outside and within the universities.

Since the 1980s, however, accusations of political correctness and the colonization of the university by the left has masked the influence on academic life by right-wing foundations, corporations, and tycoons (Soley, 1995). Indeed, many of the critics who bash the universities for being bastions of political correctness receive their funding from conservative organizations and foundations who benefit from this obfuscation.

One illustration of this ideological struggle is the "white ethnic backlash" against affirmative action, or what is often called "reverse discrimination" (Glazer, 1997). Emblematic of this concern is a federal discrimination suit filed in 1997 against the University of Michigan by Gennifer Gratz, who is white and whose father is a policeman. Ms. Gratz stated, "They are using race as a factor in admissions by weeding out students who aren't of that minority race [but who otherwise would be qualified]" (Reibstein, 1998, p. 76).

The paradoxes of this situation are, first, that most whites favor diversity and desegregation even though they tend to be against special treatment for particular groups, and second, that the concept of "reverse discrimination" itself is a perversion of what affirmative action is intended to mean and accomplish. Polls show that most Americans are ambivalent about affirmative action but not necessarily against it. They don't like "quotas" but, since the Bakke decision, rigid quotas have been outlawed and most affirmative action programs take race into account but do not make it exclusive or determinative. In effect, the idea that "affirmative action equals quotas" is propaganda of the enemies of affirmative action.

Similarly, most Americans favor the idea of racially diverse workplaces and campuses, but, as Martin Luther King (1964) foresaw, they don't like giving preferences to minorities. Even among those who oppose affirmative action, however, the overwhelming majority has not felt personally damaged by the policy, as Paul Sniderman and Thomas Piazza show (1993). Only 7% of respondents in their polls actually claimed to have been victims of "reverse discrimination" and only 16% know of someone who has. "More strikingly, most whites have no complaints about the affirmative action policies that are in effect where they actually work" (Frederickson, 1997, p. 74).

Why, then, do 8 out of 10 oppose such policies in the abstract? How can we explain the "white ethnic backlash" against diversity and affirmative action? One answer is political and media propaganda against affirmative action, as well as against women's studies, Afro-American studies, multiculturalism, postmodernism, secular humanism, and, indeed, all of the more critical or progressive activities to which universities are dedicated. For more than a decade a "culture war" has been conducted in the United States in which the actual goings-on in such programs and within universities in general are often grossly misrepresented. To cite but two examples of this, Ellen Messer-Davidow (1995) conducted systematic ethnographic fieldwork in conservative organizations and also examined financial records of prominent right-wing organizations that rail against "political correctness." Her research documents the flow of money into right-wing think tanks and, from there, the flow of "expert knowledge" into the media, courts, government agencies, and schools. Those of us who have been involved directly in the incidents reported by such sources know that the supposedly egregious aspects of such events are usually exaggerated, distorted, or falsely reported. Alice Jardine (1995) corrects one such misrepresentation made in a volume titled *Illiberal Education* (1992) by Dinesh D'Souza, who himself has been funded by some of the institutions studied by Messer-Davidow. Accusing Jardine of political correctness, D'Souza recounted that a student delivered "ribald one-liners about a man who lost his penis . . . [and] brought loud and embarrassed laughter from the professor and other students." In an exacting analysis, Jardine shows how D'Souza produced in his text an appearance of reality by using quotes from faculty and students and graphic descriptions of the people, places, and interactions. He then decontextualized and recoded them as instances of political correctness. But, as Jardine explains, the discussion about the missing penis was actually about the myth of Osiris, a deity whose body parts were scattered throughout Egypt. Osiris's wife, Isis, buried each part as she found them, but the phallus was never recovered, and to this day images of it are used in festivals and sold to tourists.

Since such ideological conflicts and confusions often have taken place within or were directed against universities, those institutions became more difficult to govern and their purposes and values more open to contest.

Interactions Between Long- and Short-Term Forces

The economic and demographic crises that have dominated American higher education since the end of the 1960s offer a sharp contrast with the ideologies of affluence that prevailed at the time. Even though schools were facing a situation of economic scarcity and even though the nation was involved in the Vietnam War and its aftermaths, many academics acted as if scarcities of resources and values did not exist.

In many universities, presidents and the boards they served saw the alliance between faculties and students as a threat to their own positions and the funding base of their institutions. Educational administrators no longer acted as leaders of a community of scholars and learners, nor as national spokespersons for enlightened values, nor even as intermediaries between the ivory tower and the fields of government and business. Instead, they became specialized bureaucrats engaged in tasks more narrowly defined. Responding now to renewed outside pressures, their primary functions became those of quelling internal dissent and securing external funds. Since such administrators often lack a vision of the cultural mission of universities, they have been unable to resolve the contradictions between the material conditions of their institutions and the ideological orientations imputed to faculty and students. Indeed, their technocratic way of thinking is inherently unsuited for cultural or moral reflection. The result has been a system that disheartens learners, teachers, and scholars and undermines any moral legitimation of their practices.

THE COMMODIFICATION OF LEARNING

Since the rise of the modern university in the mid-nineteenth century there has been a conflict between the views of universities as communities of scholars and learners engaged in "conversations of humanity" (Oakeshott, 1959), and their definition as training grounds for narrowly defined skills. Yet in recent decades commercial voices have almost totally silenced their rivals. This happens in both explicit and subtle ways. For example, American educational standards are now almost exclusively defined in purely quantitative terms, as in the use of such concepts as "credit" to mark academic progress, or "accountability" (meaning countability) to measure the effectiveness of instruction. Indeed, the obligation of students to accumulate a sufficient amount of numerically interchangeable credits in order to graduate legitimates the view that schooling is a form of economic rather than cultural capital and that the university is a factory for the production of functionaries. Higher tuition fees, the commercialization of much research, and corporate recruiting on campus reinforces this impression.

Against this mercantile backdrop, academic administrators used two seemingly divergent tactics to deal with the short-term pressures described above. One tactic expresses the rationalization and predictability of advanced capitalist systems, the other reflects the radical subjectivism of contemporary culture. On the one hand, academic leaders have lamented the decline in students' abilities and have emphasized the need to maintain standards. Correspondingly, they have required students to take specified numbers of credits of core courses in the natural and human sciences. While their stance can be read as an apparent commitment to the ideal of the university as a center of learning with its own internal standards, this is belied by the utilitarian definition of these standards and the bureaucratized quantification of measurements of learning. Such a technicist approach mainly respects predictability and efficiency of systems, not the autonomy and competence of learners.

On the other hand, administrators also have stressed the concept of relevance, in which curricular changes are seemingly made in response to personal needs and group aspirations of students, regardless of more universal cultural standards. While such accommodations are hailed in the name of equity or diversity, their ad hoc character suggests that administrators have yielded to the radical subjectivism. The maintenance of standards and responsiveness to the needs of students both are thought to help keep up enrollments. The problem, however, is not only that these two stances often conflict, but mainly that both of them respond to essentially commercial motivations. The first stance often speaks of higher academic standards while effectively subordinating the academic trajectory of students to the interests of their future employers. The second stance relies on the rhetorics of individual or group freedom in order to subordinate academic values to the market orientations of specific clusters of consumers. Both positions denigrate the validity of accumulated knowledge, favor the present over tradition, and minimize the importance of the conceptual foundations of any discipline and, indeed, of intellectual discipline itself.

Another change was in grading systems. Some students felt that the traditional letter grades were too formal and restrictive, so universities started to use the pass/fail method of grading, to assign academic credit by examination, and to employ other lenient methods. There was more off-campus work, travel or work-study programs, and supervised or unsupervised internships. There was also a movement to develop new, nontraditional learning institutions, such as universities without walls, external degree programs, freestanding professional schools, and Internet universities or research archives (Mayhew, 1977, pp. 46–67).

In sum, these new tactics of academic administrators reflect the tensions that the consumer society fosters between systems maintenance and radical subjectivism. The first stance parodies academic standards in reducing them to quantitative terms; the second mocks these standards by turning them into consumer choices. The ensuing reduction of academic work to terms imported from the marketplace demoralizes the relations between faculties and students. This can be seen more concretely in the ambiguities of the notion of relevance, the quantification of the curriculum, the bureaucratization of teaching, and the commercialization of scholarship.

THE AMBIGUITIES OF THE NOTION OF RELEVANCE

Despite their insistence on maintaining academic standards, administrators also have stressed the need to make the university more relevant to the needs and aspirations of students. As noted, however, this concept is doubled-faced, for several reasons. First, the logic of the notion of relevance implies that students should tailor-make their own educational programs. To the extent that such an option is available, as in combined majors or independent studies, it tends to attract the extremes—students who are broad-gauged, hyperspecialized, or simply seeking an easy degree. Even though the large variance within this group suggests the importance of advising and counseling, these services are labor-intensive and largely unrewarded and, hence, in short supply.

The idea of relevance can be a good marketing tactic, since it allows administrators to promise something for everyone. When taken seriously, however, as in small elite colleges or in university honors programs, personalized "relevant" instruction tends to decrease the per-capita output of professors. In response, universities offer shorter courses that are often target-marketed to the particular desires of specific student populations and taught through self-instruction techniques or by nonsalaried part-time instructors. The combined results of tailor-made courses and reduction of quality and quantity of instruction often leads to the trivialization of curricula. Minorities are especially subject to this, often unwittingly. To be sure, fuller participation of any marginal group in a mainstream institution requires special structures of support. But often specialized minority studies offered in the name of relevance and self-awareness have led to continued academic marginality.

Further, in the name of responding to the particular needs of students, grading tends to become more a private accord between students and instructors than a public assertion of universalistic standards. As an example, current policies of "privacy" require the faculty to post grades only after having removed names from the class list. In contrast to the past, when individual students were publicly lauded for their achievements or chastised for their shortfalls, it is now the faculty that is publicly accountable for protecting them from a consequence of their failures. Moreover, tighter grading fosters resentment, gripes, and formal complaints by students who have been sufficiently socialized to a mercantilist view of learning to punish such professors by grading them poorly on the students' own evaluations of their courses. Thus, few professors grade strictly, especially in departments where low enrollments impel professors to either raise body counts or lose positions and power. The "Gentleman's C" of yesteryear has become "Everyone's B" of today. Of course, universities do have an obligation to evaluate themselves and seek to improve their performance, especially their effectiveness in education and not mere socialization or training. To the extent that such "evaluation" is reduced to checkoff items on questionnaires, however, the self-reflection of universities as communities of learning is thereby reduced.

Responsiveness to students' needs may be more apparent than real. Instead of serving as the clarion for critical awareness or civic commitment, relevance has come to express the consumerist values that it initially was intended by many to oppose. Thus relevance raises more crucial questions concerning higher learning. Is education a private purchase that the learner can negotiate? Or is it an institutionalized mode of reproducing a collective cultural heritage? Are instructors agents of training, or do they act on behalf of a civilizing tradition for the community as a whole? Is graduation the receipt of a ticket to middle-class status, or is it a rite of passage that marks the conveyance of a collective trust? In practice, the American educational system has opted for the first set of choices: It has largely transformed the teacher's calling and the student's commitment into a commercial contract.

THE QUANTIFICATION OF THE CURRICULUM

Curricular reforms have involved quantitative changes in the distributions of credits that individuals must acquire in order to graduate. But these quantitative changes are rarely accompanied by parallel changes in the qualitative definition of what students are supposed to know. Students are required to take a certain number of credits, say, in French, but without any statement of the knowledge they are expected to acquire of that language and culture. Should one be able to engage in conversation, write business letters, understand the basic structure of French grammar, or read major authors in the original? Should one acquire an understanding of French history, culture, and character through the language? Is the knowledge of French expected to help students to work in international arenas, or is it supposed to contribute to the student's understanding and appreciation of English and American culture?

To address such questions requires reflection on disciplinary and departmental boundaries, thereby unsettling political and organizational status quos. Indeed, the debate over maintaining the "purity" or "professionalism" of disciplines versus making courses "relevant" to students is rarely engaged within universities or even within departments (Thompson, 1979). This forfeiture preserves disciplinary boundaries but limits inquiry just at those interstices between fields where scholarship often becomes most fruitful. Further, the absence of such self-reflection on the core conceptual requirements of disciplines renders them all the more subservient to anti-intellectual corporatist interests.

Practical measures of educational policies such as the "body count" or the "number of clients served" also express bureaucratic and free-market rhetorics that demoralize both faculty and students. Consider, for example, this comment by two leading educational specialists: "People are allocated to adult roles on the basis of years and types of education, *apart from anything they have learned in school*" (Bock & Papagiannis, 1983, p. 93, emphasis added). On the one hand, it is a largely accurate observation. On the other, it also is a self-fulfilling prophecy that excuses professors from thinking about what they should teach and how. Indeed, when the authors add that "medical knowledge as an abstract category probably possesses even less utility for society than witchcraft," they suggest that the function of medical schools is much more to *certify* that their graduates possess valued competence than to make sure that they actually *have* it. Indeed, in *The Credential Society* (1979), Randall Collins showed how professional guilds protect their monopoly privileges by using otherwise useless university degrees as a barrier to keep out competition. Despite its sociological merits, when this line of reasoning is adopted in academic circles it effectively mirrors the anti-intellectualism of American society.

Anti-intellectual views also have invaded proposals for reform of curricula. For example, the report of the National Endowment for the Humanities,

"50 Hours: A Core Curriculum for College Students," does say that students must be taught to think critically. Yet the survey of what students know, commissioned by the NEH, covered only knowledge of disciplinary content. It revealed nothing about the students' ability to solve problems, construct arguments, evaluate propaganda, comprehend meanings, or make connections. The report seemed almost happy to note that students need more facts, such as the dates of the Civil War or the author of the *Aeneid*.

Similar thinking is evident in E. D. Hirsch's bestselling book, *Cultural Literacy: What Every American Needs to Know* (1987). Hirsch's conception of "cultural literacy" reflects a view of literacy that is essentially technical, and of knowledge as depersonalized information completely alienated from human experience. Indeed, the concept of information is central to Hirsch's analysis. "Culturally literate" people possess certain bits of information that others do not have, and he even tells us what these bits should be. This is a far cry from the classical concept of education. In this now old-fashioned view, "cultural literacy" is a redundancy, since formerly to be literate *meant* to be cultured. To be cultured, literate, or educated was to push against the frontiers of one's own ignorance, to recognize one's own mortality and finitude, to enter into the "conversation of humanity" and so be able to speak of our history, our conditions, and our mandate. That is quite beyond information, and it is something that a computer cannot do. But a computer could quite easily be culturally literate in Hirsch's terms. In such thinking, civic and intellectual culture is reduced to another data tape, and knowledge to a set of facts, phrases, and allusions.

THE BUREAUCRATIZATION OF TEACHING

The reduction of teaching from a public trust to a private contract has been associated with changes in the normative definition of what teaching is about. The role of the teacher as a witness for and model of learning has been largely replaced by a belief in the objectivity of facts, the utility of findings, and the substitution of the passion for truth with the *dis*passion of method. These shifts reflect the overall bureaucratization of the university. Similarly, the universalism of knowledge is being replaced as a norm by the universalism of due process—due process in pursuing knowledge, in grading students, or in promoting professors—with less regard for the intrinsic value of learning or of scholarship. With this, professors who do too much teaching, particularly of undergraduates, are assumed to be weak scholars or inept academic entrepreneurs. The higher one's professional recognition, the less likely one is to offer large and frequent lectures, which become the domain of the most novice teachers—the graduate students.

The very concept of education has become confused with socialization, schooling, instruction, and training. Education derives from the Latin *educere*, to draw out what is latent in the auditor. As such, education is an activity based on a thesis that cannot be proven: that the achievement of fully human consciousness, even though a tragic destiny, is nonetheless the redeeming end of human existence. To deny this thesis is either to practice education in bad faith or to substitute for education activities that have other ends, such as socialization, instruction, or training. All of these are necessary for society, but only education is necessary for humanity. For socializers, the point is to reproduce the authoritative order of society; for instructors and trainers, it is to impart skills and information. The educator, by contrast, has an inherently subversive mission. Though she makes use of skills, information, and values, it is not in order merely to reproduce them, but rather to cultivate in the learner a capacity to critically assess them, to interiorize or to reject them, and to create them (Stanley, 1981, 1986). In education, then, information, skills, and values exist not for their own sake, but at the service of a permanently revolutionary conception: the exposure of the learner to a "conversation" on the nature and purpose of human existence itself.

Whatever their disciplines, this conception of education is what professors have to profess. Informed by civilizing values, the world of professional educators once was ideally governed by discretionary rules derived from the principles of noblesse oblige, civic comity, and a secularized Christian calling. With bureaucratization, however, the practice of discretion, which was part of the educational mission, has become a tool that administrators use to divide the faculty. For example, until the 1990 Supreme Court decisions, administrators invoked the right to privacy of the instructors they intended to sanction in order to prevent these victims from knowing the nature and the sources of the charges against them. Conversely, the same administrators may facilitate the selective circulation of information concerning the misdeeds of individual instructors to justify their discretionary sanctions.

The use of students' evaluations of teachers provides a case in point. Formerly, student governments and fraternities or sororities assessed instructors in order to inform succeeding classes what to expect. If done by questionnaires, these evaluations required the instructors' assent. The results were sold on campus, but were not used officially by administrators in decisions concerning academic personnel. Under the rhetorics of fairness and accountability, however, students' evaluations of instructors were introduced as components of decisions on tenure, promotion, and salary. This began in the early 1970s, just when administrators sought to break the alliance forged by students and many faculty during the Vietnam War.

The introduction of such evaluations has been demoralizing on a number of counts. First, the instruments have been devised by psychologists who have acquired copyrights. Their behavior illustrates not only the demise of the distinction between basic and applied research, but also the fragility of occupational solidarity among social scientists who do not hesitate to sacrifice their colleagues to serve the bureaucratization of teaching. Second, the use of these instruments has many conceptual confusions. For example, because the evaluation questionnaires obscure much disagreement on what "good teaching" consists of, two instructors might each have the same overall rating despite great difference in their observable methods and intended results. In one case, the student ratings may cluster in the middle, whereas in the other they may skew toward the extremes, resulting in the same median ratings for both. Yet there is no attempt to identify the better teacher. Is it the "average" instructor, who neither pleases nor dissatisfies students? Or is it the other "average" teacher, who inspires both enthusiasm and distress?

Third, the instruments also reveal neglect of construct validity. Social scientists have described the statistical preconditions that warrant combining the scores obtained by the same individuals on specific items of a questionnaire; nonetheless, evaluation specialists rarely check whether such preconditions are met (e.g., that items are clustered around a single statistical axis). Neither do they ascertain the conditions under which differences in the scores obtained by instructors are statistically significant. Thus, the "objectivity" of the questionnaires illustrates the illusions attached to the positivist reductionism of many social scientists. There is little attempt to choose items or techniques that could be cross-evaluated even in the initial design and testing of the instruments themselves. In short, despite the importance of the decisions involved, students' descriptions of their instructors are taken at face value as nearly exclusive indicators of professors' classroom performance.

Fourth, this type of evaluation also illustrates the moral contradictions of current educational policies. Thus, students themselves have lost control of the instrument used to evaluate their instructors and there is no system of checks and balances in the use that administrators make of the results. The ensuing secrecy enables administrators either to ignore or to dramatize the scores obtained by differing instructors. Such abuses are ironic in light of the overt commitment of universities to the protection of human subjects. Whereas instructors are required to obtain informed consent from the subjects of their own research, they are offered no protection against the anonymous respondents to questionnaires that affect their fates.

It is also curious that although teaching evaluations have been in use since the 1970s, no overall improvements in the scores of instructors have been reported. This seems to negate the main purpose that was widely stated when student evaluations of teachers was introduced. Perhaps this is partly because such evaluations are used in the competition for salary increases—high-scoring teachers are reluctant to share their successful techniques, and lower-scoring teachers remain silent about their need for help. Thus,

> it is never altogether clear if the drive for teaching evaluation reflects, as is usually claimed, the desire to "improve" teaching, or to rationalize teaching, or to maximize and enforce the control of teaching. In each and every case we see how equivocal these questions remain. If the replacement of old-fashioned registration in the gymnasium or fieldhouse by voice enrollment, of small classes by large classes, or of personal feedback by standardized evaluations, reflects the bureaucratization of the university, such trends are only the tip of the iceberg. (Blum, 1991, p. 28)

To summarize, the demoralization of teaching results from its deprofessionalization as a calling. This demoralization, caused by the long-term structural disjunctions in American society and precipitated by short-term demographic, economic, and ideological pressures on universities, reflects the subversion of education by a system that pushes for formal assessments of its own instrumental efficiency. As a result, education is reduced to training or socialization, and educators are disheartened and alienated from students and from one another. They cannot readily offer appropriate role models within the bureaucratized university. Nor can they easily engage in intellectual exchange with their harried, specialized, and competitive peers. It is therefore unlikely that students will identify with an academic reference group, assimilate intellectual values, and become self-motivated participants in the conversation that is expected to take place within a community of scholars.

THE COMMERCIALIZATION OF SCHOLARSHIP

The short-term pressures on universities have fostered the collapse of basic research into applied. What Robert Nisbet (1996) calls the academic dogma was the belief that the mission of the academy is the pursuit of knowledge for its own sake. This "dogma" was inherited from Athens and institutionalized in the medieval university. The measure of a university's greatness and of the stature of an individual scholar was ideally determined not by the immediate usefulness of their work, but by how much it contributed to our search for understanding and truth about humanity and nature. This indeed remained central even with the rise of research universities in the nineteenth century and their more complete fusion of knowledge and power. What has become most important today, however, is the amount of funds obtained by researchers, regardless of the civic or intellectual merits of the work proposed. This was shown, for example, in the agreement reached between American researchers and France's Pasteur Institute over the sharing of credit, information, and royalties, which clearly recognized the profits that will go to those who first discover an antidote to AIDS. As the organized production of knowledge has expanded over the past few decades, it also has been increasingly conducted in the service and pay of governmental agencies and capitalist corporations. The connections between Stanford University and the Silicon Valley or between MIT and the Boston Route 128 high-tech corridor are only the most noted, or notorious, examples (Harvey, 1989, p. 160).

Similarly, as administrators have gone after previously neglected research funds, the distinction between basic and applied research and the preeminence of basic research have faded (Gumport, 1989). Many academic administrators have ceased to worry about the appropriateness or morality of research projects, and have even hired lobbyists to go after new sources of income. In general, money brought in has become the chief criterion used to evaluate the success of programs and professors. Knowledge, which institutions of higher learning are supposed to create and transmit, increasingly has become a commodity subject to the laws of deregulated market competition.

As individual careers become dependent on the amount of monies secured, however, cupidity tends to replace curiosity, and research agendas increasingly are set by the managers of the government and corporations, rather than the intellectual community itself. The ensuing definition of research objectives calls for projects that narrowly focus on immediately useful commercial, technical, military, or administrative results.

The social sciences no less than other fields of inquiry have been affected by the needs of the corporate state and a regression toward the mean of direct utility in the topics and methods of research (Brown, 1998, chap. 8). Indeed, some research programs, such as behavioral psychology, statistical sociology, criminology, and demography, were created almost entirely as creatures of statist and corporate funding in the interest of social control. This influence penetrated to the choice of research topics and methods, even to the conceptual apparatus of the disciplines themselves (Brown,

1998, chap. 7; Danziger, 1990; Reid, 1992). By the 1970s, for example, nationally projectionable survey research had become a task so complex and expensive that only larger-scale institutes could finance, staff, and sustain it. Bureaucratic research centers emerged which had the capacity to produce, store, and exchange great quantities of data (Lyon, 1994). Politically, the "findings" of such studies become almost uncontestable. Who, after all, has $1,000,000 to verify or challenge the initial survey that was projected statistically to represent the entire nation? Who, indeed? The same sources and interests that funded the initial study.

The intellectual trivialization of a large part of research is paralleled by the trivialization of its evaluation. For example, even though sociologists of science remind other researchers that citation indexes provide information about invisible colleges and power networks, "number of citations" is used by sociologists themselves as an unequivocal indicator of the value of the work of their colleagues, regardless of whether references are positive or negative (see Fuller in this volume). As celebrity based on visibility replaces fame based on achievement, and as there is no such thing as bad publicity, academic life becomes akin to politics or show business. As a result, evaluators treat the first name to appear in a joint publication as that of the senior contributor, and consider joint publications as less significant than solos, despite the emphasis placed by the official ideology on cooperation and joint ventures. Journals also are rated according to perceived prestige. These prestige numbers, multiplied by the number of articles, discounted for co-authorship, and added to the citation index, thus yield a single figure that can be used to indicate scholarly productivity. This Taylorism of the mind enables administrators and colleagues to evaluate the quality of each other's research without ever having to read it—a good thing, too, since, given the hyperspecialization of the academy, such reading likely would not enhance comprehension.

The trivialization of evaluations of research is matched by the trivialization of much research itself. For example, in 1990 the Institute for Scientific Information, which compiles indexes of scientific papers, counted how often papers in the top 4,500 (out of 74,000) science journals had been referred to in later papers. They found that 45% of these supposedly top-quality papers, published between 1981 and 1985, received not a single citation in the five years afterward. The implication is that much of the "top" scientific work in this country, and presumably much more of the "lesser" work, is basically without significance, in the sense that it does not appear to be part of any network of scientific influence nor to have any impact on future research. Universities count for about 50% of the overall scientific research in the United States. Research conducted in the private sector or government tends to be almost entirely "applied" and without general intellectual import.

The commercialization of scholarship also can be in the marketing of professors as symbols, especially those who have

> acquired a reputation among the general public. Nobel Prize winners are espe-
> cially valuable commodities as are those professors whose journalistic skills
> lead them to be published in the daily press and popular magazines. In recent
> times, the designation Distinguished Professor has come into common use.
> Funding for these positions is provided by a philanthropic patron whose name
> is given to the professorship. While the inflationary use of this method has led
> to the appointments of undistinguished Distinguished Professors, it remains
> the executive's method of first choice, having the triple advantage of satisfying
> the ego of the patron, of creating endowments to cover the costs of a salary
> and of advertising a distinguished faculty. (Vidich, 1994, p. 664; see Crane,
> 1965; Gumport, 1989, p. 20; Noble, 1977; and, for a contrary view, Geiger,
> 1986)

This system of celebrity tends to differentiate professors into stars and deadwood, with the criteria of funds raised and research becoming pub-licized paramount over the quality of scholarship and teaching. As these "criteria are re-constituted and internalized by faculty . . . the dynamics that produce a stratified system of organizations seem to produce stratified iden-tities as well. If one is labeled as deadwood, and especially if one feels dismissed without the work actually being reviewed, one may start acting like deadwood [and] the labeling becomes self-fulfilling. . . . Thus, the star system suggests a more painful and divisive differentiation in the academic profession than the sector-specific fragmentation that other scholars have described" (Gumport, 1989, p. 25; see Alpert, 1985; Bird & Allen, 1989; Seashore, Blumenthal, Gluck, & Stoto, 1989). The paradigm that commer-cializes research also renders invisible and thus unimportant scholarship in the pursuit of justice, even though such scholarship is not inherently incompatible with the production of knowledge.

Research is demoralized because it is less and less guided by its own internal standards of excellence, including ethical concerns. Instead, what counts is the size of the funding, the celebrity of the results, and the utility of the research within the status quo, defined by governmental and corpo-rate funders rather than the researcher's capacity to deepen a tradition, inspire surprise, generate competing hypotheses, or enlighten the public. Thus, much research has become intellectually amoral, though still ac-cepted as moral because it is lucrative and not illegal. Under the guise of objectivity, value freedom, and relevance, and in response to administrative pressures and state, corporate, or foundation funding, researchers commercialize their work and avoid unpopular questions, methods, or results.

DISCUSSION AND CONCLUSIONS

One hundred years ago, Nietzsche observed that the educational systems of the Western world "share the same striving to achieve the greatest possible expansion of education and the same tendency to minimize it and to weaken it." These symptoms persist today, though in differing cultural forms. In some contexts, liberals continue to define formal schooling as the most powerful instrument of popular liberation, whereas conservatives seek to restrict the educational system to the reproduction of elites or the production of appropriately skilled and disciplined workers. In other contexts, radicals criticize universities and colleges as being elitist, whereas liberals use educational expansion to avoid changes in the underlying economic structures that generate inequality.

Increased bureaucratization and commercialization of teaching and research is typical of all highly industrialized nations, though it takes particular forms in the United States. In such societies, the reduction of any activity to mere quantitative terms minimizes the moral involvement of individual actors. Teaching is no different in this regard. It becomes just another job, rather than a calling. The same holds true of learning, as American students learn to "psych out" instructors or to focus on the number of pages required for an assignment and the proportion of the final grade it represents. Further, the stress on making education relevant to students' needs places learning experiences in the private realm, thereby limiting the role of education in social transformation. Instead, universities, colleges, and other schools tend to uncritically reproduce existing social forms, including their inequities and delusions.

All educational systems are confronted with dilemmas of autonomy versus responsiveness, access versus excellence, external control versus self-governance, or narrowly defined market skills versus general intellectual and civic competencies. But the balance between these sets of poles and the responses invented by the members of each system are culturally and historically specific. In the case of the United States, we have tried to show how the short-term demographic, economic, and ideological pressures exerted on institutions of higher learning amplify the long-term contradictions of their decentralized structures and the utilitarian orientations of American society. We have suggested how the combined effects of the bureaucratization of higher education, the diffusion of consumerism in the educational realm, and the persistence of a private and decentralized vision of universities create a malaise in the academy.

In our exploration of the links between the long- and short-term ambiguities of the American educational system, we have used the notion of reproduction, suggesting that postindustrial societies, like all societies, reproduce themselves. We have gone beyond the notion of reproduction, however, for several reasons. First, schools remain relatively autonomous of other societal institutions and are not wholly constrained to do the bidding of current elites. An example of the relative autonomy of universities is provided by an incident at the Columbia University School of Business in 1987. When one of the professors offered $100,000 finder fees to the students of his course on mergers and takeovers, he was overruled by the dean, who claimed that this was inconsistent with academic ethics. As another example, in the same year the president of the University of Rochester bowed to pressure by officials of Kodak, a lavish patron of that institution, to forbid the admission of Japanese students to the business program. Yet this capitulation was successfully resisted by outraged faculty who appealed to the board of trustees.

Of course, these two examples may be construed either as atypical exceptions or as evidence that academic administrators defend long-term ideological interests of the entire capitalist class rather than the short-term concerns of specific firms or individuals. Yet it remains the case that educational actors are selective about what components of the currently prevailing social and cultural order they choose to reproduce. Universities *are* dominated by boards composed of corporate elites and they *do* have hidden and overt curricula that promote uniformity. Yet people with more schooling still manage to acquire more democratic personalities and values than those with a lower level of educational attainment. Moreover, the many redeeming features of the system should be acknowledged—for example, that significant opportunities have been opened up for previously excluded groups, that there is a competitively high level of scholarship to be found in most fields at the top postgraduate departments, and that genuine efforts are being made to create pluralistic discourses within many colleges and universities.

Moreover, it remains true that schools are more democratic than workplaces. Women and minorities face less discrimination in schools than on the job. Students have more rights of political expression and participation than workers. Spending on different schools is more equal than differentials in workers' incomes. From a strict Marxist or functionalist perspective, this is a paradox: If schools are to prepare students for work in an unequal, repressive capitalist system, why do they have a democratic character at all? But, as Carnoy and Levin (1985) argued, in some periods the schools are influenced by egalitarian social movements, while at other times economic and cultural forces push the schools in a more conservative direction. In the American political system, schools are subject to conflicting forces. Working-class movements, the civil rights movement, and the women's movement, among others, have undercut capitalist efforts to make the schools into narrow training grounds for future employees. This in part explains the "paradox" that schools are more democratic than workplaces. Similarly,

> it is often argued, especially by those on the left, that the best universities are training grounds for children of the upper and upper-middle classes. They are being prepared for succession, for continuation of class rule. Those institutions, it is said, with some supporting evidence, are controlled by members of the ruling class and they are thought to be ardent defenders of the status quo. This might be the case with respect to governing boards, but the students in those institutions, especially those in the liberal-left fields, are likely to be receiving an education that would challenge inherited privilege. Where meritocratic practice prevents the entry of upper-class children into the best universities, they would probably fall back on the best of the liberal arts colleges where currently the liberal and leftist political orientations are [even] more strongly represented. Working-class and lower-middle class children, in contrast, are most likely to be educated by conservative and moderate professors in two-year institutions and comprehensive universities. (Hamilton & Hargens, 1993, p. 621)

Hence, we reject simplistic notions of educational superstructures being epiphenomenal of a capitalist base, or of the universities as simply a medium of social reproduction. In our view, both bases and superstructures are composed of discursive practices, and both are therefore subject to "mechanical" as well as "interpretative" forms of reproduction. Further, the distinction between base and superstructure refers both to relations between the broader political economy and the universities, and to relations between the material organization of schools and the practice of scholarship and teaching within them. Given the relative autonomy of educational institutions, the professoriate, and even disciplines, it remains open as to whether the "externalist" or "internalist" explanations will be the most fruitful to explore. Accordingly, it is not sufficient to assert only that educational strategies reproduce the structural components of the current society. The further task is to ascertain how long and by what means it takes for changes in such structural components or elite interests to be translated into new educational strategies. More pointedly, we must ask how long it takes for shifts from competitive to oligopolistic to transnational forms of capitalism to affect American educational structures and processes, and by what mechanisms and in what ways they may be so. And we must ask how more democratic forms of the relationships between capital and the academy might be achieved by popular social movements and by professors and students themselves.

Similarly, we must ask questions concerning the state's interventions in the educational realm. When does centralization stifle individual creativity and create rigid orthodoxies that discourage innovations? When does it maximize equality of access and minimize provincial fiefdoms of incompetence? Alternatively, when does *de*centralization provide the appropriate organizational infrastructure for social experimentations and fruitful competition? And under what conditions is decentralization a pretext to justify anarchic narcissism and the triumph of various cultural fundamentalisms? All these caveats and distinctions are especially important with reference to the American system of higher education, which is one of the world's most sprawling, heterogeneous, and diverse.

CONCLUSION

Our analysis highlights ambiguities in the notion of reproduction and in the policies that may be derived from it. The contradictions of higher education become most visible when economic, demographic, and ideological forces create a hiatus between aspirations of continuous progress and upward mobility, and the experience of a world of increased class divisions and ecological constraints.

The concept of reproduction becomes conceptually limited and politically retrograde when it is used to implicitly justify the *status quo ante* and to release intellectuals from their obligation to offer alternative visions to the American public of what can be known and, implicitly, what we might become. This is because we also reproduce our own practices, institutions, and selves, and we do retain some discretion in this process. And thus we can seek to reproduce our own environments as ones of critical discourse and prudent judgment that serve as models for a possible civic life. Higher education, and especially higher public education, can be about educating a public for a higher, more reflexive and self-directing democratic life.

REFERENCES

Alpert, D. (1985). Performance and paralysis: The organizational context of the American research university. *Journal of Higher Education, 56,* 241–281.

Altbach, P. (1995). Introduction. In L. Wilson, *The academic man: A study in the sociology of profession* (pp. iii–xxvii). New Brunswick, NJ: Transaction.

Apple, M. (1993). Constructing the "other": Reconstructions of common sense. In C. McCarthy & W. Crichlow (Eds.), *Race, identity, and representation in education* (pp. 24–39). New York: Routledge.

Beverly, J. (1978). Higher education and capitalist crisis. *Socialist Review, 8*(6), 67–91.

Bird, B., & Allen, D. (1989). Faculty entrepreneurship in research university environments. *Journal of Higher Education, 60*(5), 583–596.

Blum, A. (1991). The melancholy life world of the university. *Dianoia, 3,* 16–42.

Bochow, M. (1985). Review of Finkelstein (1984). *American Journal of Sociology, 89*(5), 1481–1484.

Bock, J. C., & Papagiannis, G. J. (1983). *Nonformal education and national development.* New York: Praeger.

Bourdieu, P., & Passeron, J.-C. (1990). *Reproduction in education, society, and culture.* London: Sage.

Brown, R. H. (1998). *Toward a democratic science: Scientific narration and civic communication.* New Haven, CT: Yale University Press.

Carnoy, M., & Levin, H. M. (1985). *Schooling and work in the democratic state.* Stanford, CA: Stanford University Press.

Cheney, L. V. (1989). *50 hours: A core curriculum for college students.* Washington, D.C.: National Endowment for the Humanities.

Collins, R. (1979). *The credential society: An historical sociology of education and stratification.* New York: Academic Press.

Crane, D. (1965). Scientists at major and minor universities: A study of productivity and recognition. *American Sociological Review, 30,* 699–714.

Danziger, K. (1990). *Constructing the subject: Historical origins of psychological research.* New York: Cambridge University Press.

D'Souza, D. (1992). *Illiberal education: The politics of race and sex on campus.* New York: Vantage.

Finkelstein, M. J. (1984). *The American academic profession: A synthesis of social scientific inquiry since World War II.* Columbus: Ohio State University Press.

Frederickson, G. M. (1997, October 23). America's caste system: Will it change? *New York Review of Books,* 68–75.

Geiger, T. (1986). The mass society of the present. In R. Mayntz (Ed.), *Theodor Geiger on social order and mass society* (pp. 169–184). Chicago: University of Chicago Press.

Giroux, H. A. (1983). *Theory and resistance in education: A pedagogy for the opposition.* South Hadley, MA: Bergin and Garvey.

Glazer, N. (1997). *We are all multiculturalists now.* Cambridge, MA: Harvard University Press.

Gumport, P. J. (1989). *The research initiative.* Unpublished manuscript, School of Education, Stanford University.

Hamilton, R. F., & Hargens, L. L. (1993). The politics of professors: Self-identifications, 1969–1984. *Social Forces, 71*(3), 603–627.

Harvey, D. (1989). *The condition of postmodernity: An enquiry into the origin of cultural change.* Cambridge, MA: Blackwell.

Hirsch, E. D. (1987). *Cultural literacy: What every American needs to know.* Boston: Houghton Mifflin.

Jardine, A. (1995). Illiberal reporting. In C. Newfield & R. Strickland (Eds.), *After political correctness: The humanities and society in the 1990s* (pp. 87-121). Boulder, CO: Westview Press.

King, M. L. (1964). *Why we can't wait.* New York: Signet.

Lasch, C. (1979). *The culture of narcissism.* New York: Norton.

Lyon, D. (1994). *The electronic eye.* Minneapolis: University of Minnesota Press.

Mayes, S. S. (1977). The democratization of higher education. *Journal of Educational Thought, 11*(11), 16-27.

Mayhew, L. B. (1977). *Legacy of the seventies: Experiment, economy, equality and expediency in American higher education.* San Francisco: Jossey-Bass.

Messer-Davidow, E. (1995). Manufacturing the attack on liberalized higher education. In C. Newfield & R. Strickland (Eds.), *After political correctness: The humanities and society in the 1990s* (pp. 122-151). Boulder, CO: Westview Press.

Nisbet, R. (1996). *The degradation of the academic dogma.* New Brunswick, NJ: Transaction.

Noble, D. (1977). *America by design: Science, technology, and the rise of corporate capitalism.* New York: Alfred A. Knopf.

Oakeshott, M. (1959). *The voice of poetry in the conversation of mankind.* London: Bowes and Bowes.

O'Toole, J. (1975, May/June). The reserve army of the unemployed I and II. *Change,* pp. 114-122.

Reibstein, L. (1998, December 29/January 5). What color is an A? *Newsweek,* 76-78.

Reid, H. G. (1992). Review of Bruce Weilshire's *The moral collapse of the university. Educational Studies, 23*(2), 309-315.

Rubin, B. (Ed.). (1994). *Quality in higher education.* New Brunswick, NJ: Transaction.

Seashore, K., Blumenthal, D., Gluck, M., & Stoto, M. (1989). Entrepreneurs in academe: An exploration of behaviors among life scientists. *Administrative Science Quarterly, 34*(1), 110-131.

Sniderman, P. M., & Piazza, T. (1993). *The scar of race.* Cambridge, MA: Harvard University Press.

Soley, L. C. (1995). *Leasing the ivory tower: The corporate takeover of academia.* Boston: South End Press.

Stanley, M. (1981). *The technological conscience: Survival and dignity in an age of expertise.* Chicago: University of Chicago Press.

Stanley, M. (1986). *Can American pluralism tolerate civic education? An examination of the status of civic rhetoric in America.* Unpublished manuscript, Department of Sociology, Syracuse University.

Thompson, M. (1979). *Rubbish theory: The creation and destruction of value.* New York: Oxford University Press.

Tuckman, H. P., Caldwell, J., & Fogler, W. (1978). Part-timers and the academic labor market of the eighties. *The American Sociologist, 13* (November), 184–195.

Vidich, A. J. (1994). The higher learning in America in Veblen's time and our own. *International Journal of Politics, Culture, and Society,* 7(4), 639–668.

Weiss, M. J. (1988). *The clustering of America: A vivid portrait of the nation's 40 neighborhood types—Their values, lifestyles and eccentricities.* New York: Harper & Row.

Wilke, A. (Ed.). (1979). *The hidden professoriate: Credentialism, professionalism, and the tenure crisis.* Westport, CT: Greenwood.

THREE

SCIENCE AS A VOCATION
Circa 2000

STEVEN FULLER

ALTHOUGH MAX WEBER may have been more nuanced than Karl Marx in his understanding of the relationship between economic and cultural change, he would be an easy mark for today's academic administrators, who promote a close fit between successful business firms and successful universities. Careful readers of the original 1918 "Science as a Vocation" cannot fail to detect Weber's captivation by the ideology of enterprise that characterized the United States in the early twentieth century (Weber, 1958, especially pp. 129–131). While he may have been careful to distinguish the calling of academics from that of politicians, Weber uncritically embraced the analogy between business and academia. Luckily for his posthumous reputation, Weber's critics were equally oblivious, as they fixated on the physics-based model of inquiry that was in the process of replacing the humanist-based model of *Wissenschaft*. Thus, Weber's most incisive contemporary critic, the Latinist Ernst Robert Curtius (1989), objected to a definition of science that did not require inquirers to realize the ends of inquiry in their professional lives. Curtius harkened back to the liberal arts model of the unity of teaching and research that had lost credibility with the disciplinary fragmentation that had come to be institutionalized even at the time of Weber's address.

Nowadays, equipped with 20/20 hindsight, we pretend to understand these matters much better than Weber did. But, of course, the cost of every error corrected is a new error committed. On the one hand, the spirit of enterprise that Weber found in the American academy was seen by Americans as itself a German adaptation, specifically of the Kaiser Wilhelm Institutes (today called the Max Planck Institutes), which were unique in their day in treating the research site as a crucible for forging together academic, state, and industrial interests (Conant, 1970, pp. 69–72). On the other hand, in recent years, science policy gurus have forgotten this ancient history altogether, making it appear that the industrialization of science is a product of World War II and, more importantly, that it has been largely for the better in fostering a spirit of interdisciplinary inquiry (Gibbons, 1994). Lost from this view of history is that the experimental natural sciences historically have been the main vehicle by which industrial and commercial concerns have permeated academia, largely in the face of resistance from the traditional liberal arts culture, which disdained of machinery and manual labor on university grounds. And the time lag between the establishment of laboratories at major universities in Europe and the United States and the profusion of industrial concerns on campuses is approximately one generation: from the third to the fourth quarter of the nineteenth century. We are now completing the first century of this transition, which, to my mind, is more important than the so-called Scientific Revolution of the seventeenth century.

The result is that in recent times, the academic community has embodied a paradox. On the one hand, we have persuaded many nonacademics that history has recently entered a "postindustrial" phase, whereby the endless production and accumulation of material goods are no longer the driving forces of the human condition. This is the so-called Knowledge Society that we currently inhabit. On the other hand, our professional consciousness remains very much captive to the old industrial mindset. Even an expression as innocuous-sounding as "knowledge production," which freely tumbles from academic lips, immediately calls to mind the manufacture of products—specifically books and articles: the more the faster, the better. To sound a familiar Marxist theme, the meaning of our labor has come to be identified with its products, the ultimate fates of which we are in less and less of a position to control. University administrators merely articulate this subtle form of capitalist alienation when they characterize the need to shift faculty energies from research to teaching as a reorientation of the academic enterprise from "producing goods" to "distributing services."

I shall reflect on the origins and implications of our lingering industrial mindset, the new sense of marginalization that has resulted, and what we may do about it. To capture the spirit of my argument, consider the entry that "Knowledge Society" would receive in *The Devil's Companion to Social Theory*:

Knowledge Society (K.S.). n. What advanced capitalism looks like to intellectuals, once they have been assimilated into its mode of production—a classic case of what economists call the "internalization of a negative externality." Intellectuals specialize in two sorts of activities: moralizing and criticizing, which are typically deployed against the powers that be.

However, with the right incentives, they can be just as easily deployed on their behalf. Thus, intellectuals may be made to moralize by appealing to norms that, at the same time, function as principles for reproducing the social order. They can even be motivated to criticize each other in ways that not only distract them from criticizing the powers that be, but also enable those powers to appropriate whatever survives the criticism. The roots of K.S. predate advanced capitalism, reaching back to the reconstitution of the university as the "spiritual infrastructure" of the nineteenth-century nation–state, starting in Prussia. Faced with the inadequacy of the old feudal-clerical order's response to Napoleon, Wilhelm von Humboldt came up with the inspired idea of coopting the intellectuals, many of whom had been sympathetic to Napoleon, by declaring the university the natural home of "Enlightenment." In one fell swoop, free-floating gadflies were flattened into civil servants. Over the course of the century, the critical spirit of Enlightenment metamorphosed into a guild right under the rubric of "academic freedom," which was most definitely not to be confused with the sort of "license" that would be routinely censured in the public sphere (see Weber, 1958). An important turning point was the Franco–Prussian War of 1870-71, in which Germany's victory was widely attributed to the rapid conversion of its industrial base for military use, which was in turn attributed to its relatively high level of technically skilled personnel who could be mobilized at a moment's notice. This led to periodic calls across the industrialized world (usually made in anticipation of wars) to increase the level of scientific and technical training in the general public. The universities duly expanded to meet the new demand, and soon academics were in the business of administering "aptitude tests," standardizing school curricula, and certifying the credentials of an increasing number of people in fields of employment. They became quality control checkpoints for the new military–industrial order. In addition, educational achievement became the "democratic" principle of social structure that eroded traditional class and status barriers to social mobility. This principle was most celebrated as "meritocracy" during the Cold War period of the 1950s through the 1970s, the time when K.S. is first formally identified. However, with the end of the Cold War, K.S. ideology has begun to buckle under the strain of capitalist expansion. Two general signs stand out: (a) Credentials have gone the way of other forms of social discrimination. It is slowly becoming clear that just as race and class were never especially good performance indicators, neither is the possession of academic credentials. The point is not obvious because formal education has permitted social advancement for an unprecedented number of previously excluded groups, but at the cost of eliminating alternative paths of advancement, including on-the-job experience. However, if total war no longer seems likely and "the market" gets its way, the credentials monopoly currently enjoyed by universities may be punctured by corporate-sponsored training centers, perhaps as part of an omnibus devolution of the welfare state to private sector agencies. (b) Ironically, a surfeit of academically qualified people has given the competitive edge to those who possess nonacademic, specifically entrepreneurial, forms of knowledge. This is no more evident than in the sciences themselves. The "expert" scientist enters and exits lines of research just ahead of the pack, invests in skills and equipment that are usable in the widest variety of projects, and constructs her knowledge products so as to extract a certain "tribute" (be it an attribution in a citation list or a financial tribute in patent royalties) from their users. At the limit, "knowledge engineers" design computers that simulate a field's expertise and thereby eliminate still more academic competitors. The raw material for the simulations is experts who gladly sell their knowledge in the face of eventual obsolescence.

  Related Concepts: 1. *Credential Society*—used somewhat cynically to refer to K.S. in its latest, decadent phase of credential inflation. 2. *Information Society*—used by both boosters and critics of K.S. to highlight technology's role in the construction of K.S.; boosters tend to focus on the high-grade (and very impersonal) knowledge it takes to program computers and other electronic media, whereas critics focus on the low-grade (but very personal) knowledge that is collected and distributed on such media. 3. *Postindustrial Society*—used somewhat obscurantistly to suggest that because Marx failed to predict the end of capitalism, he was therefore wrong about the relentless expansion of capitalist logic into every sphere of social life (Harvey, 1989). 4. *Risk Society*—used to capture the management of uncertainty, be it in terms of distributing potential costs and benefits across various social sectors or creating a generalized sense of risk on the basis of which authority is challenged.

SCIENCE AS POLITICS BY OTHER MEANS

Higher education in the twentieth century has made great strides to incorporate people who have been historically marginalized on the basis of gender, ethnic background, and ideological persuasion. In most of these cases, the marginalization had been more or less intended. However, the upscaling of the academic enterprise since World War II and especially during the 1960s and 1970s—the increasing numbers of people who have become professional academics along with the enormous resources that have been lavished on university-based pursuits—have brought on a more insidious form of marginalization, insidious because it is an unintended consequence of the academy's newfound expansiveness. In fact, this form of marginalization is so insidious that it is now just as likely to affect straight white males from Oxbridge and the Ivy League as colleagues with contrary qualifications. I am speaking, of course, of the marginalization that results from one's published work going unread, undiscussed, uncited—and even when cited, cited in an omnibus fashion, as part of a list of names whose company the author had perhaps taken great pains *not* to keep.

When Weber delivered "Science as a Vocation," he stressed the subtle but real personal satisfaction one could derive from a life of scholarship, even knowing that one's work would be surpassed by future scholars. Of course, Weber was assuming that scholarly work would be *read*. However, this is an all too big assumption to make these days, a deceptive tale that we continue relating to aspiring academics. Epistemologists who like to see the pursuit of inquiry in Darwinian terms are inclined to think that today's research is born into a world where survival depends on a process of critical scrutiny that resembles natural selection. It is expected that few pieces of research will survive intact across a variety of critical environments. But this is perhaps to misconstrue the relevant analogue. For it would be truer to our current predicament to say that most of today's research fails to survive because it perishes once it is published—stillborn, as it were—never quite connecting with an environment long enough for other scholars to subject it to critical scrutiny. I resort to such grim metaphors in order to impress on the reader that being ignored is not a sophisticated form of criticism, however much our radical fantasies may tell us otherwise.

As with so many of the other ailments of contemporary academic life, the natural sciences have displayed the most exaggerated symptoms of the marginalization I describe. But the social sciences and humanities are following close on their heels. Credit for uncovering these symptoms in the 1960s belongs to the sociologist Robert Merton (1973, part 5) and the historian Derek de Solla Price (1978). Unfortunately, they interpreted the emerging behemoth as speaking to the health, not the illness, of what Price called "Big Science" (cf. Turner & Chubin, 1976). To appreciate this point, consider the lengths to which Merton, Price, and their followers have been willing to go to portray the pursuit of knowledge as a massive industrial enterprise—but one that exhibits only the positive features of scientific and technological progress. Their most concrete legacy is the *Science Citation Index (SCI)* and the attendant use of citation counts as indicators of quality, relevance, and influence. Even humanists and social scientists find it difficult to resist measuring their careers in terms of the droppings left at the foot of other people's articles.

SCI discriminates between research contributions in rather crude ways for reasons that have largely to do with the massive labor costs originally associated with compiling and processing the citations (Fuller, 1997, p.

69ff). Normally attention is focused on the distribution of citations among those cited. Generally speaking, the harder the science, the more easily identifiable the research frontier, as an increasing percentage of citations concentrate on a vanishingly small group of authors, virtually all of whom are currently active contributors to the field. Yet, to understand the social psychology of the citation process, we must examine the role of *citers,* the vast majority of whom are anonymous and ultimately forgotten in the great mass of unread material to which their efforts unwittingly contribute. Regardless of how much they are cited by others, an author who cites 30 works in her article exerts 10 times more influence over the final citation count than one who cites only 3. This is a rather curious result for an enterprise like science, which has been periodically advertised as the paradigm case of democracy in action.

In most democratic theories of voting, whenever one can vote for more than one candidate, the votes are treated as fractions adding up to one, so that each voter formally exerts the same influence over the electoral process, and voters with distributed allegiances are not privileged. The only major exception is the system of multiple voting for university dons and graduates that John Stuart Mill advocated until everyone met (what Mill regarded as) the basic educational requirements for full political participation. However, Mill would have been shocked by the kind of multiple voting permitted—and perhaps even encouraged—by *SCI* citation counts. In essence, authors who acknowledge a large number of scholarly debts—as measured by the citations they bestow on their colleagues—exert a disproportionate control over the structure of knowledge in their field. Imagine a polity that by its electoral system discourages its citizens from being economically self-sufficient and ideologically focused. This, then, is the sense of scientific self-governance implicitly promoted by *SCI.*

The reader may regard what I have just described as a formula for producing the kind of "dependency culture" that is the dark side of the welfare state. Certainly, from an economic standpoint, a debtor-driven market looks less than rational. Whereas debts usually accumulate around those whose capital assets can be independently assessed, in science one's capital assets grow in proportion to the number of colleagues who perceive it in their interest to openly acknowledge a debt. This is an instance of Pierre Bourdieu's (1990) "symbolic capital" at work with a vengeance: The size of your capital is determined exactly by the degree to which others recognize it. Of course, this is not entirely a case of backward causation and spontaneous judgments of whose work is likely to matter in the long run. There is a material basis, but it will remain obscure as long as systematic correlations between citation counts and research finances (including not only outright grants but also the fixed capital embedded in university infrastructures) continue to be regarded in poor taste. At this point, it is easy to imagine how Bronislaw Malinowski (1984) must have felt when he tried to present the Trobriand Islanders with naturalistic explanations for why rain dances seem to bring about rain (when they do).

Are less explicitly political accounts any more rational in their explanation of scientists' citing practices? I am afraid not. There is a school of thought that regards the bestowal of citations as less an act of affiliation than of *differentiation*. Though often associated with evolutionary theory, in practice it looks more like a mutant form of cell division theory—a "carcinomic" model of science! Both the historian Thomas Kuhn and the sociologist Niklas Luhmann have had their names attached to such euphemistically entitled "autopoietic" or "self-organizational" models of scientific change. Central to the plot of both is that science becomes autonomous from the larger social environment sometime in its history (say, with the founding of the Royal Society)—not merely in the sense of science being protected from ambient social pressures, but more importantly in terms of science's development being defined exclusively in the scientists' own terms. In practice, this means that the invisible hand of peer review miraculously discriminates important from unimportant research as the overall result of a set of privately taken decisions in referees' reports. Autonomy in this sense enables science to simulate the frictionless medium of thought that philosophers since Plato have considered ideal to the pursuit of knowledge. Consequently, neither Kuhn (1970) nor Luhmann (1995) has much to say about the material requirements of scientific knowledge. Rather, they present a seemingly irreversible, if strictly nonteleological, story of functional differentiation of the scientific enterprise as inquirers encounter impasses in the day-to-day business of puzzle-solving that force them to divide their efforts in order to clarify the overall direction of their inquiries.

These impasses are registered as acts of differentiating oneself from previous researchers. And to be sure, the more citations you give to others in such an act, the more focused your own contribution to the knowledge system appears. But for that very reason, the less significant your contribution will likely appear in the long run, precisely because you have defined it so narrowly. Indeed, given the vagaries of institutional memory that collapse the complexity of the historical record of any generation into a few distinguished inquirers, the ironic long-term consequence of your careful efforts at differentiation will simply be to raise the citation counts of those from whom you distinguished yourself. Your own contribution will probably be lost in the process. The easiest way around this eventuality is to cite yourself a lot, and hope that the self-promotion will drive others to promote you—at least by attacking what you cite so frequently! A subtler course of action is to become part of a mutual citation network: that is, to cite others who cite you. Once *SCI* defined the "impact factor" of a journal in terms of the frequency with which articles published in the journal are cited, it turned out that *Social Studies of Science,* the premier journal in the sociology of science, scored consistently highest in this factor. Could this be because the editor decided to apply one of the field's key findings to itself? If so, it would provide further evidence of the time-honored maxim that "If you can't beat 'em, join 'em," since arguably the original aim of the sociology of science was to expose the sources of science's power to critique (for further elaboration, see Fuller, 1999, chap. 7).

Most democratic theories presume that voters cast their ballots fully realizing that their vote is a scarce resource: to give to one is to withhold from another. Of course, scholarly citing practices are no less strategic, but scarcity does not play quite the same normative role. When each citation, but not each citer, is weighted equally, it becomes impossible to detect the deliberate enhancing or withholding of credit. The received view is that scientists cite simply because their knowledge claims demand that they do. The implied image of the citing scientist is one devoid of agency, which in turn creates the impression that a science is a spontaneously self-organizing field of activity that can be monitored as one would any other object of enquiry; hence, the expression *science of science.* Moreover, although *SCI* formally masks the strategic character of citing behavior, once the citation counts are made public, the scientists can adjust their citing strategies. In a political system that enables one to cast a nonexclusive vote for a candidate, there will be a tendency to err on the side of voting beyond one's preferences, that is, to vote for every minimally acceptable candidate, so as to ensure that someone tolerable is elected. The corresponding tendency is for scientists to cite anyone who might have a hand in the fate of their article (or anyone whom such people would expect to see cited), lest the article be ignored and their next grant proposal go unfunded. Here we find Merton's fabulously mystified "communist" ethic, according to which scientists cannot tell the difference between protection money and selfless sharing. Be that as it may, by adhering to this norm, scientists end up inflating the citation counts of their colleagues who are regarded as even marginally powerful, which in turn enhances the power of those colleagues, as *SCI* indicators are fed into the larger science policy process.

Can anything be done about scientific citing practices to prevent Big Science's slender grip on democracy from dissolving into mafiosism? My recommendation here is to make the analogy between citing and voting as explicit as possible, so that both authors and readers of scientific texts are clear about the strategic character of situating one's work in a body of research. This would include restricting the number of citations that authors are permitted to make, and forcing them to allocate a fraction to each citation's significance so that the fractions assigned to all the citations add up to one. (That authors are already disciplined to conform to word limits bodes well for this stricture.) I would even go so far as to urge that both positive and negative citations be allocated from this single vote, so that authors are forced to decide whether they wish to be counted more as supporting certain claims than opposing others. One obvious consequence of taking this advice to heart is that citations can no longer be used as an "unobtrusive measure" of the overall trajectory of scientific research. However, as we shall now see, that might not be such a bad idea.

SCIENTIZING THE POLITICS OF SCIENCE

Soon after scientists started conspicuously using *SCI* to orient their research, science policymakers started using *SCI* to orient themselves to the scientists. Indeed, as an instrument of policy, *SCI* became an "unobtrusive measure" of the pace and direction of scientific activity that worked to check scientists' own self-interested testimony on these matters. Policymakers can justify funding decisions that go against the wishes of the scientific community by arguing that they are merely trying to promote tendencies already present in *SCI*-based indicators. In other words, actions that may appear disruptive at the local level of the individual scientist or research team reappear as supportive at the level of the "knowledge system" that *SCI*-based indicators are "about." The French postmodern philosopher Jean Baudrillard has coined the useful term "hyperreality" for a representation that, once extracted from the represented object, can be used as a standard against which to judge and shape that object, even though it is, strictly speaking, a fiction constructed by selectively attending to only some of the object's characteristics. In that sense, the knowledge system is a hyperreal entity. To gauge the full sense of *SCI*'s impact, we need to go deeper and plumb the industrial unconscious of the Knowledge Society.

Price operationally defined "science policy" as investment strategies for producing the largest number of highly cited articles. He coupled this assumption with an interesting statistical fact, namely, that the clearest economic indicator of scientific productivity (as measured by number of papers published per scientist) is national electrical consumption (as measured by kilowatt-hours per capita), which is in turn related to economic productivity (Gross National Product per capita) by a power of 3/2 (Price, 1978, p. 87). The coincidence was impressive: The top 10 producers of scientific knowledge are also the top 10 consumers of electrical energy, with the United States accounting for 25 to 35% of total production and consumption, respectively (see Olsen, 1992, for more recent confirmation). Price then proceeded to treat this correlation as the basis for an analogy, one that has served to legitimate the indefinite and perhaps even profligate growth of scholarly production in all the disciplines. Just as more customers can get cheaper electricity with a larger power station, Price reckoned, so too a scaled-up knowledge enterprise increases the likelihood that more scientists would produce citable papers—Price's measure of scholarly relevance and quality. The policy advice that followed was obvious: Increase the number of people and effort devoted to the production of scholarly papers.

Price's analogy highlights the extent to which science itself consumes resources, thereby reversing the economists' image of science as exclusively a "factor of production," a perpetual motion machine. By drawing attention to consumption patterns, Price unwittingly brought into the focus the question of waste in the scientific enterprise. Here I am reminded of Michael Polanyi's (1964) famous definition of free inquiry as the ability to waste resources with impunity in the name of truth. However, it is worth recalling that these resources include not only money, paper, machines, and energy, but most especially people. This point is papered over in what Robert Merton has euphemistically called science's "principle of cumulative advantage" (also known as the "Matthew Effect"), which, like capitalism's "invisible hand," is presented as a situation that appears cruel to individuals but eventuates in long-term systemic benefits. Accordingly, in science, those who are rewarded earlier (say, in terms of elite training, early posts, and publications) are rewarded more and longer, with the difference between the initially advantaged and disadvantaged increasing rapidly over time, such that two-thirds of scientists give up on publishing altogether after their first article.

As Social Darwinists of science policy, Merton (1967) and Price (1959) never suggested that this tendency should *discourage* the recruitment of new scientists, which would in turn downsize the scientific enterprise so that more of its participants would have a better chance of having their contributions recognized. On the contrary, Price stressed "economies of scale" as improving the overall quality of science. In other words, an ever-widening field of competitors would keep all scientists on their toes, which would in turn ensure their best performances, leading to an increase in the overall percentage of quality publications—not to mention an increase in the absolute number of unrecognized scientists "wasted" by the system. (The same argument can be taken back a step to justify scientists acquiring Ph.D.s before starting their careers. If credentials provide at least an indirect measure of likely achievement, and this fact is widely known, then all competitors will meet the highest standard they can, which of course will raise the quality of the average applicant while diminishing the advantage gained having that credential.) Merton went so far as to argue that if indeed genuine contributions to knowledge are likely to go unrecognized, disadvantaged scientists should try to get advantaged scientists to promote the findings as their own.

The idea of channeling enormous talent in the single-minded pursuit of inquiry was not itself a new idea. Precedents for its efficacy could be drawn from World War II, when many and diverse technical personnel were sequestered in secret locations for the purpose of achieving a specific large outcome in a race against time—most notably, the atomic bomb. Yet one might have reasonably thought that with the war won and the urgent backdrop to research removed, scientists would simply return to their original, smaller-scale enterprises. But because the atomic bomb was regarded by most people as a mixed blessing at best, there was a concerted effort by various American politicians and social scientists to ensure that such research would never be done again, and that the natural sciences would be made to serve exclusively peaceful purposes.

Many natural scientists saw the prospect of government regulation as ending the freedom they enjoyed during their years of federal patronage. True, the scientists behind the U.S. atomic bomb project were focused on goals not of their own making, but at the same time, they did not have to account for their activities on a day-to-day basis and, in fact, overran their budgets with impunity. The original goals were indeed achieved, and the instruments of destruction were wrought. Now if only this model could be sustained in peacetime! At least, this was what the defenders of natural sciences were hoping to pull off. And, for the most part, they did. How they did it is perhaps most persuasively presented in *The Endless Frontier* (Bush, 1945/1985), the report that Vannevar Bush wrote in support of the establishment of a National Science Foundation, a document that has set the tone for American science policy in the post–World War II period. The success of this document and attendant efforts lay in presenting the heavy industry model used to organize scientific labor for the war effort, not as a creature of expedience and urgency, but as a promethean principle with the potential to accelerate the course of inquiry in all the natural sciences. And with the work of Price and Merton, the model was presented as extendable to all scholarly endeavor.

ACADEMIA STRIKES BACK:
DISECONOMIZING THE SCALE OF SCIENCE

Let us look at Price's original analogy a little more closely. Efficiency is a relative notion, and the large-scale utilities that fascinated Price so much are efficient only in a very particular sense. Big plants produce more power but at a big cost to the environment, especially when measured in terms of the resources consumed by such plants that could have been used for other purposes, perhaps at another time. These are what economists call the "opportunity costs" of producing energy in this so-called efficient manner. As ordinary folks, we experience the costs as pollution and waste.

All of these observations apply analogically to the fates of the people who are pumped into a scaled-up knowledge enterprise. As more of the highly cited articles are produced, the difference between the number of citations garnered by such articles and by all the other articles also increases—and there are, of course, more of those other uncited articles in the knowledge system. Indeed, the long-term tendency is for larger knowledge enterprises to produce more articles by more people that fail to be cited in the articles of those diminishing few whose articles are cited frequently. One is reminded here of the income disparities between rich and poor—what used to be called "uneven development"—that are exacerbated when Third World countries go through a period of rapid industrialization. In academia as elsewhere in the capitalist world, the rich get richer and the poor get poorer. Indeed, it has become almost second nature for sociologists of science to speak of the social stratification of science in terms reminiscent of world-systems theory: a "core set" of front-line scientists, on the one hand, and a "peripheral" set of client-scientists, on the other (e.g., Pinch, 1990).

In addition to this bird's-eye view of the political economy of science, there is also a corresponding personal ideology whereby one learns to welcome the prospect of the more prominent knowledge producers presenting as their own the ideas of the less prominent knowledge producers. After all, so the ideology goes, this would seem to show that the knowledge system is ultimately just, since the really good ideas do manage to survive even if their originators quickly fade into oblivion. In fact, Merton has even suggested that given how the system works, truly selfless knowledge producers would turn over their best ideas to the people who they know will most likely draw attention to them.

By now we have charted a perverted course from Weber's humble toiler in the groves of academe. But the story takes even more tortured turns for the knowledge producers who manage to keep their citation counts high. Consider the steady stream of ignorable articles that are dumped into the knowledge system. Their presence threatens to overwhelm the knowledge producer's ability to detect the few articles that are worth citing in his or her own research. What is the knowledge producer to do? Well, basically, one circumvents the noise in the publication network by adopting alternative forms of communication. Just as the rich are able to solve the problem of pollution to their personal satisfaction by moving to cleaner neighborhoods, so too the major knowledge producers avoid the morass of journal literature by participating in so-called *invisible colleges* that circulate work in prepublication form, thereby enabling the relevant colleagues to get a head start on positioning their research programs and grant proposals.

In the natural sciences, the maneuvers of these epistemic cartels, these invisible colleges, have much of the character of insider trading in the stock market, where the stakes are very high indeed. Failure to equip one's lab with the right instruments and personnel within a limited amount of time can automatically eliminate the scientist from the cutting edge of research. More to the point, a failure to update one's research interests and skills in light of an ever-shifting research frontier can consign even a highly cited scientist to the academic backwaters. In this regard, one of Price's more memorable correlations is the index that bears his name. According to Price's Index, the "harder" a science is perceived to be (where physics is the hardest science of them all), the lower the average age of the literature cited in its articles. (In contrast, characteristic of literary criticism is that Plato is cited about as regularly as Stanley Fish.) It would seem that in the hard sciences, attention is just as difficult to sustain as it is to acquire. Here it is worth recalling that hard things are often the most brittle, and that science is no exception.

As to be expected, the career trajectories of scientists have adapted to the accelerated pace of inquiry, which an uncharitable soul might call "planned obsolescence." Each new scientific growth area calls for the mastery of new techniques and discourses that take more experienced researchers farther away from the intellectual capital they accumulated in graduate school. Rather than continuing to fight the uphill battle to remain in the front lines of research, scientists at ever-earlier ages—nowadays in their early 40s—shift over to the less technically demanding (though often just as stressful) work of full-time teaching or administration. But scientists are never formally instructed in these new academic roles; instead, they ease into the roles over time, operating on the hopeful assumption that competence in teaching or administration is a natural byproduct of having impeccable research credentials. Indeed, despite the sharp rise in the number of students matriculating in universities since 1945, the education they receive depreciates more quickly than ever before. This planned obsolescence enables more people to enter the system, secure in the knowledge that they will be uniquely qualified to tackle the problems of the day—that is, the problems of the day they graduate and perhaps the next few months!

BREAKING THE CHAIN OF HERMENEUTICAL COMMAND

So far my comments on invisible colleges have been limited to the services that their members perform for each other. However, these virtual institutions also act as opinion leaders that influence the spin that "lesser" knowledge producers end up giving to the journal literature they read, for even those who are not themselves part of an invisible college need some way of sorting through the surfeit of publications. The spin doctoring offered by an academic opinion leader is therefore welcomed and often actively sought. However, it has had some significant long-term effects on the reading and writing practices of inquirers, effects to which humanists have yet to give adequate reflection, even as these effects have begun to infect their own practices.

As indicated earlier, the hard sciences have distinctive textual practices that appear even at the level of citations. If an article is frequently cited, it will be cited for the same reason, which is usually localizable to a particular section of the article: its theoretical framework, its review of the literature, its research methodology, its data, or its analysis of the data. By contrast, highly cited articles in the softer sciences are cited for a variety of reasons in a variety of contexts (Cozzens, 1985). How is such a citing practice stabilized in the hard sciences? Some may wish to believe that these sciences are getting at some objective reality upon which all reasonable inquirers can agree. This would be nice if it were true. A much simpler hypothesis is that there are, as it were, fairly strong "chains of hermeneutic command" in the harder sciences. Readers are specifically told to read certain articles for certain things that are worth emulating or attacking—and to ignore the rest of the material in that field. Consequently, an article's entire contribution will be stereotyped in terms of one of its parts, which can then be easily fitted into an ongoing disciplinary narrative. Keep in mind that I am speaking here about the treatment given to the *highly* cited pieces.

Of course, these reading practices affect the writing practices associated with knowledge production, in particular, the increasing reliance on "boilerplate," those moveable modules of text that are sufficiently self-contained to appear anywhere in a given article and perhaps even in any article in a given field at a given time. Discussions of research methodology are perhaps most susceptible to the boilerplate treatment, but the onset of word processors has made virtually any kind of scholarly writing servable as boilerplate. From the reader's standpoint, the result is an article that is stitched together in a sequence of parts that conforms to local disciplinary conventions. However, enough seams show through the stitching to absolve the reader of any guilt she might feel should she decide merely to sample the article here and there without reading it in the order in which it is presented—let alone in its entirety.

It is no exaggeration to say that the disciplines that are typically taken to excel in the rigor of their methods and the reliability of their findings are also the ones that fail the most abysmally by the criteria that humanists most respect: namely, attention to the construction and reception of a text, including a thoughtfully critical response to the claims that the text makes. The fact that in the last few years rhetoricians and other humanists have managed to elicit interesting and often surprising readings of scientific texts when they treat them as works of literature or public address merely reinforces the point that this is *not* the way those texts are normally read or even written to be (cf. Gross & Keith, 1995). This is an important point that I fear is often lost on humanists, who suppose that all knowledge producers attend to each other's texts with the care that humanists often lavish on them. Please do not misunderstand me. I find these humanist readings of scientific texts most enlightening as accounts of how such texts *ought* to be read. I stress the normative dimension of the humanist enterprise because, as my depiction of Big Science makes clear, the way one treats texts is intimately tied to the way one treats the people who author these texts. A social ethic is implicit in careful readings that does not correspond to the actual circulation patterns of scientific texts among the scientists themselves—certainly in our own time, but perhaps even from the first moment that writing became the core practice of knowledge production in our culture. Several years ago, Gerald Graff (1992), a historian of American literary institutions, declared that academics have a duty to "teach the conflicts" in which so-called canonical texts have been embedded. While Graff had the humanities in mind, I would extend his call to critique to the sciences. In most cases, this will be to ask our students to behave much better toward the texts they read than the original authors behaved toward each other.

We should be disturbed by the ease with which the hardest of the sciences—the ones in which so much of our material and human resources are invested—can so easily yield to the rubrics of "opinion leaders," "spin control," "boilerplate," "planned obsolescence," and "product life cycles." These categories define the analytical matrix of mass communications and consumer culture. Their presence in quantitative social studies of science— "scientometrics"—is perhaps the clearest sign that the market mentality has penetrated the heartland of organized inquiry, rendering postindustrialism simply industrialism raised to the second order (De Mey, 1992, pp. 111–172). In fact, not postindustrialism, but *meta-industrialism* is a more apt expression for science's epistemic plight, which all inquirers increasingly share.

The ultimate irony of *SCI*'s metamorphosis from postindustrial research tool to meta-industrial policy instrument is that scientists invited the move by their own image of self-organizing communities of inquirers who are oriented exclusively toward each other. It follows that a summary of the judgments reached by such a body could be taken as a definitive record of its activities. In other words, *the ideology of autonomy facilitates external control.* Because the humanities and social sciences are known to be routinely susceptible to forces beyond their control—such as the day's events, ambient ideologies, and public opinion—few have imagined that any neat set of unobtrusive measures could encapsulate their activities. Consequently, policy incursions into the "soft sciences" have always appeared high-handed and messy, reflecting only one of many possible perspectives from which the development of these fields may be regarded.

CODA: BEWARE OF EVOLUTIONISTS BEARING GIFTS

Things analyzable by the categories of consumer culture are often faulted for debasing some value system or other, if not all value systems, often in the name of "commodification." Should the same conclusion be drawn about Big Science's impact on the value of knowledge and its producers in our supposedly knowledge-intensive postindustrial society? And if that conclusion is drawn, then what should those of us concerned with the politics of the academy do about it (Fuller, 1993)? A life of inquiry is now officially available to more people than ever before in human history. However, the *quality* of the life one leads in that pursuit is changing rapidly and probably declining—if the rise of contract-based research and teaching in universities is any indication. At the very least, we should critique narratives of progress, especially the seductive evolutionary models of knowledge production (Campbell, 1988, is probably the best of the lot).

The persuasiveness of evolutionary models often rests on an ambiguity: Is the evolution in question supposed to be *unique* or *repeatable*? For example, does Kuhn (1970) model the stages through which *the* history of science as a singular global phenomenon passes, or rather the phases through which specific sciences pass in any of a variety of times and places? Were Kuhn to have intended the former, his model would have approximated a literal application of evolution to epistemology. But then he would have been forced to confront how the initial scientization of certain fields at certain times and places—specifically, experimental physics in seventeenth-century Western Europe—set constraints on later developments, even in remote fields, times, and places. In other words, how does the prior existence of certain forms of inquiry constitute the environment against which subsequent forms of inquiry are selected? Clearly, Kuhn has not been read in this way, but rather as having advanced a multiply repeatable, perhaps even universalizable, model of scientific change that is just as relevant to, say, sociological inquiry in the 1960s as physical inquiry in the 1660s. It is ironic, given Kuhn's reputation for having "historicized" the history and philosophy of science, that his model should be applied in such a mindlessly ahistorical fashion.

Nowadays it is often assumed that because science does not follow the same path in all times and places, it must therefore follow different, unrelated paths that can be explained only by citing local factors. This inference, characteristic of the "ethnographic" or "postmodern" turn in social and cultural studies of science, constitutes a false dilemma. It overlooks that the evolution of scientific knowledge may be *exactly* like biological evolution in being a single and unrepeatable trajectory that encompasses the entire world. This is, of course, compatible with a considerable degree of variation across local environments, which can in turn be explained by the differential impact of earlier events of common ancestry. My model here is Lenin's theory of imperialism, according to which the logic of capital expansion enables the first industrializing nations to force latecomers into a position of subservience, either as mere providers of raw materials or as consumers of goods produced by the early industrializers. In this way, a "core–periphery" relationship is perpetuated—that is, until the Communist Revolution (if it occurs).

Whatever its own shortcomings, Lenin's theory managed to eliminate the "metaphysical residue" in Marxist political economy, namely, the idea that the essence of economic development was first manifested in Western Europe's transition from feudalism to capitalism and would subsequently be reproduced by the rest of the world, largely without change. (The most systematic scholarly elaboration of Lenin's perspective—albeit without Lenin's apocalyptic outcome—is *world-systems theory*: Wallerstein, 1991.) Even Lenin's "bourgeois" critics, while questioning the inevitability of imperialism, nevertheless conceded that one needs to consider the world-historic environment that defines what often turns out to be a narrow band of possibilities within which development can occur in a given time and place. For example, while late developers have often industrialized more quickly, they typically have to supply local substitutes for the institutions of the originators (Gerschenkron, 1962).

Kuhn's theory of scientific change retains just the sort of metaphysical residue that Lenin endeavored to purge from Marx's theory. Not surprisingly, Kuhn has been eagerly embraced by the most famous recent metaphysician of economic development, Francis Fukuyama (1992, pp. 80–81, 352–353), who regards the inviolate "logic" of scientific inquiry as described by Kuhn to be the motor of economic progress that will eventually lift all nations to the standard of living currently enjoyed by the United States. One need not be a Leninist to find bioevolutionarily relevant reasons for doubting Fukuyama's prognosis. The average American already consumes six times more energy than the average earthling. Barring a breakthrough in the design of artificial environments, that alone precludes the U.S. from providing the basis for an ecologically sustainable political economy. As my earlier critique of Price and Merton revealed, the same applies to American science as a model for world science. However, compared with the idea of limits to economic growth (Arndt, 1978), limits to scientific growth have been rarely touched upon (an exception is Rescher, 1984).

The closest that Price and Merton got to specifying the "ends of science" was the indefinite accumulation of highly cited scientific articles. As a metric of progress, this is about as primitive as measurements of wealth prior to Adam Smith, when it was commonly thought that a nation increased its wealth simply by accumulating more bullion in its treasury than its neighbors. Smith proposed that the range of living standards and the organization of labor be taken as alternative indicators of a nation's overall wealth. We have yet to take the "Smithian Turn" in our understanding of science, whereby progress would be judged more by the quality of its people than its papers. Taking this turn would require merging what evolutionists call the "selection environment" for science (Campbell, 1988) with that of the surrounding political economy. Consider the case of science's "invisible" tendency toward elitism via Merton's principle of cumulative advantage. As research becomes more "advanced" (i.e., specialized), it becomes more expensive in almost every respect and hence subject to various problems of scarcity (of skills, equipment, etc.), which are then resolved by concentrating resources in a few researchers and institutions. Yet when this relatively unproblematic observation is set against the backdrop of science's contributions to labor-saving devices and other forms of technical efficiency, it would seem that science helps economize on other social activities only to make room for more lavish expenditure on its own activities, as measured not only by the number of researchers but also by the time the general population must invest in acquiring credentials for any scientific line of work. Certainly, this is one (uncharitable) way of interpreting the growing presence of "knowledge-intensive" activities in the economy at large.

An interesting historical precedent for this line of thought is Schlick (1974, pp. 94–101), written shortly after founding the Vienna Circle. He argued that the advance of civilization is marked by science gradually reversing its role from being a means to other ends in life to an end pursued in itself, and ultimately the only end worthy of unconditional pursuit. But to regard science as an "unconditional pursuit" is to forgo any scrutiny of its return on investment. Many would argue that this is as it should be, since science's returns are typically "intrinsic," "deferred," or "diffuse" in ways that defy normal accounting procedures. However, the very use of the en-quoted terms concedes the elusiveness of the boundaries that define science's selection environment.

But there is more to worry about here. Consider the expression "functional differentiation," which is supposed to structure the ever-expanding scientific enterprise. At first glance, this suggests that the pursuit of inquiry is becoming more efficient, as each scientist does what only she can do and then collaborates with her fellows to get the entire job done. Adam Smith would be pleased. And while such an image may well capture the microdynamics of the research team, it has virtually no bearing on the sense of "division of labor" that operates at the systemic level of scientific activity. At this level the issue turns more on *entitlement* than efficiency, namely, the settlement of jurisdictional disputes between competing inquirers, which then becomes the basis for relations of mutual deference and trust. This image of science as an abstract sort of real estate presupposes that over time the access that any individual scientist (or scientific discipline) has to reality becomes more circumscribed and mediated, so that most of what a scientist knows about a given field may be based almost entirely on whom she trusts for reliable information. Again seen in strictly economic terms, this puts us in the realm of brokered exchanges, whereby potential buyers no longer know firsthand what is for sale and hence must rely on third parties. A situation of this sort arises in the "informal economies" of the former Soviet Bloc countries, which have experienced the breakdown of socialism without yet installing market mechanisms that reliably transmit price information. Do we really want to call such a state of affairs "functional"?

Evolutionary theorists of science have great difficulty envisaging the decline or corruption of science as a long-term consequence of science having been developed symbiotically with, say, capitalism or the nation-state. However, the pressures on governments today to divest their massive funding commitments to science suggest that we may not be so far from a world that would force this awareness upon us. In a fascinating essay on the collapse of the great ancient civilizations, the archaeologist Joseph Tainter (1988) argued that these societies eventually became too complex for their own good, as the cost of governance exceeded the benefit that accrued to either the governors or the governed. Collapse came in the form of either a simplification of the administrative apparatus or a fragmentation of the regime itself. If our highly "functionally differentiated" science system is like one such ancient civilization that let its material development go unchecked, then we might expect *epistemic collapse* to come from, on the one hand, the elimination of disciplines and specialties (say, through the reorganization of the university) and, on the other, the privatization of knowledge in the form of intellectual property. These "developments" are already upon us, and as critical intellectuals, we have a duty to theorize them as signs of decline, not progress, in a hypertrophic knowledge system.

REFERENCES

Arndt, H. W. (1978). *The rise and fall of economic growth*. Chicago: University of Chicago Press.

Bourdieu, P. (1990). *In other words: Essays toward a reflexive sociology*. Stanford, CA: Stanford University Press.

Bush, V. (1985). *The endless frontier*. New York: Ace Books. (Original work published 1945)

Campbell, D. (1988). *Methodology and epistemology for social science*. Chicago: University of Chicago Press.

Conant, J. B. (1970). *My several lives: Memoirs of a social inventor*. Cambridge, MA: Harvard University Press.

Cozzens, S. (1985). Comparing the sciences. *Social Studies of Science, 15,* 127-153.

Curtius, E. R. (1989). Max Weber on science as a vocation. In P. Lassman & I. Velody (Eds.), *Max Weber's science as a vocation* (pp. 70-75). London: Unwin Hyman.

De Mey, M. (1992). *The cognitive paradigm* (2nd ed.). Chicago: University of Chicago Press. (Original work published 1982)

Fukuyama, F. (1992). *The end of history and the last man*. New York: Free Press.

Fuller, S. (1993). *Philosophy, rhetoric, and the end of knowledge*. Madison: University of Wisconsin Press.

Fuller, S. (1997). *Science*. Buckingham, UK: Open University Press.

Fuller, S. (1999). *Being there with Thomas Kuhn: A philosophical history for our times*. Chicago: University of Chicago Press.

Gerschenkron, A. (1962). *The relative advantage of backwardness*. Cambridge, MA: Harvard University Press.

Gibbons, M. (1994). *The new production of knowledge*. London: Sage.

Graff, G. (1992). *Teaching the conflicts*. New York: Norton.

Gross, A., & Keith, W. (Eds.). (1995). *Rhetorical hermeneutics*. Albany: State University of New York Press.

Harvey, D. (1989). *The condition of postmodernity: An enquiry into the origin of cultural change*. Cambridge, MA: Blackwell.

Kuhn, T. (1970). *The structure of scientific revolutions* (2nd ed.). Chicago: University of Chicago Press. (Original work published 1962)

Luhmann, N. (1995). *Social systems (writing science)*. Stanford, CA: Stanford University Press.

Malinowski, B. (1984). *Argonauts of the western Pacific*. Prospect Heights, IL: Waveland Press.

Merton, R. K. (1967). *On theoretical sociology: Five essays, old and new*. New York: Free Press.

Merton, R. (1973). *The sociology of science*. Chicago: University of Chicago Press.

Olsen, M. (1992). The energy consumption turnaround and socioeconomic well-being in industrial societies in the 1980s. In L. Freeman (Ed.), *Advances in human ecology* (Vol. 1, pp. 197-234). Greenwich, CT: JAI Press.

Pinch, T. (1990). The sociology of the scientific community. In R. Olby, G. Cantor, J. Christie, & M. Hodge (Eds.), *Companion to the history of modern science* (pp. 87-99). London: Routledge.

Polanyi, M. (1964). *Science, faith, and society*. Chicago: University of Chicago Press.

Price, D. J. de S. (1959). Contra-Copernicus. In M. Clasett (Ed.), *Critical problems in the history of science* (pp. 119-142). Madison: University of Wisconsin Press.

Price, D. de S. (1978). Toward a model for science indicators. In Y. Elkana (Ed.), *Toward a metric of science* (pp. 69-96). New York: Wiley-Interscience.

Price, D. de S. (1986). *Little science, big science . . . and beyond*. New York: Columbia University Press.

Rescher, N. (1984). *The limits of science*. Berkeley: University of California Press.

Schlick, M. (1974). *The general theory of knowledge*. Berlin: Springer-Verlag. (Original work published 1925)

Stehr, N. (1994). *Knowledge societies*. London: Sage.

Tainter, J. (1988). *The collapse of complex societies*. Cambridge, UK: Cambridge University Press.

Turner, S., & Chubin, D. (1976). Another appraisal of Ortega, the Coles, and science policy: The Ecclesiastes hypothesis. *Social Science Information, 15,* 657-662.

Wallerstein, I. (1991). *Unthinking social science: The limits of 19th century paradigms*. Cambridge, UK: Polity.

Weber, M. (1958). Wissenschaft als Beruf [Science as a vocation]. In H. Gerth & C. W. Mills (Eds.), *From Max Weber* (pp. 129-156). Oxford: Oxford University Press. (Original work published 1918)

FOUR

INTELLECTUAL DISCOURSE IN THE ACADEMY AND SOCIETY
Interpretation, Legitimation, and the Rise of Management Talk

KARL-MICHAEL BRUNNER, JOHANNA HOFBAUER, AND GERALD PRABITZ

WE ADDRESS the question of academic knowledge and political power—how these two key terms connect to each other. In our discussion of the role of intellectuals inside and outside the academy, we develop two complementary and interdependent themes or problematics: first (part one), we describe academic knowledge as situated action within a field of power and confronted by the challenge of domination by nonacademic, economic pressures; second (part two), we outline the possibilities and problems of reflexive modernization. We then focus both themes on the position of intellectual discourse within both the academic field and the larger civic and capitalistic society. "Intellectuals," in our context, refers primarily to the *scientific intelligentsia,* the experts, less than to literary persons, artists, and the like.

By studying the significance of buildings and offices, academic titles, classification systems, and various practices of working scientists, we suggest not only the extent to which power is part of the everyday life of academics within their scientific fields, but also that practices infused with power are vital in the creation of knowledge (cf. Brown, 1998b; Hodge & Kress, 1988). After discussing the *world of the academy* and its symbolic and institutional power relations, we address the decentering of intellectuals and notice a shift in the *hegemony of discourses.* We claim that the role and position of intellectuals in society has changed. They are no longer able to impose their truth claims, but must compete with other social groups over the definition of legitimate knowledge—which today often means "useful" knowledge or information. The knowledge of intellectuals does not necessarily imply power (as was the case in the age of the Enlightenment). Since knowledge is no longer a good in its own right but has been commodified during postindustrial capitalism, intellectuals have to struggle for a position in a market for cultural goods. In this market, the discourse of managers and technocrats has gained significance. Academics now are expected not only literally to produce knowledge but also to raise funds for it, promote it, and sell it. Yet this process of the production and sale of knowledge is dependent on scientific progress. Science, technology, and the economy therefore have been in a constant state of tension and mutual dependency. During the last decades certain forms of critical self-awareness or *reflexivity* have emerged within the sciences, however, which adds another dimension to the knowledge/power relation.

Our analysis of power structures as well as of managerism and technocratic tendencies in our society should lead not so much to disappointment about the decline of the traditional image of the intellectual, as to a sense of encouragement that we have the ability to criticize ourselves from various discursive standpoints. And in the process we may not only be able to avoid self-destructive illusions, but also to strengthen our capacities for a more vigorous and self-reflective democracy.

ON POWER AND MANAGERISM

Universities as Cultural Monuments and Situated Action

The physical locus of the academic universe, the space most consecrated to intellectual life and work, is the university. At first sight, what one perceives of the academy, as a physical place, is a cluster of large and impressive buildings, usually approached up a broad staircase. You open one of the big, heavy doors and enter a hall that bears all the signs of a venerable institution. You tacitly know what the building represents, what the institution stands for. You notice the traditional pillared hall, adorned with the busts of pillars of society (the honorable men of science of whom the university is proud), and the epigraphs in Latin inscribed in stone, often with gold leaf. Or perhaps it is a modern building that sacrifices dignity for practicality. Whether in traditional or modern shape, the building is obviously more than material with a functional purpose. It is also a "monument," a device of cultural memory (Flusser, 1989) that reminds the visitor of the fact that the university is a stronghold of knowledge. And there are many other signs of this, from salaried positions to letterhead stationery.

As we continue to journey through the university halls, we encounter other signs and dimensions of power. We perceive how different modes of dress, speech, and comportment are organized hierarchically and not only distinguish academic from administrative personnel but also classify subgroups of the scientific community. The office doorplates suggest that every department is also a symbolic pyramid—a classification of titles is a distribution of rights and duties—with professors on top, down to graduate teaching assistants. Like the location and size of the offices, furniture also is graded in terms of comfort, cost, and back height. Some offices have seating accommodation for visitors, or better views or light; others do not (Hatch, 1990). The academic world, in that respect, is not much different from other organizations.

Of course, the production of knowledge is not monopolized by the academy. It never has been. There have always been educated individuals, intellectuals, who have spoken from outside the university walls. But between these "free" intellectuals and the intellectuals who claim one of the titles the academy so carefully bestows, there runs a symbolic and material border. It is this line of distinction that divides the orthodox representatives of science from the nonorthodox. In the extreme case, scientific freelancers are autodidacts without institutional affiliation who therefore lack the symbolic devices that can work miracles for fundraising or publishing. The distinction between institutional and free (or freelance) intellectuals is but one instance of power structures within the intellectual universe. Still, this first rough distinction identifies the university as a social monument that also is a symbol and system of power, organizing the distinction between both insider and outsider discourse,[1] and also between official frontstage versions of science and the actual backstage practices of knowledge production.

In a lively and penetrating analysis, Bruno Latour (1987) has juxtaposed official philosophies of science with scientific practices in action—the everyday rituals of scientific inquiry, the control and craft use of apparatus and machinery, the rules of the publishing game, the rhetorics for connecting what is going on within the laboratory to the outside world, the forming of coalitions and networks, all helping in securing the flow of funds, producing reputation, and accumulating competitive advantages. For example, looking more closely at power within the academy, you also will distinguish various practices of academic politics, as in departmental reviews, tenure and promotion committees, and activities related to acquiring funds and publishing research papers. You will get to know about the subtle differences that are made between this or that journal or publisher, and the frequency with which one is expected to publish.

These are only a few of the elements that count in the definition of academic power relations. Central to these, however, is the competition for resources, acknowledgment, and influence, in short, the competition for power in which the members of the scientific community are involved, whether they like it or not. Of course, there is no single competition for power. In practice, we have to deal with a plurality of competitions and the forms of power that they embody and reproduce. An anthropologist's look at the tactics and strategies within scientific laboratories, for example, is provided by Woolgar and Latour (1986)[2] and Pickering (1992). Further examples appear in Pierre Bourdieu's reflexive sociological account of academic life, *Homo Academicus* (1988), in which he classifies various fields of power according to the form(s) of capital at stake in any given competition. Bourdieu develops two ideal types of academic actors: on the one hand, the "politician-type," who in the first instance is provided with and disposes of social and economic capital and uses them as symbolic assets; on the other hand, the "intellectual or scientist-type," who primarily invests in and deploys cultural capital—mainly his or her knowledge and status as an expert scientist.

The notion of power is also fundamental because power permeates the entire process of knowledge production, not just questions of resource distribution and social ranking within the academic universe, but the very production of knowledge itself. Or, more precisely, resource allocation, ranking, peer review, decisions on contracts and grants, and status competition within the laboratory all are relations laden with power through which knowledge is produced. Karin Knorr-Cetina (1981) calls this process the social "manufacture of knowledge" and thereby refers to the micropolitical and strategic dimensions of the formation of scientific findings. The thrust of her argument, which is confirmed by many other researchers in recent sociology of science, is that scientific findings are not telling an absolute "truth" about "reality," but rather are constructions of reality that come to be taken as true through persuasive argumentation within that scientific field. As soon as we accept that any process of validating perceptions as accurate or theories as true is a process of constructing a reality through certain rhetorical practices, then there are plenty of potential truths, only a few of which "make it" socially within that scientific community. Or, putting it conversely, there is no one absolute or ultimate truth, but only more or less legitimated answers to the questions of science.

Our suggestion that power is part of everyday academic practices is hardly surprising if we consider that society has organized scholarly life to produce the subjects and objects of knowledge within the institutionalized framework of universities, research centers, and the like. These institutions of organized research are part of our "Society of Organizations," and as such they operate accordingly. Thus, the everyday life of academics is ruled both by numerous structural devices from within the whole span of bureaucratic forms and hierarchical orders, and by competition and evaluation of scientific performance. In this sense, academics are enmeshed in diverse forms and relations of power that are realized in fairly direct and specific ways.

The consequence of this argument is that the process of "formation of scientific findings" can no longer be seen merely from a "progress of reason" perspective. At the least, to understand the practical efforts of scientists to construct scientific findings, we have to keep in mind the struggles that go on to validate certain observations as "findings," and certain findings as "significant." Moreover, scientifically active academics must participate in these struggles—struggles through which status, standing, or merit as a scientist is gained—because nonparticipation involves facing all the risks of the freelancer, forfeiting one's symbolic assets and legitimate interactions with those who have decided to stay. The formal and, to a lesser extent, the informal rules of the game are always largely particular to a certain historical moment. But by staying in the system, one may become one of the lucky or talented ones who not only know these rules but also know how to play them like a virtuoso. This higher and more difficult game within the game may subvert the constraints of form, at least temporarily and locally. But to play it presupposes an unusual degree of social knowledge and political insight, as well as ambition and other personal traits. Moreover, it will be of central importance for the intellectual or research-oriented scholar (as distinct from the politician) to understand and make use of one's own position within the scientific community and of its often brutal criticism of the presumptive contributions of its members.

Priests and Prophets, Legislators and Interpreters

The name and position of intellectuals have always been contested, especially by intellectuals themselves, since they have been central in the production and criticism of classifications, definitions, and categories by which social, natural, and supernatural worlds are defined. One need only think of the conflicts between two groups of intellectuals that marked the coming into existence of modern sociology: critical essayists and novelists on the one hand and early social scientists on the other (cf. Lepenies, 1988; Williams, 1982). Both were interested in providing influential interpretations of modern capitalism, and therefore both were rivals for public support. Or, more recently and in the United States, one might think of the growing tensions between neoconservative defenders of the status quo (and their mighty allies in politics, corporations, and the media) and critical left-wing intellectuals, a tension of which Noam Chomsky, for example, is both an actor and a symptom (cf. Herman & Chomsky, 1988).

Different social settings enable different dominating ways of world-making. Seen ahistorically, there have always been heated disputes between defenders of intellectual traditions and those who would open them. These controversies have been characterized with the biblical image of the conflict between priests and prophets. The priests, defenders, and functionaries of the established order are challenged by the new visions and rigors of prophets—whether their visions are progressive or reactionary. In more modern times, these age-old tensions have been articulated in the rivalry between the defenders of the Enlightenment project of unrestricted use of reason, and those who aim to limit the relevance and scope of reason and thereby preserve or retain the "enchantment of the world," to use Max Weber's phrase. This latter strategy has been articulated by recourse to traditions and morals, by romantic retreatism, by various kinds of absolutisms, and by invoking myths of unanimity to impose assertions rather than encourage participation in deliberative public debate.

What has been crucial in such conflicts, however, is whether priest or prophet was able to dictate the terms of trade of intellectual exchange, for they both shared the same field of discourse. Priest and prophet were always heavily dependent on each other, could not exist without their respective opponents, and operated within and reproduced a discourse of God and the revelation of His will. For our purposes, however, we move past these schisms for a moment and label both priests and prophets as intellectuals whose task was to maintain the supply of categories and of discourse through their very talk and argumentation. The social construction of reality was in large measure dependent on their symbolic power. The construction of their discourse included selection of the individuals supposed and allowed to participate in that language game, the type of relations this involved, the stakes of the game, and the structure of legitimate representation. In these terms, the premodern position of intellectuals regarding symbolic expression and self-understanding was a culturally hegemonic one.

This has been changing in late modern (or postmodern) society, and today, instead of supplying the legitimate vocabulary for the interpretation of the social world *ex cathedra,* intellectuals themselves are subject to a managerial discourse that to a large measure is not their own. Zygmunt Bauman (1987) has tried to make sense of this changing condition by introducing yet another distinction within the intellectual universe: the dichotomy of legislators and interpreters. These two intellectual attitudes are described as appropriate strategies within two different social settings. The legislator emerges as the typical intellectual role in a stable modern society like Europe and the United States until the nineteenth and early twentieth century. The legislators' judging and superior attitude, their issuing of authoritative statements, has nowadays, in this postmodern world, given way to the more hermeneutic intellectual strategy of interpreting, which "consists of translating statements, made within one community based on tradition, so that they can be understood within the system of knowledge based on another tradition" (p. 5).

Intellectuals and Managerism

The removal of intellectuals from their former central position started some 200 years ago with the transformation of an absolutist society into a civic society. The reaction of intellectuals against this threatening devaluation was always ambivalent, to say the least. As is known of Germany and Austria at the turn of the century, for example, most intellectuals reacted with ontological fundamentalism, moral rigorism, dogmatism, and a longing for authority and order—an authority which was, of course, invoked in order to stabilize these changing societies in the name of intellectual abstractions such as nature, blood, nation, or community and thereby guarantee intellectual supremacy.

A further shift from traditional to modern and postmodern roles for intellectuals is visible today in Austria and elsewhere in the discursive formation that we call "managerism." And it becomes visible as a trespassing. This means that the relation between intellectuals and politics, or the power/knowledge equation, to use Foucault's term, is again being questioned. Knowledge has never been an easy and homogenous category. There have always been different kinds of knowledge, legitimate discourses, power/knowledge relations of diverse kinds, both legitimate and illegitimate. What we mean by managerism is that a certain conception of knowledge, new typical kinds of emphases, new arguments and associated practices, are in the process of replacing older discursive formations, which will lose their former status.

This time, however, the questioning does not only take place as one more quarrel between intellectuals, but is also directed against intellectuals from the outside. The intellectuals' position, nowadays described as theorizing or as idle contemplation within an ivory tower, is challenged by a rhetorical strategy of practicability and efficient intervention in society's affairs; in short, by a managerial discourse. This shift occurs in two ways. On the one hand, this shift of emphasis is the contemporary version of the old "internal" battle described in the initial section of this chapter: New generations of intellectuals challenge older ones in the name of current status aspirations and current intellectual obsessions. On the other hand and at the same time, the intellectual sphere is being threatened by an outside force. This second intervention can best be described as a process of unification (operating against the Weberian process of differentiation) in the course of which social systems that until now were differentiated are being subjected to one hegemonistic subsystem: the economy. The economic subsystem—that is, corporate ideology, practices, and power—is increasingly infiltrating formerly autonomous or semi-autonomous subsystems such as the academic world, the political sphere, or the ordinary lifeworlds of citizens. The major consequence of this shift (as described, for example, by Brown and Clignet in this volume) is that power is turning against intellectuals and changing their position both materially and symbolically.

What is at stake here is the emergence of a new type of brain-worker. We have already spoken of their workplace, which differs sharply from idealistic accounts of the intellectual world. This new infiltration of an economic rationale into the academic world seems to be one of the latest effects of a longer process. Capitalism, it has been said, is a liquidating device, a machine that breaks up all frozen relations (to use the famous Marxian image), that does away with all "venerable prejudices and opinions" so that "all that is solid melts into air." Marshall Berman (1982) has used this image from the *Communist Manifesto,* together with the Goethian image of Faust, to provide a lively interpretation of the "experience of modernity." One is also reminded of Deleuze's and Guattari's (1983) image of capitalism as a deterritorializing machine. Such a breakup of established orders is not sparing any area of social and cultural life.

At the end of World War II, Theodor Adorno and Max Horkheimer coined the term "culture industry" to make it clear that capitalism does not leave the cultural sphere untouched. On the contrary, in their opinion, culture has become one industry among many. The old ways have gone, they mournfully assert, and nowadays culture is the standardized and typified product of a highly profitable industry. In his *Negative Dialectics* Adorno (1973) goes even farther and states that in our time even *theory* does not escape the *market process,* since every theory can be construed as merchandise and has to prove its worth in a capitalistic world, which selects from an inventory of possible theories. The old categories of production are replaced by an emphasis on reproduction and consumption, not only outside but also inside the symbol factory, the university. Or, to formulate this point as a question: Is there any remaining difference between a university department and the bureaus of an insurance firm?

The reactions to this phenomenon are manifold. Some see new possibilities of symbolic gain and hence are adopting the managerialist ways. Nevertheless, with the loss of an older symbolic power and the need to express oneself in the new language of "management-talk," the more decisive transformation is the dissolution of the earlier intellectual. Increasingly the new-speak requires everyone to reframe problems and positions in terms of funds to be raised, projects to be offered, interests to be served, and performance evaluations and productivity controls to be met. Not only is such a discourse antithetical to that of the more traditional intellectual; in addition, it redirects intellectual energy toward new problems, it imposes the necessity of new procedures and research strategies, and it requires new ways of argument and justification.

Until recently, management talk, skills, and practices operated in discrete arenas. Now this specialized talk and experience have massively entered into worlds other than those of commerce or government, thereby replacing an older vocabulary of intellectual discourse (intellect, fundamentals, theory, and the linking of the abstract with the concrete), the necessity of which had been accepted as self-evident. How did this transformation occur?

The theory of business administration (in the German-speaking countries) was a rather abstract language, determined to find the laws of industrial production, formulated ideally in mathematical symbols and relying heavily on statistics, decision-calculus, and what today is called operations research. But not only in Austria and Germany. In their bestselling *In Search of Excellence,* Peters and Waterman (1982) recall that in the 1960s and 1970s the prevailing mood at universities, in MBA programs, and within top executive circles was infused by the "rational model." This was characterized by a fixation on mathematical investigation, a firm belief in planning, quantitative methods, the creed of numbers and ratios, and the dominance of accounting practices and methods, in a word, the undisguised adherence to instrumental reason and to a quantitative, naturalistic approach to human affairs.

Beginning in the mid-1960s and increasing rapidly, German-speaking business administration took over several trends and ideas from other spheres of inquiry and thereby transformed itself completely. These intellectual acquisitions included the incorporation of sociological, psychological, and anthropological findings within their explanatory schemes; the import of management theory as a social theory of decisionmaking and leadership (in contrast to the logical decision-calculus that it replaced); the shift of theoretical emphasis from production to marketing; and the problematization of organizational dynamics, evolution, and culture. With this, a rather new preoccupation with so-called "soft variables" more and more replaced the old rationalistic and calculus-fixated approaches.

At the same time, for a number of reasons and partly because of these eclectic and often thinly disguised incorporations of common sense, business talk became popular in the United States. Two sets of reasons are usually held responsible for this change in climate and popularity. The first is centered around the economic and political crises of the 1970s. This series of events (Vietnam, Watergate, weak dollar, stagflation) produced a favorable climate for new approaches. Perhaps more important, by the 1970s the economics of Europe and Japan, which had been devastated during World War II, were now fully recovered and in full competition with that of the United States. For example, the U.S. share of world trade, which was 48% after World War II, had fallen close to its prewar level of about 25%. In the face of this competition, many felt that U.S. business needed to intellectually retool itself. As the old technical skills and devices of management did not fulfill expectations and could not secure U.S. supremacy in world markets, the incorporation of fashionable "soft variables" became possible. Out of this prevailing mood, business administration started to produce bestsellers. These bestsellers were written in a lively and enthusiastic tone, exuded optimism, displayed trust in the American economy (in the name of neoliberalism and Reaganomics), were entertaining, and coped with the needs of frustrated practitioners (for all this see Prabitz, 1996).

This popularization meant and means that managerial language and habits of thought are now almost universally available. What had been the specialized means of articulation for a small group of economists and managers became the vulgate for the many, including professors. Management talk is now a lingua franca in social intercourse. Business people are of course affected by this redefinition, but so are intellectuals and the university system. For example, small semifeudal university departments, competition-free bureaus and programs, and administrative and professorial positions now must design their messages in conformity with consumer expectations, rationalize their organization, and use universalistic, ethically and intellectually neutral managerial language when selling and justifying their practices, budgets, and projects.

Ironically, however, when management talk becomes an omnipresent official language it no longer is the exclusive metalanguage of specialists. Indeed, the urge to quantify, evaluate, comply, and perform is no longer the vocabulary of the avant-garde business managers. Just as management talk has become pervasive in the universities, corporate executives have come to speak of attitudinal adjustment, meditation, dream work, human resources, creativity, and sensitivity training, and are concerned about emotions, motivation, and culture. Thus the talk that has spread to the universities is a popularized and vulgarized version of hard-core management talk of more than 20 years ago.

Concluding, we note that for specific historical reasons, intellectuals in the Western world were held in high esteem and shared the table of the powerful. Since the eighteenth century, they have ridden the waves of change. But in the course of several developments during these 200 years, their position has changed. Our thesis has been that the central transformation is not so much an internal reconfiguration but a decisive reshaping of the intellectual and of the intellectuals' relationship with other actors in the social system. We also consider whether intellectuals can remain critics of power; or are they so engaged in power games and management talk themselves that they are simply another set of combatants? Is discursive reason a means to escape the predicament of capitalistic commodification, or are language and discourse not already always part of the capitalist universe?

REFLEXIVE SCIENTIZATION AND THE "USE" OF INTELLECTUALS

Although the processes of commodification and industrialization of science and of scientific practices have been much noted, it is less obvious whether this is a unilinear tendency toward economical hegemony and technocratic discourse. There are some indications that modernization processes have always been and are increasingly becoming contradictory and reflexive, and that science is part of this "reflexive modernization" (cf. Beck, Giddens, & Lash, 1994), which opens up new opportunities for intellectuals to foster critical discourse and to promote a democratization of scientific knowledge. In the remainder of this chapter we would like to elaborate the concepts of *reflexive modernization* and *scientization* and thereby try to produce a multifaceted image of intellectuals and power in postmodern societies.

Scientization of Society

Max Weber described the process of modernization as one of rationalization (see, for instance, Weber, 1993). He characterized cultural modernity as the separation of substantive reason expressed in religion and metaphysics into three autonomous spheres: science, morality, and art. This differentiation was made because the unified worldviews of religion and metaphysics fell apart. Scientific discourse, theories of morality, jurisprudence, and the production and criticism of art were institutionalized and became the domain of professional specialists. As a result, the distance between the culture of experts and that of a larger public increased. Science played a very important role in Weber's analysis of the process of rationalization because it helped to destroy traditionalism and paved the way for the development of capitalism. In this sense, rationalization and scientization went hand in hand. Similarly, in an early essay on "Technical Progress and the Social Life-World," Habermas (1971) addressed the problem of scientific civilization.

His question was how the relationship between technical progress and the social life-world can be reflected upon and guided by rational or deliberative discussion. Today, the scientization of modern society often means the hegemony of positive sciences and technology in modes of economic production, social control, and public conversation. Science and technology nowadays have become the basis of our life. Instrumental rationality has marginalized other, more substantive forms of rationality. Today, science and research have been coupled with production and administration in the industrial system of labor and, as discussed, science itself has become an industry (cf. Aronowitz, 1988; Brown, 1998b; Ravetz, 1995). Engineering, and subsequently social engineering, have come to power.

Thus the problem can be stated as one of the relation of science, technology, and democracy. The key questions are: How can the power of technical control be brought within the range of the judgment and decisionmaking of citizens? How can this be done in the light of the hegemony of the scientific-industrial complex? Can there be a democratization of science and technology, and can there be a democratic mediation of relations between scientific and technical progress and the social life-world? Or perhaps the idea of progress itself has to be questioned? If it is true that modernity promised control over nature through science, material abundance through superior technology, and effective government through rational social organization, then this belief in progress (peace, equality, and happiness for all) has turned out to be a betrayal. Indeed, as Richard Norgaard (1994) argues, several promises of progress through science were either unfulfilled or had ironic outcomes: scientific culture has fostered materialist madness, imprisons people in bureaucratic gridlock, accelerates the depletion of resources and the degradation of the environment on which progress depends, pits people against people in a multitude of regional wars, and makes political, economic, and nuclear hostages of a sizeable portion of the global population.

Dissemination of Scientific Knowledge

The hope of Francis Bacon that science and progress would walk hand in hand has become ever more dubious (cf. Böhme, 1991; Brown, 1998a). Although the achievements of scientific-technical progress are still welcomed, the negative sides of the scientific-technical civilization are increasingly the focus of public criticism as, for example, in the environmentalist critique. As the legitimacy of science is increasingly challenged, the much-vaunted neutrality and value freedom of science gives way to a politicization of the sciences, as the right has it (cf. Weingart, 1983), or the revelation that science has always been political, as in the view of the left. This politicization (or awareness of the political) is a result, on the one hand, of a crisis of scientific- and technical-based modernization and, on the other, of the broad dissemination of critical social scientific knowledge. Not only have the natural sciences spread throughout society, but the social sciences also have been adopted in social and political life. In this sense, to speak of a marginality of the social sciences is no longer plausible. Sociology, for instance, has not only spread in the universities in the last 30 years with new departments and integration into other disciplines; it has also penetrated nonacademic discourses. Indeed, generally speaking, a dissemination of scientific knowledge has taken place, often in connection with processes of professionalization in different spheres of action.

This dissemination has had ambivalent results for both the relationship between science and society, and the relationship between intellectuals and politicians. In the 1960s, leaders of student movements sought to politicize and democratize the university and the sciences; likewise, intellectuals were seen as the avant-garde for the oppressed. This model of revolutionary advocacy is no longer so relevant, partly because of its illusory and antidemocratic conception of "speaking for the masses." By contrast, in the 1970s the idea of a scientific politics reemerged—that the social sciences should no longer be regarded as revolutionary, but instead should help to make politics more rational and to foster societal reforms through scientific knowledge. It was thought that academic knowledge should provide the basis for more rational political decisions, and that the intellectual should serve as consultant to the politician, in either the mode of social engineering or the mode of enlightenment (cf. Bauman, 1987).

These interpretative models turned out to be too simplistic. Studies of applied social sciences have shown that the process of "applying" social sciences is quite different from that envisioned in the models of social engineering or enlightenment. The intromission of social science expertise into other fields of practice depends on the specific character of each field and its particular rationalities and irrationalities. There are both opportunities and risks in applying social knowledge; in seeking to enhance social control, one can also lose it. One risk lies in the very "professionalization" or "academization" of knowledge itself, which not only gives greater authority to academic experts, but also separates academic from public discourse, and academics from social and political actors (cf. Böhme & Stehr, 1986; Wagner, Wittrock, Whitley, 1990). In sum, the transfer of academic discourse to public issues, like the communication of scholars with political leaders, is problematic. It can help open new directions in social criticism, or it can support mechanisms of social control. Similarly, social scientists may treat their research activities in either a pure "positivistic" or a pure "critical" manner. In both cases, however, they tend to forget that they are political actors by way of their very involvement in the scientific construction of reality and their classification and evaluation of social phenomena.

In times of societal certainty, academic knowledge is often dominated by a positivistic conception of knowledge and the authority of expertise. But in times of uncertainty, even expert knowledge may become controversial and risk a loss of both legitimacy and its legitimating function. "It is in such periods of search for new orientations that social science discourse systems are relatively open to other kinds of knowledge and discourse systems" (Nowotny, 1990, p. 31), for instance those put forward by social movements. Then critical, interpretive, "orientation knowledge" may become more important than the application of technical knowledge. Not the mere expert is required in such a situation, but the expert as intellectual who makes contributions to developing orientation knowledge that can enhance critical interaction between social, scientific, and political publics, and encourage societal learning instead of reinstalling the status of the expert. In sum, in times of uncertainty, discourse systems of social sciences are relatively open for mutual interaction with other kinds of knowledge and discourse systems, thereby highlighting the need and role of the intellectual not as legislator but as interpreter.

Reflexive Scientization

In his book *Risk Society* (1992), Ulrich Beck has made a distinction between "primary scientization" and "reflexive scientization." Following Max Weber (1993), simple scientization refers to the rationalization of the world and the domination of a certain type of knowledge (instrumental or technical-scientific rationality), linked with the idea of unilinear progress. Primary scientization expresses the idea that science is "applied to a 'given' world of nature, people and society. In the reflexive phase, the sciences are confronted with their own products, defects, and secondary problems, that is to say, they encounter a *second creation in civilization*" (Beck, 1992, p. 155). Primary scientization gains its dynamism from the contrast of tradition and modernity, of lay people and experts; the application of scientific results takes place in an authoritarian fashion.

By contrast, reflexive scientization expresses the idea that progress itself has become a problem. The idea of cumulative scientific and technical progress is publicly attacked, and consensus about the basic directions and interpretations of the world begin to vanish. The helplessness of experts and politicians after the nuclear accident in Chernobyl provides an example for these emerging threats, uncertainties, and doubts. As the authority of science becomes more and more questionable, the lay addressees of science become more and more interpreting subjects rather than passive objects of information.

Reflexive scientization also means that the sciences "are now being confronted with their own objectivized past and present—with themselves as product and producer of reality and of problems which they are to analyze and overcome. In that way, they are targeted not only as a source of solutions to problems, but also as a *cause of problems*" (Beck, 1992, p. 156). Beck speaks of a "process of demystification of the sciences," in the course of which the structure of science, practice, and the public sphere will be subjected to a fundamental transformation that opens up new chances for "democracy beyond expertocracy" (Beck, 1995, p. 109). The loss of legitimation of science can be the basis of politicization in the sense that nonscientific actors can more easily impose their political values and aims on the scientific community. Although academic knowledge still retains a very high standing in society, political conflicts and societal antagonisms have begun to influence and deconstruct expert discourses (cf. Brown, 1998a).

For men and women of knowledge, that is, intellectuals, such a delegitimation of positive science and expertise provides a privileged moment to participate in this search for orientation. As there are other discourses in society beside the scientific ones, it also is the moment to form productive relationships between these different forms of discourse. The mystique of scientific knowledge can now be publicly questioned. Thus the gap between academic and public discourse should not be regarded as an eternal one. If intellectuals can link scientific knowledge (especially in the social sciences) to the social life-world, they may be able to arrest the reduction of reason to instrumental calculation and revive marginalized forms of knowledge. This does not require thinkers to flatten the differences between scientific talk and everyday knowledge, but instead to understand knowledge not only as the results of instrumental reason, but also as culture—as the formation of symbolic orders (Pickering, 1992). This also involves communication about the direction of societal development, and about how to limit or cope with the disadvantages of so-called scientific-technical progress. Here the intellectual as "interpreter" can make his or her contribution as a mediator between science, management talk, and democracy.

A society based on exchange value and commodification is dependent on the specialist or expert. Indeed, academics have already started to reshape their position by becoming the officially acknowledged interpreters of various specialized fields. In this transformation, intellectuals have lost irretrievably their former position of the all-powerful legislator. But they have gained or are in the process of acquiring a position as producers of certain highly valued entities: arguments, vocabularies, interpretations. In a word, they become *shapers of knowledge and skills useful to lay citizens*—and in that way contribute to a *deconstruction* of economical hegemony and technocratic discourse. This function seems to be all the more urgently justified with the growing strength of technicist discourses or management talk in contemporary societies.

NOTES

1. The truth, as Michel Foucault says, also can be articulated by outsiders. But generally only those who speak within the institution, who follow the rules of a "discursive police" (Foucault, 1972, p. 25), and who reinstate these rules with every fresh discourse are "within truth" (Foucault, 1972, p. 25). According to Pierre Bourdieu, " . . . a language is worth what those who speak it are worth, i.e. the power and authority in the economic and cultural power relations of the holders of the corresponding competence" (Bourdieu, 1977, p. 652).

2. A fictional account of what is going on within academia and university departments as opposed to ordinary proceedings within an industrial plant is provided by David Lodge in his novel *Nice Work* (1990).

REFERENCES

Adorno, T. W. (1973). *Negative dialectics.* New York: Seabury Press.

Aronowitz, S. (1988). *Science as power. Discourse and ideology in modern society.* Basingstoke, UK: Macmillan Press.

Bauman, Z. (1987). *Legislators and interpreters.* Oxford: Polity Press.

Beck, U. (1992). *Risk society: Towards a new modernity.* London: Sage.

Beck, U. (1995). The world as laboratory. In U. Beck (Ed.), *Ecological enlightenment: Essays on the politics of the risk society* (pp. 101-110). Atlantic Highlands, NJ: Humanities Press.

Beck, U., Giddens, A., & Lash, S. (Eds.). (1994). *Reflexive modernization: Politics, tradition and aesthetics in the modern social order.* Cambridge, MA: Polity Press.

Berman, M. (1982). *All that is solid melts into air: The experience of modernity.* Harmondsworth, UK: Penguin.

Böhme, G. (1991). Am Ende des Baconschen Zeitalters. In G. Gamm & G. Kimmerle (Eds.), *Wissenschaft und Gesellschaft* (pp. 202-223). Tübingen: Edition Diskord.

Böhme, G., & Stehr, N. (Eds.). (1986). *The knowledge society.* Dortrecht, Austria: Reidel Publishing Company.

Bourdieu, P. (1977). The economics of linguistic exchanges. *Social Science Information, XVI*(6), 645-668.

Bourdieu, P. (1988). *Homo academicus.* Cambridge, UK: Polity.

Brown, R. H. (1998a). Modern science and its critics: Toward a post-positivist legitimation of science. *New Literary History, 29*(3, Summer), 521-550.

Brown, R. H. (1998b). *Toward a democratic science: Scientific narration and civic communication.* New Haven, CT: Yale University Press.

Deleuze, G., & Guattari, F. (1983). *Anti-Oedipus: Capitalism and schizophrenia* (R. Hurley, M. Seem, & H. R. Lane, Trans.). Minneapolis: University of Minnesota Press. (Original work published 1972).

Flusser, V. (1989). *Gedächtnisse.* In *Ars electronica, Philosophien der neuen Technologie* (pp. 41-57). Berlin: Merve.

Foucault, M. (1972). *L'ordre du discours.* Paris: Gallimard.

Habermas, J. (1971). *Toward a rational society.* London: Heinemann.

Hatch, M. J. (1990). The symbolics of office design: An empirical exploration. In P. Gagliardi (Ed.), *Symbols and artifacts: Views of the corporate landscape* (pp. 129-135). Berlin: Walter de Gruyter.

Herman, E. S., & Chomsky, N. (1988). *Manufacturing consent: The political economy of the mass media.* New York: Pantheon Books.

Hodge, R., & Kress, G. (1988). *Social semiotics.* Oxford, UK: Polity Press.

Knorr-Cetina, K. (1981). *Manufacture of knowledge: An essay on the constructivist and contextual nature of science.* Oxford: Pergamon Press.

Latour, B. (1987). *Science in action: How to follow scientists and engineers through society.* Cambridge, MA: Harvard University Press.

Lepenies, W. (1988). *Between literature and science: The rise of sociology.* Cambridge: Cambridge University Press.

Lodge, D. (1990). *Nice work.* Harmondsworth, UK: Penguin.

Norgaard, R. B. (1994). *Development betrayed.* London: Routledge.

Nowotny, H. (1990). Knowledge for certainty: Poverty, welfare institutions and the institutionalization of social science. In P. Wagner, B. Wittrock, & R. Whitley (Eds.), *Discourse and society: The shaping of the social science disciplines* (pp. 23-41). Dortrecht, Austria: Kluwer Academic Publishers.

Peters, T. J., & Waterman, R. H. (1982). *In search of excellence: Lessons from America's best-run companies.* New York: Harper & Row.

Pickering, A. (Ed.). (1992). *Science as practice and culture.* Chicago: University of Chicago Press.

Prabitz, G. (1996). *Unternehmenskultur und betriebswirtschaftslehre: Eine untersuchung zur kontinuität betriebswirtschaftlichen denkens.* Wiesbaden: Gabler.

Ravetz, J. R. (1995). *Scientific knowledge and its social problems.* New Brunswick, NJ: Transaction.

Wagner, P., Wittrock, B., & Whitley, R. (Eds.). (1990). *Discourse and society: The shaping of the social science disciplines.* Dortrecht, Austria: Kluwer Academic Publishers.

Weber, M. (1993). *The sociology of religion.* Boston, MA: Beacon Press.

Weingart, P. (1983). Verwissenschaftlichung der gesellschaft—Politisierung der wissenschaft. *Zeitschrift für Soziologie, 3,* 225-241.

Williams, R. (1982). *Culture and society.* London: Hogarth Press.

Woolgar, S., & Latour, B. (1986). *Laboratory life: The construction of scientific facts.* Princeton: Princeton University Press.

FIVE

LEISURE AND THE INTELLECTUALS
The End of the Legislator?

HANS MOMMAAS

THE OPPOSITION between *modernity* and *postmodernity* not only represents tendencies in some "objective" or "outside" reality; it also reflects a
transition in the self-perception and social position of those whose profession it is to make some sense of that reality, whether they are called intellectuals, scientists, researchers, social commentators, critics, or whatever.[1]
Zygmunt Bauman (1987, 1992), who perhaps more than anybody else explored this double hermeneutic dimension of the postmodern, termed this
a transition from *legislators* to *interpreters*. In "the good old days," intellectuals were regarded and regarded themselves as privileged explorers of a
yet-unknown world of processes, mechanisms, and laws. The more they
would be able to chart this *terra incognita,* the more they would become
guardians of a powerful knowledge that could guide humanity on an inse-
cure but in the end successful journey toward greater wealth, a more refined culture, and increased happiness.

The intellectuals involved made it their job to spread their message
among the masses. Not that they expected that the uneducated would understand what they were talking about: Adequate knowledge of the laws of
nature, including human and social nature, was an exclusive privilege for
those with a long educational training that conferred, among other benefits,
the moral competence necessary to rightfully use the knowledge gained. By
contrast, popular education aimed at generating the necessary sentiments in
the broader public for the intellectuals to be regarded as intellectuals—the
acceptance of the humanist culture of rationality. In order to accept the
intellectual's authority in matters of nature and society, it was necessary for
people to adhere to the worldview of science. Based on their administrative
capacities and their institutional power within universities, intellectuals had

already gained entrance to the bureaucracies of the newly formed nation-states, which represented an important financial and cultural resource. State bureaucracies and intellectuals partly shared a common fate: the establishment of a national culture based upon the rule of rational "surveillance."

According to Bauman (1987, 1992), talk about a postmodern world reflects, for one thing, a change in this configuration between the intellectuals, the state, and society. On the one hand, in their home countries the spreading of the gospel of rationality has been so successful that the intellectuals have made themselves redundant. Their knowledge is potentially available to all (Giddens, 1991). On the other hand, on a global scale, changes in the power balance between continents have transformed other cultures into something more than just laggards in a common march to an ever-modernizing world. And if that's not enough, the state doesn't seem to be in need any longer of some "grand design" that precedes practice. The result of all this is that intellectuals have lost their social position as "legislators." Instead, in the plural world we live in, intellectuals have turned into "interpreters," mediating different, often foreign, cultures. Meanwhile, the scientific worldview has been turned into one model of social order among many others.

In this chapter I would like to illustrate and sharpen Bauman's thesis concerning tendencies in the position of Western intellectuals. I believe that a history of long-term changes in the way social scientists have problematized and analyzed people's "free time" or "leisure" is useful for this purpose. From its creation as a product of modernity onwards, people's "free time" was an object of a more or less constant and nervous debate among intellectuals, circling around the proper use the masses were expected to make of it. Central to the intellectual's formation of the issue of free time were notions of culture and taste, refinement and enlightenment, rationality and civilization. From the beginning, the social sciences were heavily involved. They not only provided the information necessary to evaluate educational projects, but they also took it as their job to formulate a moral standard that could transcend political debate and thereby legitimate and neutralize the relation between the intervention and the interventionist: a moral foundation that could give the intervention a pastoral character, as Foucault (1980) has termed it.

For the sake of this chapter, in presenting the history of the involvement of Dutch scientists in the public representation of free time, I will restrict myself to three published academic research articles as exemplars of more general research conventions in the periods distinguished. These periods embrace respectively the 1930s/1940s, the 1950s/1960s, and the 1980s/1990s. Together they reflect a long-term and in detail more complicated turn from the nineteenth-century mixture of humanism and evolutionism to modern (that is American) postwar sociology, to the current contextualism and pluralism. I will end this history by confronting my research with Bauman's thesis about the transformation in the role and self-image of Western intellectuals.

THREE EXEMPLARS

In 1936 the results were published of the first nationwide research project organized in the Netherlands with regard to the free-time activities of unionized workers (see Blonk, Kruijt, & Hofstee, 1929). The initiative for the project came from the *Instituut voor Arbeidersontwikkeling* (Institute for Workers Education), an association founded in 1924 by Social Democrats. Its aim was to organize educational activities and cultivated pleasures for workers in order to enhance their free time. The organization wanted to know why the large majority of workers didn't participate in the activities organized for them (Beckers, 1983). By the time of the publication of the research report, the project was taken over by the *Maatschappij tot Nut van 't Algemeen* (Society for Public Welfare), an association involved with popular education and already founded in 1784 by enlightened factions of the Dutch bourgeois.

Responsible for the project were two academic researchers, both more or less at the beginning of their rather successful academic careers, A. Blonk and J. P. Kruijt. The account of the way the workers spend their free time was partly based upon a series of local ethnographic studies done in various villages and neighborhoods throughout the country. In addition, the study contained a quantitative survey (621 questionnaires) and a time-budget analysis (226 time budgets) of workers.

The free-time activities of laborers were categorized into 17 groups, some of which seem rather peculiar to us. Besides categories such as hobbies (e.g., taking care of plants and dogs "just for fun") and listening to the radio, we find distinctions such as those between (a) going to lectures, instructive meetings, museums, and excursions, (b) visiting theaters, cinemas, concerts, performances, and festive meetings, (c) attending balls and dances, or (d) visiting cafes ("for company or games"). The authors also differentiate between visiting relatives and friends without playing games or doing so for the purpose of playing games.

The conclusion of the research is reassuring. The increase in free time has resulted in "more involvement of the father with his child, a strengthening of family ties, decreased alcoholism, a strong expansion of educational work among grown-ups, a spreading of the daily press amongst the deepest layers, an exodus by foot or on bicycle to the countryside, a strong expan-

sion of many branches of sports, an enormous expansion of social life"
(Blonk et al., 1929, p. 73). However, one-third of the organized workers
still did not touch a book, a fact clearly proving to the authors that more
work remained to be done. Besides, the competition to more cultivated or
healthy activities from cinemas, dance halls, sport events, and the radio was
increasing.

Following a national representative study on radio listening and free
time in the winter of 1955–56, the Dutch *Centraal Bureau voor de Statistiek* (Central Bureau for Statistics, a government institute, 1958) initiated an
ambitious project to study the way the Dutch population spent its free time.
Two sociologists, J. Lammers and P. Thoenes, were responsible for this
project, both of whom belonged to a new and still young postwar generation whose aim, as they proclaimed it, was a "modernization" of Dutch
social theory and research. Their academic careers would be successful, as
would the project of the modernization of Dutch sociology. Again, the study
involved a survey and a time-budget analysis, this time, however, not restricted to workers but aimed at the entire population (a change that signals
the generalization of the issue of free time in the period considered). The
data were generated through a national representative sample of 7,200 people, supplemented with 3,300 interviews with representatives of smaller
subcategories of the population and 250 in-depth interviews. While doing
in-depth interviews, researchers also had to observe people's home interiors
and social relations. Thus, a combination of quantitative-correlational and
qualitative-narrative research methods was used.

The aim was to get a simple and straightforward representative national
overview of the ways in which people spent their free time, mainly in order
to learn how various sections of the Dutch population made use of an increasing number of public provisions that were financed by the state (e.g.,
theaters and music halls, radio and television, sports facilities, and libraries).
The investigators hoped to portray the "cultural structure" of Holland and
to explain it by analyzing relations between people's professional, family,
and recreational life. Of special interest were the effects of the increasing
differentiation, mechanization, and automation of labor and the commercialization of recreation.

The authors were very careful not to evaluate things in moral terms.
One of the researchers critically typified the term "passive recreation" as
"a perhaps slightly dubious term" (Centraal Bureau voor de Statistiek, 1957,
p. 27). In the same spirit, his colleague placed hierarchical classifications
between inverted commas: "In total, the free time behavior of the 'lower'
social milieus is dominated by the element of amusement. Striking, however
is that this amusement generally is more of a 'middle' and least of a 'low'
quality" (Centraal Bureau voor de Statistiek, 1958, p. 20). One of the conclu-

sions of the research was that its findings would correct a lot of mistaken presumptions that figured in public debates about people's use of free time. As the Dutch are a family-minded and industrious people, the researchers only occasionally were confronted with situations that differed from mainstream middle-class culture. These exceptions were typified as resulting from some adaptational problem: "The cosmopolitan, not used to life in a quiet rural town, the farm worker going to work in a factory, the worker not used to the rhythm of life in shift work, the working wife, just married, that has to adjust itself to 'her' household and loneliness during the day" (Centraal Bureau voor de Statistiek, 1958, p. 84).

In 1991, following a conference on Dutch cultural history, a collection of papers was published under the title *Fragmenten van Vermaak* (Fragments of Pleasure; Kalb & Kingma, 1991). The collection brought together recent research on pleasure and free time, done by, again, relative newcomers to the Dutch academic field. The studies are based on a wide variety of methods, from research of records to in-depth interviews and participant observation. The studies deal with a variety of topics, among them a history of *De Zandstraat* in the center of Rotterdam from around the turn of the century, in its most infamous period the working area of hundreds of prostitutes, but in 1911 doomed to be replaced by a new town hall and post office. (What better symbol of the victory of bourgeois culture can you get?) There also is an analysis of the attitudes among a local labor aristocracy around the turn of the century regarding the leisure activities of cobblers in the south of the Netherlands. The collection also contains an analysis of the time regime oriented toward tasks, which until the turn of the century was common among peasants living in Markelo, a village in the eastern Netherlands. There also is a postwar history of the censorship of films in Tilburg, an industrial town in Brabant, and a history of the changing configuration of hunters and poachers in the Netherlands during this century. The study finishes with an exploration of the legitimacy of bingo as an object and resource of pleasure in postwar Holland, especially among players themselves.

The introduction to this collection of essays doesn't provide the reader an idea of its intended societal function. Neither does the conclusion, because there is none. But then one could say that this book was not primarily aimed at policymakers but at "anyone with a more than everyday interest in cultural studies," as the cover says. The editors are skeptical about whether it is possible to write a history of pleasure: "What we do have are varying reconstructions of groups, practices and experiences" (Kalb & Kingma, 1991, p. 5). The only possibility yet found for the academic incorporation of popular culture is "the explication of the field of tension between the subcultural and individual construction of a meaningful existence and the possibilities and constraints posed by more extensive and more subtly divided societies" (Kalb & Kingma, 1991). As the studies particularly focus on cultural preferences of "common people," the editors present them in the context of other studies that emphasize conflicts of class, ethnicity, gender, or generation; confrontations between elite and folk culture; and ambivalences and power differentials.

FROM CIVILIZATION TO INTERPRETATION

Of course, I have collected these exemplars of 60 years of academic reconstruction for a purpose. Indeed, by using other research projects and presenting them differently, an alternative history could be suggested. For instance, one could probably tell a story of growth and maturation, a story about how the study of leisure in Holland, young as it is, gradually turned into a serious science, given certain indicators of what that means. One also could show how the study of leisure gradually detached itself from bourgeois myths about people's leisure and developed its own frame of reference and interpretation. Or one could argue that in the course of time it developed more rigorous research methods or formulated its hypotheses more sharply. On the other hand, one could probably also present a history of decline, that is, of how over time the study of leisure lost its explicit cultural aims or of how, after a brief period of "normalization," in Kuhn's terms, centrifugal tendencies surfaced again.

The above is meant to indicate another "real" tendency that only will reveal itself when we detach ourselves a bit from the academic field and its codes of scientific progress and decline. That is the tendency suggested by Bauman's thesis of the transition of intellectuals from legislators to interpreters. In the course of time, the academics involved abandoned their "extraterritorial" (cf. Bauman, 1992, p. 19) legislative position, instead to accept cultural diversity and their inescapable embeddedness within it. For a better impression of that tendency we have to take a look again at our cases and see what they exemplify in more detail, especially in terms of the intellectual sentiments that inspired them and the social aspirations that they expressed.

CIVILIZATION AND EVOLUTION THEORY

Along with everything else, our first research project, published in 1936, is characterized by the self-confident way in which the researchers judged other people's leisure. This is expressed openly in evaluative remarks, but also more implicitly in the categories used to classify free-time activities. We can find this in many other research projects on leisure of that period. Of course, one could connect this to some political-moral *zeitgeist*. The prevailing conventional bourgeois mood is revealed in the attention payed to the sort of literature workers read, the clubs they went to, the radio programs they listened to, and their habits of drinking and dancing; and also in the way in which these activities were classified, such as in terms of the sensational versus the serious, the passionate versus the rational, the pleasurable versus the educated, the vulgar versus the cultivated, or the superficial versus the committed.

However true that may be, the academics concerned also were keen about the strictly objective and autonomous status of their scientific profession, clearly to be demarcated from morality, ethics, and law. Hence the question arises as to what opinions about science and what social theories informed this (for us) contradictory mixture of objective science and moral intervention. Perhaps it is not so much the relation between morality and science as such but, first of all, the historical variance in what these two poles actually stand for.

The investigators who were responsible for this research project belonged to the so-called sociographic school. At stake is a rather Dutch version of sociology developed in the Netherlands by S. R. Steinmetz, who until 1933 was a professor at the Municipal University of Amsterdam. In methodological terms, doing sociography originally implied that researchers described the situated life of local communities in all its material, physical, geographical, demographical, social, and moral details. This could be done by analyzing all kinds of available local sources, such as historical travel reports, newspaper archives, regional novels, memorial books, police archives, and local statistics; by talking to local spokesmen such as priests, social workers, policemen, and union officials; and by observing local relations and customs. Simply speaking to the local population itself was considered unscientific. It took a learned mind to observe things properly (see Steinmetz, 1942).[2]

For Steinmetz, sociography aimed not only at detailed descriptions of the situated life of people, but also at a general theory of human civilization. Inductive classifications and comparisons of the situated life of people living in various places should in the end lead to an explanation of their type and stage of civilization. Civilization here stood for a rationally formulated, empirically traceable, and scientifically explainable phenomenon. It depended upon two indicators, on "the possession of which enormous depends, that more than anything else influences the entire social and cultural life" (Steinmetz, 1942, p. 115). These indicators were "the nature of thinking" and "the foundation of the means of sustaining life." Both functioned as an indication of the position of a people on the developmental axis between "natural societies" and "cultural societies." A naive associative sort of thinking, little strength of mind, and a primitive sort of maintenance, namely gathering, characterized the first group. The second group was blessed with a critical and systematic sort of thinking and a high industrial economy (Steinmetz, 1942, pp. 115–122).

It is perhaps clear now what was at stake. Dutch sociography was one of those many twentieth-century heirs of a colorful nineteenth-century European social-evolutionist tradition. According to Mandelbaum, in those days social evolutionism was so popular that "Even for those who did not regard social evolution as part of a single evolutionary process, and even when its truth was not taken to be a corollary of Darwin, it was widely believed that the only scientifically correct way of understanding man's history was through the use of comparative methods, in which societies were seen as representing stages in human development" (Mandelbaum, cited in Manicas, 1987, p. 71). Evolutionist works such as those of Spencer (*The Principles of Sociology,* 1879), Darwin (*On the Origin of the Species,* 1859/1970), Bachofen (*Myth, Religion, and Mother Right,* 1861/1973), and Tylor (*Primitive Culture,* 1877) are quoted by Steinmetz, and he is especially critical about a too extreme organic analogy and naturalism. Nevertheless, the project of sociography remained within the broader definition of social evolutionism, very much inspired by the work of Herbert Spencer.

Contrary to what one would expect, however, this interest in Spencer's social evolutionism did not result in some *laissez-faire* viewpoint. Instead, the academics involved committed themselves strongly to the humanist project of popular education and the social democratic goal of workers' emancipation. Indeed, such dyads as theory and practice, objective science and popular education, rationality and humanism, came together in the person of Steinmetz himself. He was not only the founding father of sociography, but also an initiator of the so-called *Volksuniversiteit* (Popular University), both of which aimed at the distribution of popularized scientific knowledge among the Dutch population. At the occasion of the opening of the first Popular University in 1913 in Amsterdam, Steinmetz said, "Teaching the higher sciences may perhaps be unfeasible. However, also knowledge achievable for many is of great value; it turns people into better national citizens, gives them the capability to judge and value more fairly, gives spiritual independence and a heightening of the most noble delights" (Steinmetz, cited in Gastelaars, 1985, p. 70). What is interesting about this quotation, besides the link that is made between nationalism, rationalism, morality, and aesthetic appraisal, is the suggested aim of the project of popular education. Despite the proclaimed "natural" relation between race and culture, popular education is considered worthwhile. It will not close the gap between the cultivated and the uncultivated, but it could bring people to an understanding and acceptance of the rationalist worldview involved. As a consequence, measures necessary to reach a higher level of civilization would also become acceptable, even if these would be of an eugenist character (see also Steinmetz, 1917).

Thus a tight configuration was established between public education, moral evaluation, and science, with science as the base. The cultivation of "wild cultures" (Gellner, 1983) was legitimized and given direction by a scientifically traceable and rationally quantifiable civilizing process. At the same time, the public project of popular education formed an important cultural resource and base of support for scientific practice. In between there was the interpretation and evaluation of people's leisure activities, framed in a theory of history that at the same time reflected the self-image and aspirations of a class and a profession, positioned in terms of the opposition between culture and pleasure.

ENGINEERING AND FUNCTIONAL ANALYSES

In the second half of the 1950s, a new generation of social scientists got involved in the study of free time. As said above, the members of this generation actively aimed at what they proclaimed as a modernization of the social sciences. This implied that distinctions such as those between active and passive, cultivated and vulgar, or culture and pleasure came to be looked upon as a part and reflection of localized status aspirations. The way people spend their free time is the expression less of a level of civilization and more of relations of sociocultural inequality. What dominates the research on leisure far into the 1970s is the issue of the social differentiation of free time behavior. As one member of this generation put it, questions asked in this period concerned the relations between people's work (work time, work environment, and prestige) and their free time; the relations between social structure (social status, sex, age, origin, education, and religion) and free time; group-specific values regarding free time and their mutual relations; and relations between free time and the structure of Dutch geography (Heinemeijer, 1959, p. 99). But what above all had to take place was a transformation of the relation between science and morality. The social ontology of political and denominational elites had to be considered as such, and become the object of what was called a process of "demythologization." What took place was no less than a radical reformulation of the older enlightenment project. Researchers now thought that former generations had not gone far enough, that they mistook what in effect were situated moralities and ideologies for universal categories. A more detached and more rigorous social scientific enterprise would be able to demarcate science and value more precisely, with the result that people's free time would appear less of a moral threat.

From the perspective of the intellectual field of leisure studies, this transformation in the social analysis of free time can be connected to two mutually related developments: a turn toward American sociology, and a growing interest in issues of social stratification.

For a postwar generation of sociologists, speculative social theory was no longer attractive. German social thought came to be regarded as a product of traditional Europe, as "classical" social theory. Instead, America appeared to be not only the place of nylon stockings and Lucky Strikes, but also of a totally new, more open, and truly "scientific" brand of sociology that also was better suited to the task of constructing a modern, more open, socially mobile, and rationally planned society. The Dutch postwar field of social theory gradually became dominated by the intellectual triangle of Parsons, Merton, and Lazarsfeld. Central in this was the combination of various versions of functional analyses, coupled with a methodology derived from experimental statistics. As far as free time was concerned, what dominated the intellectual field were analyses of the functional relations between free-time behavior and a wide range of other social and psychological factors. These analyses could be based on a "strong" version of functionalism (in which functionalism was used as an explaining device in itself) or on some "soft" version (in which functional relations were seen as relations of correspondence, in need of some further causal explanation).

Integral to American functionalism, however, was also a neo-evolutionist interpretation of history. Human evolution was seen as having "unfolded" along a succession of stages of differentiation and integration, in the course of which societies became capable of an increased adaptation to and thus control over their natural and cultural environments. On top of this history of modernization, of course, stood the United States, with its idealized flexible and mobile labor market, secularized and rationalized culture, democratized politics, educational revolution, and open stratification structure.

This issue of changing patterns of social stratification captured the attention of sociologists in the Netherlands. The social stratification of Dutch society became heavily debated and researched, with many references made to Burnham's (1960) concept of the Managerial Revolution or Riesman's (1950) and Bell's (1973) idea of the coming of postindustrial society. This orientation provided the new generation of sociologists with a new intellectual and public platform, while also linking their intellectual interests to new public concerns and resources. The topic of social stratification stood at the center of debate between "modern" and "classical" social theorists, and at the same time offered a new sort of public authority and recognition in a period of major societal reconstruction. Not only the social sciences, but Dutch society in general had to be "modernized," to free itself from the remainders of a stratification system based upon particularistic values and relations of social honor and prestige. Working-class deviancies from mainstream middle-class aspirations were evaluated not as possible cultures in themselves, but as relics of a former class society, with those involved as part of a "proletarian rear guard" soon to be dragged into a new social realm of value openness and social mobility. As one of the leading sociologists expressed the mood later, "Of course, against progress there is decline, one has to do with unbridgeable gaps. But that was not popular in those days. Things of a subcultural nature, we even related that to racism, to heredity, it was a reactionary notion" (Van Doorn, cited in Bovenkerk, 1984, p. 8). Subcultural differences were a phenomenon from the past, soon to be incorporated and neutralized in the overall openness and individualism of postindustrial, mass middle-class society.

Within this perspective, there was no room any longer for particularistic values concerning the correct style or the correct way of spending one's free time. Instead, particularistic interests were seen as a hindrance to social mobility because they monopolized educational or cultural resources. Wasn't it Parsons himself who had typified the cultural pessimism of writers such as Ortega y Gasset and T. S. Eliot as a sign of a further secularization, now not only effecting religious thought, but also classical social theory itself? (See Parsons, 1977, p. 194.) Modernization needed a more open and plural value system, based upon generalized notions of rationality, democracy, equality of opinion, and individual responsibility.

Of course, this had major consequences for the scientific foundation of social critique. In his introduction to the report of the Central Bureau for Statistics, published in 1957, Thoenes distinguished between two principles that could lead to a scientific valuation of people's activities, the principle of "harmonic man" and the principle of "adjustment." The former, based upon a Greek and Renaissance heritage (and especially found in circles of popular and physical education, the Popular University, and the library system), had become redundant. The reason given is significant: "Scientifically" the harmonic man is "difficult to approach. In our pluralistic world there are almost as many images of ideal harmony as there are world views" (Centraal Bureau voor de Statistiek, 1957, p. 8). Because there are no longer any cultural models that can claim universal supremacy, the only possible foundation that remains of use is the idea of adjustment: "Here existing structures outside the realm of free time are thought of as unassailable and it is the function of recreation to absorb, divert or sublimate the tensions and unsatisfied needs elsewhere" (Centraal Bureau voor de Statistiek, 1957).

Thus what remained of value in the scientific assessment of people's free-time behavior was the notion of functional integration, a notion in fact directly related to the project of modernization itself. A clear example of this is given by Wippler (1968), another adherent of "modern sociology" but from a later generation. He defines free time as a social problem in so far as the value pattern of a society is not adjusted to its social structure. In the United States, he noticed, a traditional ascetic value system is replaced by a more hedonistic one. This mirrors a transformation in the social structure of the United States, from production to consumption. In the latter case, continued adherence to puritanism would lead to social frictions. The value relativity promoted was far from absolute, but bounded by considerations of social order, and thus still grounded upon an "external" scientific foundation.

In line with this change in social theory, a transformation took place in the social position and orientation of the intellectuals concerned. Whereas in previous periods they had linked their intellectual projects to "public reason" and to the edification of a well-informed public, during the postwar years, their social orientation moved from civil society and culture to the managerial state based either on Merton's model of the social engineer, with its ideal of functional rationality, or upon Mannheim's model of the *freischwebende Intelligenz*, with its ideal of substantive rationality. In both models, however, social scientists placed themselves above political debate, as administrative functionaries and experts of an expanding state seeking to fulfill the new social rights of the citizens who were now, ideally, universally middle class. Thanks to a growing affluence and an increased social welfare, political-ideological conflicts of any importance would cease to exist. Attention thus could be concentrated on the equal distribution of resources.

As far as leisure was concerned, research and policy aimed at the removal of economic and cultural barriers prohibiting equal access to an increasingly differentiated domain of free time, in order to enhance the individual freedom of choice of citizens, at least insofar as this did not hinder generalized social interests. For social scientists the task remained to investigate the stratified leisure needs of the population and to monitor and evaluate the use that different segments of the population made of various facilities and provisions. Both stratification and resource use were important tropes in legitimating policy decisions, which were based as much on "what the system needs" as on "what the people want." At best, scientists could also investigate the social mechanisms responsible for the social differentiation of free-time behavior. Given some knowledge of these mechanisms, scientifically legitimated measures could be taken to enhance equal access and personal self-fulfillment in leisure.

INTERPRETATION AND CONTEXTUAL ANALYSES

In the 1970s something like a leisure research profession with its own theories and methods established itself in the Netherlands. A small but steady stream of resources developed. It flowed from welfare-state institutions to research departments, and was based on a continuous administrative interest in people's free-time activities, in their cultural participation, recreational activities, sports participation, and the like. This, together with the expansion of programs and bureaucracies necessary to administer a growing number of provisions, formed an important stimulus for the emergence and proclamation of a free-time research profession that would also develop its own professional organizations.

At the same time that something like a research tradition developed, however, a next phase in the "demythologization" of the scientific absorption of free time also appeared, again carried along by attempts of new generations to position themselves in the academic field.

A first inspiration for this new approach to the study of leisure is derived from German neo-Marxist theory. Although critical theorists provided a foundation for an extensive critique of modern leisure (e.g., Horkheimer & Adorno [1947, p. 14] saw free time as the modernized domain of "pseudoindividuality" and "aesthetic barbary"), the deployment of their thought in Dutch leisure studies was first of all as a critique on what was called the ideological content of established research practices. Behind its value-free pose, established research conformed to, ideologically supported, and was often funded by a hegemonic order. Three factors may explain this. First, of course, the focus in this approach on issues of (mal)adjustment and hence on functionalism led to a validation of established social order. Second, its association of free time with free choice and its corresponding methodological individualism led it to ignore how established power relations actively constitute leisure. And third, its objectivist positivist research design encouraged it to overlook people's own definitions of their situations in favor of, again, established middle-class worldviews. In terms of Habermas's differentiation of system and lifeworld, in the second half of the 1970s, research became oriented toward people's everyday life, and the issue of free time was turned into the issue of the protection of the lifeworld from the world of market relations and technocratic policies of the state. A more qualitative, subjectivist, actor-centered approach was developed, stimulating a search for a social reality beyond middle-class definitions and administrative perspectives, that is, for the reality of the "common" people. For the first time, attacks were made on researchers taking an exclusively state-based focus on leisure. In the studies themselves, the model of "action-research" became popular. This was developed in Germany in the wake of critical theory as a research model that could stimulate people to present their own interests, through research, to the state institutions responsible for their welfare.

During the 1980s, this orientation toward German critical theory was supplemented and partly replaced by another orientation, one that stressed even more the study of free time in its larger social context. In this period, there is a growing interest in issues of culture and pleasure and hence of free time. This interest was stimulated by economic and political transformations in the 1980s, which among other factors led to a boom in consumer culture and a restructuring of codes of morality, taste, and style again. The economic crisis of the late 1970s delivered a decisive blow to the self-evident optimism that had accompanied modernization theory and its related theoretization of the postindustrial and free-time society. In response, a more contextual or situated approach to issues of pleasure and free time surfaced. This was stimulated by critical theory, by the British tradition of cultural studies and social history, by cultural anthropology, and also by inspirations derived from authors such as Elias (e.g., 1970), Bourdieu (e.g., 1972), and Giddens (e.g., 1976). Like other areas of social life, leisure was now to be regarded as a domain of ambivalences, distinctions, competitions, conflicts, and dominations. Free-time activities were now studied as situated events, whether the focus was on the unemployed or youth, the use made of leisure as a means to revitalize inner cities, gambling, the censuring regulations of films, the noble pleasures of a hunting elite, the transformation of women's participation in pop music, the culture of health and fitness, commercially organized sports, the hanging out of youth, the creation of tourist attractions, and other issues. In general, these developments could be said to honor Geertz's (1973) preference for "thick descriptions," Giddens's (1976) taste for discontinuity and contextuality, a rediscovery of hermeneutics, or even, if you like, a postmodern appetite for the fragmented, reflexive, or the other. Indeed, theories and approaches that do not situate themselves in time and space have become suspect. And one of the leading sentiments is to uncover what has remained invisible because of middle-brow, or white, or male perspectives, methods, and research agendas that had prevailed thus far.

Along with these initiatives, there also are avoidances. Attempts are no longer made to formulate general validations of people's leisure based upon some social theory of reality. The self-confidence with which a former generation judged and classified other people's leisure activities has disappeared, to be replaced by a distrust of any classifying practice whatever. After the pluralization of cultural models had toppled the ideal of the Greek-Renaissance "harmonic man" from its scientific pedestal, the ideal of social harmony or equilibrium, with its notion of adjustment and maladjustment, also has been deprived of its self-evident scientific status. In a globalizing world, with its pluralization of cultural models and contexts of life and its diffusion or diversification of "authorities" (cf. Giddens, 1991), leisure also comes to be viewed as a plurality of practices, not to be related to each other any longer in terms of relations of high and low, culture and pleasure, or normality and deviancy, but in terms of strategies and relations of power, of social distinctions and identities. Categories of high and low, good and evil, culture and pleasure are removed from the realm of social theory and put back into the realm of social reality, an "objectified subject" turned into a "subjectified object."

THE END OF THE LEGISLATOR?

At first sight, the history of leisure research in the Netherlands seems to be an instance of Bauman's thesis. Whereas in the 1930s researchers primarily looked at people's free time as something to be mastered or even captured, as a frontier of civilization against barbarism (military analogies weren't unusual), today academics seem to take free time as a cultural reality in its own right, as "an object for study, something to be mastered only cognitively, as a meaning, and not practically, as a task" (Bauman, 1992, p. 23). Instead of the self-confidence with which a former generation once classified and validated people's leisure, today every classification is suspect, potentially the object of a critique with regard to its "objectified," "middle-class," "reified," "ideological," or "ahistorical" character. True, the concept of free time has long been an object of debate leading those still thinking in terms of Kuhn's model of scientific normality to conclude that "leisure studies" is still a "young" or "multiparadigmatic" science. Nonetheless, today any attempt to suggest some theoretically active, generalized concept of free time is immediately liable to critique as a possible essentialization or reification. At the same time, however, the role of the interpreter seems to offer academics a new opportunity for social respectability now that administrators no longer need "grand designs." Whereas our first exemplar of leisure research oriented itself predominantly to "civil society" and our second example aimed at the central state, our third example flirts with the market, not in order to deliver some "grand design," but to help market actors navigate a more complex and fast-changing flow of products and images.

Beside this overall resemblance to Bauman's model, however, certain qualifications are necessary to put the so-called "crisis of the intellectual" in the right perspective. First, of course, the turn of intellectuals away from the role of legislator can be contested from various sides. From a political angle, some intellectuals would like to see the social sciences actively carrying on their foundational function, either for the sake of neoliberal or radical politics or for the sake of some generalized notion of social order. From a more theoretical angle, others still adhere to the conventional positivist promise that the social sciences can deliver universal laws of social development and, in the case of the study of leisure, can explain people's leisure with the help of some unequivocal logic or objectivity. Of course we witness a pluralization of leisure practices, but for positivists such a pluralization can be studied by turning from institutionally oriented theories to more individualistic ones. Hence the popularity today in the study of leisure of versions of rational-choice theory and of psychological theory in general. In research in the Netherlands (see Knulst, 1991), this turn to rational-choice theory is legitimated with the explicit argument that in a plural society leisure can no longer be explained by the social conditions in which people live. Instead, leisure has to be understood as the result of the interchange between the relatively stable preferences and competencies of individuals and changing temporal and financial conditions. In the meantime, people's leisure activities are still categorized into objectifying classifications, clearly reflecting definitions that emerge from policy considerations rather than actors' lifeworlds.

Second and more principally, the turn to the role of interpreter does not preclude academics from joining public debate as such. On the contrary, one could say that academics are back again. Whereas during the era of the social engineer, academics turned away from their classic public role of the intellectual to that of the state-oriented expert, today they gain academic respect by taking part in public debates in journals or magazines, appearing on talk shows, or keynoting public conferences. As intellectuals, academics do not seem to be able to remove themselves from the field of cultural entrepreneurship. Today, the cognitive mastery of leisure, culture, and consumption has become something of a task in itself, a task in which academics share and compete with loads of other professionals such as journalists and marketeers. Ultimately, however, within that domain of cultural reflexivity, academics tend to present themselves not just as interpreters among others, but as authorities. Within "reflexive modernity" (cf. Giddens, 1991), the practice of interpretation has become a new domain of intellectual legislation. As Bauman himself also seems to acknowledge (see Bauman, 1992, p. 22), in the end academics have not so much lost the legislative role as they have found a new domain in which to play that role, the domain of the interpreter. Nowadays academics regard themselves and are regarded as masters of reflexivity and interpretation. Because of their academic training and the theoretical capital thereby gained, they are the best equipped to make available in discourse what otherwise would remain hidden from view in the mundane and unreflective flow of everyday routines and interests.

NOTES

1. This chapter is largely the result of a project that aimed at the recollection of sixty years of social research in the Netherlands concerning people's free time. The results were published in Beckers and Mommaas (1991). In addition, they formed part of a broader European research project (see Mommaas, Van der Poel, Bramham, & Henry, 1996). I would like to thank Richard H. Brown for his detailed comments on an earlier version of this paper, which certainly improved its accessibility.

2. When in 1936 research workers themselves were interviewed, that was truly an exception. In fact, this is the first example of survey research in the Netherlands. But then these were organized, involved laborers, and thus better equipped to observe things "rationally."

REFERENCES

Bachofen, J. J. (1973). *Myth, religion, and mother right: Selected writings of J. J. Bachofen.* Princeton: Princeton University Press. (Original work published 1861)

Bauman, Z. (1987). *Legislators and interpreters.* Cambridge: Polity Press.

Bauman, Z. (1992). Legislators and interpreters: Culture as the ideology of intellectuals. In Z. Bauman (Ed.), *Intimations of Postmodernity* (pp. 1-26). London: Routledge.

Beckers, T. (1983). *Planning voor vrijheid.* Wageningen, The Netherlands: Landbouwhogeschool.

Beckers, T., & Mommaas, H. (Eds.). (1991). *Het vraagstuk van den vrijen tijd, 60 jaar onderzoek naar vrijetijd.* Leiden, The Netherlands: Stenfert Kroese.

Bell, D. (1973). *The coming of post-industrial society: A venture in social forecasting.* New York: Basic Books.

Blonk, A., Kruijt, J. P., & Hofstee, E. W. (1929). *De besteding van de vrije tijd door de Nederlandse arbeiders.* Enschede, The Netherlands: Tubantia.

Bourdieu, P. (1972). *Esquisse dune théorie de la pratique.* Geneva: Librairie Droz.

Bovenkerk, F. (1984). Havemann en Van Doorn over de ongeschoolde arbeider. *Sociodrome, 1,* 3-9.

Burnham, J. (1960). *The managerial revolution.* Bloomington: Indiana University Press.

Centraal Bureau voor de Statistiek. (1957). *Vrije-tijdsbesteding in Nederland, Winter 1955/56, Dl. 1, Methodologische inleiding.* Zeist, The Netherlands: De Haan.

Centraal Bureau voor de Statistiek. (1958). *Vrije-tijdsbesteding in Nederland. Winter 1955/56, Dl. 8, Sociaal milieu en vrije-tijdsbesteding.* Zeist, The Netherlands: De Haan.

Darwin, C. (1970). *On the origin of the species.* New York: Harmondsworth, Penguin. (Original work published 1859)

Elias, N. (1970). *Was ist soziologie?* Munich: Juventa Verlag.

Foucault, M. (1980). *Power/knowledge: Selected interviews and other writings 1972-1977* (C. Gordon, Ed.). New York: Pantheon.

Gastelaars, M. (1985). *Een geregeld leven: Sociologie en sociale politiek in Nederland 1925-1968.* Amsterdam: Sua.

Geertz, C. (1973). *The interpretation of cultures.* New York: Basic Books.

Gellner, E. (1983). *Nations and nationalism.* Oxford: Basil Blackwell.

Giddens, A. (1976). *New rules of the sociological method.* London: Hutchinson.

Giddens, A. (1991). *Modernity and self-identity.* Cambridge: Polity Press.

Giddens, A. (1992). *The consequences of modernity.* Cambridge: Polity Press.

Heinemeijer, W. F. (1959). De sociologische bestudering van de vrije tijd. *Sociologische Gids, 6/2,* 89-109.

Horkheimer, M., & Adorno, T. W. (1947). *Dialektik der aufklärung. Filosofische fragmente.* Amsterdam: Querido Verlag.

Kalb, D., & Kingma, T. W. (Eds.). (1991). *Fragmenten van vermaak. Macht en plezier in de 19e en 20e eeuw.* Amsterdam: Rodopi.

Knulst, W. (1991) Vrijetijd, een kwestie van kiezen of delen. In T. Beckers & H. Mommaas (Eds.), *Het vraagstuk van den vrijen tijd, 60 jaar onderzoek naar vrijetijd* (pp. 265-277). Leiden, The Netherlands: Stenfert Kroese.

Manicas, P. T. (1987). *A history and philosophy of the social sciences.* Oxford: Basil Blackwell.

Mommaas, H., Van der Poel, H., Bramham, P., & Henry, I. P. (Eds.). (1996). *Leisure research in Europe: Methods and traditions.* Oxon, UK: CAB International.

Parsons, T. (1977). *The evolution of societies.* Englewood Cliffs, NJ: Prentice-Hall.

Riesman, D. (1950). *The lonely crowd.* New Haven: Yale University Press.

Spencer, H. (1879). *The principles of sociology.* New York: Appleton.

Steinmetz, S. R. (1917). *Eugenese als ideaal en wetenschap, in: De toekomst der Maatschappij. Negen voordrachten.* Amsterdam: De Maatschappij voor Goede en Goedkoope Lectuur.

Steinmetz, S. R. (1942). *Inleiding tot de sociologie.* Haarlem, The Netherlands: De Erven F. Bohn.

Tylor, E. B., Sir. (1877). *Primitive culture: Researches into the development of mythology, philosophy, religion, languages, art, and customs.* New York: H. Holt and Company.

Wippler, R. (1968). *Sociale determinanten van het vrijetijdsgedrag.* Assen: Van Gorcum.

SIX

ACADEMY AND ASYLUM
Power, Knowledge, and Mental Disability

JOHN P. RADFORD

TO A DEGREE that is disguised by the apparently separate social worlds they occupy, the modern university and the custodial mental disability asylum emerged in parallel.[1] Both are in a sense creations of the Enlightenment, representing its positive and negative personae. The modern university evolved as a seat of learning and scholarship. At its best it has been a champion of truth, outward-looking and cosmopolitan, its self-image increasingly identified with a secular search for knowledge and truth in the interest of human progress. The asylum represents its antithesis, a closed world of ignorance and failure. While this applies to asylums in general, it is especially true of those established to confine people labeled mental defectives.

The university, increasingly in modern times the seat and symbol of supposedly rational thought, has usually been highly visible. Centers of learning, whether situated in the great urban centers or in their own exclusive college towns, have characteristically occupied privileged locations. Many of the early asylums aspired to this kind of status, their buildings designed to act as symbols of progress and therapy, but such notions were soon eclipsed. Asylums became hidden places, located outside major population centers. These contrasting geographical locations parallel the differing social positions of university and asylum, one at the crux of modern society, the other at its margin.

While the asylum remains on the edge of our consciousness, however, the writings of Erving Goffman (1961), Michel Foucault (1979), and others have shown that it occupies a central position in power–knowledge relations. What is found in the asylum, they suggest, is not confined to the spaces within its walls but is relevant to, and perhaps diagnostic of, wider society. The asylum, in a sense, epitomizes modern society. Its calculated marginalization redounds with instruction on the meaning of the Enlightenment.

The emerging asylum can be seen as part of what Max Horkheimer and Theodore Adorno (1969, p. xiii) described as the Enlightenment's "recidivist element," the dark side inherent in its fundamental dialectic. Other authors have recognized this dark side of the Enlightenment's legacy. Among recent commentators, David Noble (1997) attacks its enchantment with technological salvation, while John Ralston Saul (1992) warns that the pursuit of reason has left us with a void in our system of values. In contrast, the sociobiologist Edward O. Wilson (1998) has once more reasserted his faith in Enlightenment ideals, and predicts a "consilience" of knowledge around the methods of the natural sciences as the errant ways of the social sciences and humanities become more apparent.

The diverging paths of university and asylum reflect an Enlightenment dialectic. Ironically, as the ideals of these two institutions became more incompatible in the nineteenth century, certain academic disciplines and related professions, especially law, education, medicine, and psychology, assumed authority over the asylum.

One aspect of increasing professionalism was the development of a field distinct from that dealing with mental illness and concerning itself with a set of diagnoses variously referred to as "mental deficiency," "feeble-mindedness," "mental handicap," or "mental retardation." Today, members of such professions serve people who are often described as having an "intellectual or developmental disability" or as being "intellectually challenged." This modern separation between mental illness and mental disability represents the formal professionalization of the legal distinction between lunacy and idiocy dating from the medieval period. Of the two fields, mental disability has received much less scholarly attention, and the significance of its social history is only now beginning to become widely understood. It is no coincidence that while the academy has expressed few reservations about incorporating the study of mental illness into its curriculum, it has an uneasy relationship with the reality of intellectual disability. While professional attitudes toward the curability of mental illness have varied, belief in the potential curability of at least a significant proportion of patients has produced strategies and agendas attractive to Enlightenment perspectives. The mentally ill might offend rationality, but they were rarely viewed a priori as totally beyond redemption. The apparent incurability of intellectual disability, by contrast, challenges the very foundation of the Enlightenment ethos.

While the academy has produced significant studies on the definitions, causes, prevention, and measurement of mental deficiency, these investigations have tended to be pursued on the margins of established disciplines: in *special* education, or on the fringes of psychology and medicine. The concept of mental deficiency has consistently implied a degree of deviance. This has been reinforced by the fact that until recently almost all "scientific" studies were done on incarcerated populations, the conclusions then being projected onto others. Moreover, the dominant philosophy within the professional-academic mainstream has tended to pronounce mental deficiency a lost cause, and its victims "hopeless cases." It is this hopelessness that the closed, custodial mental handicap asylum came to represent. Despite physical deinstitutionalization (which has in any case been more slowly implemented than in mental illness), the ontology of intellectual disability has yet to enter a postasylum era. Attitudes remain embedded in a murky past.

I argue in this chapter that the stigmatizing forces operating on people with an intellectual disability have in the past been given powerful legitimation by the academy. For over a century university researchers with any interest in the issue overwhelmingly and consistently supported negative views of people diagnosed as mentally deficient. It was generally held, for example, that they were a naturally defined group apart, that they were biologically inferior, that their condition was largely incurable, and that collectively they represented a genetic and social threat. The university lent powerful authority to arguments asserting the necessity for the incarceration of so-called mental defectives for the social good. In doing so, it legitimated the custodial mental handicap asylums (later called "training schools" in many jurisdictions). Thus the academy and the asylum, despite following apparently divergent paths in the modern era, were in fact closely interconnected.

In addition, I confront the commonly held view that, while it acknowledges the rampant stigmatization of people with a mental disability by academia in former times, asserts that there has in recent years been a reversal of opinion. The implication of this view is that the writings of previous generations of university researchers are of historical interest only, and are irrelevant to an understanding of recent trends. I argue, on the contrary, that attitudes that prevailed earlier within the academy are still persistent and deeply embedded, and that although there have been changes, these have followed rather than led those in wider society. The examples that can be cited of progressive university-based programs of education, care, and community living directed at people with an intellectual disability tend to emanate from the margins even of those few disciplines that profess an interest. The cores of these fields remain much closer to an academic mainstream wherein even those who identify with a view of social science that celebrates the differences of gender, ethnicity, and sexuality overlook disability, especially mental disability. Progress in integration is also stunted by a general disinterest elsewhere within the academy, and the presence outside it of professionals previously inculcated by the academy with professional norms that are incompatible with institutional change.

Most of the progress in integration made in the past 30 years, then, has come from outside the academy and often from nonprofessionals, mainly in the voluntary sector. In cases where the academy's role has been progressive, this has stemmed from the unusual energy and determination of a relatively small number of people. In other words, it has come not because of university research agendas, but in spite of them. This says more about the culture of the modern university than it does about the nature of mental disability.

MENTAL DISABILITY AND THE ENLIGHTENMENT

The Enlightenment project penetrated the university surprisingly slowly, not impacting it significantly until the second half of the nineteenth century. In Britain the foundation of the University of London did not, for example, seriously challenge the clerical domination of Oxbridge and Durham. Not until the Redbricks were established, mainly after 1880, was the monastic ideal substantially replaced by a desire for relevance to the requirements of an industrial society (Lowe, 1983, p. 39). Yet once embraced, and especially since the turn of the century, modernist ideas have permeated the curriculum. Significant developments in higher education occurred in the United States before the Civil War, but here too the great expansion and transformation both of private and state universities came in the second half of the century. In both countries the new thinking also encouraged a closer association between the universities and the professions (Engel, 1983), a situation that was matched by experience elsewhere in Europe, especially Germany (McClelland, 1983). While national models in Europe varied greatly, the nineteenth-century reform movement was a pervasive one that cut across national and regional boundaries (Thelin, 1982, pp. 67–81).

Some academic disciplines were affected more than others by these trends. Many owe their very existence to Enlightenment thought, and it would be difficult to identify a discipline that had not been influenced by its ideas by the early decades of this century. At one level this is laudable, since in many cases it has enabled universities to be in the forefront of the acquisition of knowledge and its applications. At the same time, the dominance of reason has led to a blinding insensitivity to certain groups in society, and none more than the intellectually disabled, that most vulnerable of groups. However misguided or bizarre the various treatments of mental illness may have been, for example, they were at least founded in the possibility of a cure, or at least control of the affliction. But even rudimentary optimism was quickly abandoned in cases of so-called mental deficiency. The authority inherent within professional and disciplinary structures was exerted against the interests of such people to a degree that remains too little appreciated. Once the stigma of mental deficiency had been embedded in the culture, it was used as a trap to ensnare "undesirables" of all kinds. The diagnosis mentally deficient, especially when supported by the whole armory of statistical manipulations, was convincing evidence for the necessity of removing the "afflicted" from free society. By the early years of this century, people were routinely being incarcerated in custodial mental handicap asylums for reasons that had nothing to do with intelligence and everything to do with their social undesirability. In addition to those specifically diagnosed as feebleminded, the asylums were populated by people described simply as "inefficients," judged too dull to keep up with the requirements of modern society.

As the Enlightenment bent on its course toward individual progress and rationality, no human type was more perplexing to it than the "idiot." True, the lunatic was also a deviant, as were the criminal, the inebriate, and the pauper, but the idiot was condemned several times over. In an age that celebrated beauty and perfection almost as much as intelligence, the idiot was considered dull, flawed, and defaced with stigmata. Apparent incurability made the individual's plight even worse. John Locke articulated the distinction in blunt terms: while the lunatic had lost his mind, the idiot never had one. Whereas a lost mind might be restored to normality in some way by coaxing or shocking it out of its disorder, what had never existed could not (according to Locke) be artificially created. While the criminal might be reformed and the poor rescued, the idiot represented hopelessness.

But there was another completely opposite view that flourished briefly among a reforming elite in the 1850s and 1860, only to evaporate during the closing decades of the century. This period of intense optimism produced the earliest mental handicap asylums. Imbued with the most positive of Enlightenment traditions, the optimism revolved around new ideas about the educability of mentally disabled children. These may be traced, particularly in the new English asylums, to Guggenbuhl's home for cretins on the Abendberg in Switzerland, but the major actor was undoubtedly Eduard Seguin. A pupil of Itard, the physician known for his studies of the "wild boy of Averyon," Seguin was an enthusiastic supporter of Saint-Simon's views on the industrial state as directed by modern science (Scheerenberger, 1983, p. 68). He believed in the educability of all children and advocated the intensive use of sensory-motor activities as a route to learning. In

1844 the Paris Academy of Science declared that he had solved the problem of idiot education (Baumeister, 1970). Following the revolution of 1848, Seguin left France for Massachusetts and became influential in the establishment of numerous institutions in the northeastern states. He was the principal organizer of the American Association on Mental Deficiency, founded in 1866, and his text *Idiocy and Its Treatment by the Physiological Method* (1866) became the standard work in the field. The early asylums, established to educate mentally disabled children, especially those from poor families, relied heavily on Seguin's method. Their founders considered them educational establishments, confident that most of the children accepted into their programs would benefit from the training provided and would graduate to relative self-sufficiency in the outside world. Only a minority unable to respond would require a permanent institutional home.

Such institutions were founded during the middle decades of the nineteenth century in several western European nations. Often, as in England, they were private institutions (Radford & Tipper, 1988). Elsewhere, as in most U.S. states, public money was appropriated. An article published in the *Edinburgh Review* in 1865, apparently written by Edwin Sidney, noted the work of Guggenbuhl and Seguin as well as Langdon Down at the Earlswood Asylum in England, and Samuel G. Howe and others in the United States. Sidney noted the "remarkable uniformity of principle and practice" internationally. Although "a few years since schools for idiots would have been classed among the wildest of projects," there was now, he reported, "a universal sense of hope for their efficacy" (Sidney, 1865, p. 50). The new institutions had been conceived in the conviction that, if given special training, "all idiots can be improved . . . all their habits may be amended . . . all their moral feelings amended."

A sense of hopelessness was to be found underlying even the most enthusiastic rhetoric. Some of this can be detected in the work of Langdon Down, who, as medical officer of the Earlswood Asylum, embraced the optimism of the age and fully supported the asylum's role as an educational institution. According to Sidney, who toured Earlswood in 1859 and again in 1861, Down "had fitted up numerous neat cabinets with specimens of natural productions, and these are used as objects for lessons to be described in simple language, and the class is questioned on them, which tends very much to increase the powers of inquiry and observation" (Sidney, 1865, p. 53). Classes also used colored wooden shapes for counting and for fitting together. Carpentry, gardening, farming, and other activities were encouraged. Unlike some who thought such efforts a waste of time and resources, Down did not question the humanity of the people in his care.

Yet a few years after conducting Edwin Sidney on his tour of Earlswood, Down published the paper for which he is best known (Down, 1867), a paper so imbued with determinist notions of class, race, and intelligence that it stands as an artifact of contemporary culture. Down was seeking a framework within which to interpret the meticulous observations he had made of the physical and behavioral characteristics of the children in his care. Noticing in some children a set of recurrent stigmata, notably the shape of the head and ears and the presence of an epicanthic fold, he suggested that these were atavisms. A predisposition to the notion of recapitulation (the notion that "ontogeny replicates phylogeny") convinced him that they evidenced the appearance of Mongolian features (one step down the supposed racial hierarchy) in a Caucasian family. It was in such terms, blissfully unaware of the depth of his own biases and trusting in the objectivity of his science, that Down explained the "physical and psychical" characteristics of this particular group. The associations he articulated became fixed for a time in the genealogy of mental disability, and the labels "mongolian idiot" and "mongoloid" remained part of its lexicon for more than a century, which makes it ironic that the condition came to be known as Down Syndrome. As Stephen Gould has emphasized, these postulated links between human evolution, race, and intelligence were not made by an isolated eccentric, but were an "earnest attempt to construct a general, causal classification of mental deficiency based upon the best biological theory (and the pervasive racism) of the age" (Gould, 1980, p. 135).

The implications of the continuing scientific study of intellectual disability from an evolutionary standpoint were enormous. The "fool" whom the medieval church had seen as an object of pity or a holy innocent was now revealed by science as a biological freak, and thus inevitably a social deviant. Meanwhile, firsthand experience in asylum praxis was already beginning to suggest that the early optimism on the question of educability had been ill-founded. Asylum staffs were frustrated by what they perceived to be intractable obstacles, the "idiot" having failed to respond to perfectly reasonable methods of training and education. The blame for this failure was placed on the victim. As with the "insane asylums" a decade or two earlier (Scull, 1991), the asylum ideal in the new so-called "idiot asylums" began to atrophy almost as soon as it was born.

By the last two decades of the century, the rationale of the asylum had shifted from education to control. Harvey Simmons has described a sequence of four policy models that can be traced in Britain and North America, each one largely superseding its predecessor without entirely obliterating it (Simmons, 1982). On top of the original educational model was grafted a true asylum model: institutionalization for the protection of the disabled themselves. This gave way to an overlay of social welfare, onto which in turn was superimposed a custodial model: incarceration for the supposed benefit of the rest of society. The result was a policy palimpsest, the earlier layers of which could barely be discerned beneath the later ones. During the last quarter of the nineteenth century the custodial model took prominence, and custodialism clearly dominated the policy landscape.

THE ROLE OF THE ACADEMY

Science in general and the academy in particular (especially its disciplines of medicine and the social sciences) provided legitimation for this sequence of events. The construct of mental deficiency or feeblemindedness was set in place and its association with the desirability of custodial segregation was established. Two sets of "scientific" underpinnings were then positioned beneath this construct, anchoring it so securely that its residues remain even a century later. First, a revitalized eugenics movement made mental deficiency its major preoccupation. Second, the idea became widely accepted that intellectual capacity could be precisely measured, and that such measurements should form the basis of social policy.

These two thrusts were first integrated by Francis Galton. Following Darwin (a cousin), Galton argued that the success of medical science in Western nations had artificially prolonged the average life span of mental deficients who were now being kept alive well into their reproductive years. This situation required the application of appropriate correctives based on scientific inquiry. Galton pursued both the social question of correctives and the "scientific" inquiry. When he gave the Herbert Spencer Lecture at Oxford in 1907, for example, he treated the audience to a lesson in basic statistics (a lifelong source of fascination) before turning to a discussion of control measures (Galton, 1907). In the same year he created the Eugenics Laboratory, and on his death in 1911 endowed a chair in eugenics at the University of London, the first occupant being Karl Pearson, who was succeeded by H. A. Fisher and Lionel Penrose (Mazumdar, 1992). The entrenchment of quantitative definitions of intelligence at the University of London was solidified by two successive occupants of the chair in psychology at University College: Charles Spearman and Cyril Burt.

Eugenic ideas and the measurement of intelligence were effectively brought together in the American literature by Robert H. Goddard, whose invention of the "moron" is a powerful illustration of the power of the construct of mental deficiency. This label, which Goddard created in 1910 to describe people who were "mildly deficient," produced a threefold hierarchy of feeblemindedness: moron, imbecile, and idiot.[2] Morons, Goddard argued, could only be detected by the trained observer. They had no physical stigmata or unusual behavior patterns, but were nevertheless of low intelligence and bad moral character. Since they reproduced much more rapidly than ordinary folk, he argued, the intellectual capital of the nation was in peril of being dragged down to the lowest common denominator.

The invention of the moron stemmed from Goddard's work at the Vineland Training Center for Feebleminded Girls and Boys in New Jersey, where his brief was to discover the causes of feeblemindedness. His field researchers fanned out into the community conducting family surveys that contributed to his 1914 book, *Feeble-mindedness: Its Causes and Consequences.* In the course of this work it became apparent that a particularly rich body of data was available on the family of one eight-year-old resident, and a researcher named Elizabeth Kite was assigned the task of compilation. The result was the publication, two years before the major survey, of a study of this family, to whom Goddard gave the pseudonym "the Kallikaks." *The Kallikak Family* (1912) was only one in a whole genre of pedigree studies. As far back as 1877 Richard Dugdale (1910) had published *The Jukes,* which purported to demonstrate high fertility rates among the feebleminded, and the enormous costs incurred to society through the provision of relief. *The Kallikak Family,* however, exerted an authority that could be imparted only by its acknowledgment as science. In essence, Goddard and Kite claimed to trace the family of Deborah Kallikak, a pupil at Vineland, back several generations to a transient relationship between Martin Kallikak and a woman (whom Goddard 150 years later diagnosed as feebleminded) during the American Revolution. The descendants were portrayed as beset with a high incidence of crime, idiocy, and poverty. A second line of the family, stemming from Martin's later marriage, had no such problems, being full of solid citizens and property owners. The book contained elements to capture both professional and popular attention. Not only was it standard material in psychology texts into the 1950s, it also became a sort of primal myth in subsequent discourses of intelligence (Smith, 1985, p. 170).

Goddard's testing of World War I military recruits, which discovered horrendous levels of supposed intellectual deficit, and the part played by educational testing in restricting immigration during the 1920s are well documented. Yet, as Gelb (1986, 1987) has pointed out, Goddard's role has often been exaggerated to the detriment of a full appreciation of the general acceptance of the notions he presented. The tests merely operationalized a long-felt need, and Goddard's claims for their results were in fact more modest than proponents of the "menace of the feebleminded" theory were content with. The same forces were evident in Britain, where the "borderline feebleminded" were regarded by eugenicists as especially dangerous because they could "pass as normal" unless exposed by the Binet tests (Searle, 1976, p. 104).

The impact of eugenics on social thought in the early decades of this century, and the interconnections between North America, Britain, and Germany, have become apparent in recent years (see especially Chase, 1980; Kevles, 1985; McLaren, 1990; Mazumdar, 1992; Miller, 1996; Radford, 1991; Trombley, 1988). My purpose here is simply to stress only two points: the pivotal symbolic role of the mental handicap asylum, and its legitimation by the academy. The custodial asylum was a concrete manifestation of the same forces that fueled the eugenics movement. As intellectually handicapped persons were viewed less as objects of pity and more as a social threat, asylums lost their roles as agents for progressive reform and became places of last resort (Ryan & Thomas, 1980). Existing asylums were transformed, and many new ones were constructed. Goddard's invention of the "moron" provided a pretext for the institutionalization of all kinds of perceived deviants in the name of preserving the race from degeneration. The imperative was inexorable, and only the huge costs of opening and maintaining permanent facilities prevented the incarceration of more of the large numbers of "defectives" unearthed by the tests.

To confront these mounting costs, eugenicists increasingly called for state-sponsored sterilization programs. Some advocated involuntary sterilization of "defectives," while others wrestled with proposals for supposedly voluntary programs. Coercive sterilization programs began in the United States in 1907 and had been implemented in 30 states by 1958 (Scheerenberger, 1983, p. 155). This trend did nothing to reduce the significance of the asylum, partly because most of the sterilizations took place within asylum walls. By 1941 more than 38,000 people had been sterilized in American institutions (Reilly, 1991, p. 97). To the extent that sterilization was a precondition to release it was, in effect, a cost-effective extension of the segregation model. Before World War I the sterilization programs in the United States were the most ambitious in the Western world. They became even more widespread after the 1927 Supreme court decision in *Buck vs. Bell,* a case made infamous by the opinion of Justice Oliver Wendell Holmes that "three generations of imbeciles are enough."

The thread that links these sterilization programs with similar ones in Germany in the 1930s is clear (Chase, 1980; Miller, 1996; Smith, 1985; Trombley, 1988). The Nazi Hereditary Health Law of 1933 was based directly on a model law drafted by Harry Laughlin of the Eugenics Record Office that had been designed to evade U.S. constitutional objections. For his contribution Laughlin accepted in 1936 an honorary doctorate of medicine from the University of Heidelberg, which, he wrote, represented "a nation which for many centuries nurtured the human seed—stock which later founded my own country" (correspondence reprinted in Smith, 1985). Several other Americans were likewise recognized (Reilly, 1991, p. 108). The National Socialist regime's sterilization measure was just one step on the road to a systematic extermination program of "persons worthless to live," along lines that had been advocated in the 1920s (Kane & Rojahn, 1981). The philosophy, personnel, and equipment used to kill disabled persons evolved into those employed in the devastation of Europe's Jews (Wolfensberger, 1972). The U.S. state laws provided precedents for similar statutes in two Canadian provinces (McLaren, 1990) and most northern European countries (Reilly, 1991). Although Britain never got around to enacting a law for compulsory sterilization, a serious proposal from the Brock Commission of 1934 targeted some 3.5 million people for supposedly "voluntary" sterilization (Trombley, 1988, pp. 125–127).

Segregation and sterilization, then, both centered on the custodial asylum, and were complementary measures aimed at a common purpose: the supposed prevention of the transmission of presumed genetic defects to future generations. The academy's role in legitimating this was paramount from the beginning. The influence of Galton, Pearson, Spearman, Burt, and their successors at London was profound, and until 1930 university geneticists overwhelmingly supported the eugenic viewpoint (Haller, 1963). Indeed, eugenic ideas permeated the prewar British literati even more thoroughly than its equivalent in the United States, embracing every shade of political opinion from high Tory to Fabian socialist. Viewed in this context, the eugenic rantings of H. G. Wells (Coren, 1992) seem little more than forceful expressions of a conventional wisdom. Yet the British eugenicists envied the success of their American colleagues in getting eugenics laws onto the statute books. Frequently grafted onto the Wisconsin idea of progressive government through experts, eugenic legislation in the United States was formulated with a dispatch unknown in a British political culture less open to "rational" solutions to social problems (Kevles, 1985).

Academic backing for eugenic ideas in the United States ranged from scientists on the campuses of major universities to bizarre ventures like the establishment by John Harvey Kellogg of Battle Creek College as a base for eugenics education. Support for sterilization legislation came from many quarters, including physicians in state institutions, many lawyers and journalists, and prominent philanthropists such as Mrs. E. H. Harriman and John D. Rockefeller (Reilly, 1991). A number of scientists and university officials (David Starr Jordan of Stanford was prominent in both categories) lent credibility. The academy provided on cue the new procedures of vasectomy and salpingectomy that facilitated cost-efficient sterilization programs. It was also the main repository of expertise for studying mental deficiency and developing testing procedures. Researchers were based at some of the most prestigious research universities in the United States: Columbia, Chicago, Stanford, Princeton, Johns Hopkins, and others. Clark University's president G. Stanley Hall, the most eminent psychologist of the opening years of the century, was particularly influential. Hall supervised the doctoral dissertations not only of Goddard, whom he recommended for the position at Vineland, but also Lewis Terman and Fred Kuhlman. Researchers such as these were substantially aided by a number of foundations. The Carnegie Institute, for example, funded the Station for Experimental Evolution at Cold Spring Harbor from 1904 onwards, and underwrote the Eugenics Record Office until 1939, when it withdrew its support and repudiated its association (Reilly, 1991, p. 70). With the authority of scientific backing, custodialism was established between 1910 and 1938 as the norm. Although in most jurisdictions only a small proportion of people regarded as mentally deficient were ever institutionalized, it became axiomatic that in any well-regulated society anyone suspected of deficiency belonged in an asylum.

The eugenic imperative did not go unchallenged within academia. Some of the most prominent social scientists spoke out forcefully against it, but many more accepted it as an acceptable perspective, if not one they necessarily shared. Mainstream geneticists were sometimes privately contemptuous of some of the eugenicists' claims, but in the 1930s even a reform geneticist like Julian Huxley—a prominent personality as well as a leading scientist—could argue repeatedly in favor of segregation and sterilization of mental deficients (Trombley, 1988, p. 99). A few other geneticists did speak out in opposition, but most were preoccupied with their fruit flies and their careers (Reilly, 1991, p. 112). To most lay observers, including public policymakers, therefore, the eugenics movement appeared to be validated by the full authority of science.

The intelligence testers rapidly became deluded by the apparent efficacy of their techniques. Goddard was convinced that his Vineland staff, working at Ellis Island in 1913, could identify feeblemindedness in potential immigrants more accurately than the immigration physicians were capable of doing. Yet his estimates of the incidence of feeblemindedness in the general immigrant population were ludicrous, ranging as high as 87%. Published extracts from the field workers' records continue to amaze readers unfamiliar with the hegemony of the construct of mental deficiency during this era. An oft-quoted but quite typical entry records a Jewish tailor with five years of schooling and a knowledge of three languages as testing on the Binet scale with a mental age of 12, and therefore being declared feebleminded (Smith, 1985). Although Goddard decided that these scores should be scaled downward, he never seems to have doubted the fundamental efficacy of his methods, not even in his so-called retraction (Goddard, 1928). On the contrary, his ideal society remained one governed by an asylum-like regimen of discipline and authority (Smith, 1985, pp. 129–134).

The potency of the test scores was rivaled only by that of the labels they imposed. The diagnosis "mentally deficient" or "feebleminded" was one from which it was virtually impossible to escape. A striking illustration of this is provided by Steven Gelb (1989), who traced inmates of institutions who were recruited into the armed services during the manpower shortage of the World War II era. Some of these did well in the military, and a few were even promoted. Their home asylums often recorded their achievements with pride. But with the end of the labor shortage after 1945, their marginality and abnormality were reasserted.

POSTWAR TRENDS

It is commonly assumed that in the aftermath of World War II a fundamental reversal took place in the policies and attitudes that had prevailed during the first half of the century. There is much evidence against such a position. In most jurisdictions in Europe and North America, for example, custodial institutions continued to expand for a quarter-century after 1945. Some historians (for example, Haller, 1963) have argued that the eugenics movement was constantly on the defensive from attacks, especially from genetic science and the Catholic Church, and was already in decline by 1930. Other observers of eugenic trends, however, regard the World War II era as one of transition rather than decline. Chase (1980) argued that the movement has so successfully survived decades of exposure of its dogma that the postwar brand of scientific racism has been more virulent than its predecessors. In the years since Chase wrote, the human genome project has emerged, giving rise to new concerns over genetics and individual rights. Much current thinking is summed up in Mazumdar's (1992, p. 267) metaphor: "The virus [of eugenics] has mutated, and we are not as well immunised as we thought."

Outside a relatively narrow Holocaust literature, the resemblance between the prewar policies in several countries and the events specific to Germany has gone largely unacknowledged. Fortunately, one major exception to this generalization has proved to have a huge impact on public policy in mental handicap services: the emergence of the movement known as normalization. The concept was first expressed in Denmark in 1959, but the earliest academic paper appeared 10 years later (Nirje, 1969), followed by a comprehensive statement (Wolfensberger, 1972). Both Nirje and Wolfensberger, the major academic founders of this movement, were profoundly influenced in their advocacy of normalization by their revulsion at the horrors of the Third Reich. Together they laid the basis for the widespread adoption of the idea that it is in the provision of a normal environment that people with an intellectual disability are enabled to attain their potential. By "normal," they meant simply whatever is the norm for people within a particular culture. The concept emerged in direct opposition to historical notions of the intellectually handicapped person as a deviant (Wolfensberger, 1972, pp. 13–29).

As the idea of normalization began to spread rapidly throughout western Europe and North America in the 1970s, it was possible to be sanguine about a new era for mental disability, to believe that the momentum of progressive change was diffusing through society at large. The movement lent powerful support to policies such as mainstreaming and deinstitutionalization. Policy reformulation had in any case been rendered unavoidable by a series of asylum scandals that had stirred public attention. Asylum closure programs were adopted, and community living became the fashion, even though the reality fell short of the ideal. The various publications of the President's Committee on Mental Retardation, a product of the Kennedy era, disseminated the normalization message widely. Client services expanded rapidly as the number of professionals willing to serve intellectually handicapped people increased.

The new optimism did not entirely bypass the universities. Several integration programs were initiated with considerable success—the Milwaukee Project, probably the best known in the United States, and the Sheffield Experiment in Britain. Moreover, on campuses everywhere, intelligence determinists were on the defensive; William Shockley, Richard Herrnstein, and Arthur Jensen were challenged wherever they spoke. Leon Kamin, alerted to the intelligence issue by his experience in arranging a speaking engagement for Herrnstein (Fancher, 1985, p. 206), developed a critique that precipitated a clash with Jensen. He also began to topple the throne of Cyril Burt by exposing some of his fundamental research on twins as fraudulent, a process later completed by Leslie Hearnshaw (1979).

Yet, surveying the history of intelligence testing to the mid-1980s, Fancher (1985) was struck by the way in which the issues contested by Jensen and Kamin were little different from those that had separated Francis Galton from J. S. Mill. He was able to report two trends: a wider acceptance that intelligence is not a single factor, and greater stress being laid by many on the importance of environment in intellectual development. Both trends are reflected in successive editions of standard psychology texts over the past two decades. They are also fundamental to the work of psychologists such as Sternberg (1985), who states unequivocally that intelligence and intellectual ability are multifaceted phenomena, and calls for a contextual view in which classes of behavior are seen as intelligent in a given environment. This he sees as part of a renaissance in intelligence research since the 1970s.

Yet even Sternberg argues that previous work on intelligence was not misguided, simply incomplete. While most of the current literature is less dogmatic in tone than its predecessors, there is little evidence of a major shift in perspective among academics. Support for this view comes from an unlikely source: Snyderman and Rothman's (1988) apologia for IQ tests. I question their portrayal of the nonprofessional educated public as duped by a press interested only in extremist views. But they are correct when they write (in a rather superior tone) that "expert views have not undergone the fundamental change characteristic of the attitudes of the informed public. . . . [S]cholars with any expertise in the area of intelligence testing . . . share a common view of the most important components of intelligence, and are convinced that it can be measured" (Snyderman & Rothman, 1988, p. 250). By the same token, a medical student relying on the text edited by Robbins and Cooper (1988) could be forgiven for assuming that doubts about the measurability of intelligence have long since been resolved and that the major challenge today is to ensure that practitioners are sufficiently numerate to interpret test scores correctly. In reality, the greater problem is that practitioners are prone to accept test results as definitive, even though they may proclaim a contextual view of intellectual ability. Such an approach resembles what Walter Firey (1978) identified in the urban theory of his day as an "empirically compromised rationalism."

Events in the 1980s indicate that the sterilization issue was still unresolved in many jurisdictions. Government officials in Britain continued to make speeches about the desirability of sterilization (Trombley, 1988), and involuntary sterilization of certain groups was still legal in 19 states in the U.S. as late as 1985 (Reilly, 1991, p. 148). More broadly, the Thatcher-Reagan-Bush era brought tight budgets and the cost-driven closing of asylums. Liberal arguments against asylum environments were welcomed in many jurisdictions as providing justifications for closure, and there were brave pronouncements about the transferability of revenues to community programs. Yet such programs were almost everywhere under severe strain. Successful ventures depended on the efforts of voluntary associations and parental groups, and to the extent that this support has not been forthcoming, homelessness and deprivation became epidemic. Normalization was distorted in the service of enforced "independence."

ACADEMIC KNOWLEDGE AND INTELLECTUAL DISABILITY IN THE 1990S

Advocates for people with an intellectual or developmental disability have moved on from normalization to embrace a human rights perspective. Significant gains have been made in establishing rights to medical treatment, education, and human services. In this endeavor, advocates have received the support of individual lawyers, physicians, and educators. Yet, even today, the gains are being made largely without the institutional support of the academy. The intellectually disabled remain outsiders, and the academy remains part of the problem. That there should be academic requirements for students entering colleges and universities—conceived as communities of the knowledgeable and wise—is readily understood. The telling charge against the academy is not so much that it has marginalized people with a mental disability, but that it persists in marginalizing the holistic study of intellectual disability as a phenomenon. This it does largely by allowing its intelligence specialists to privilege one particular tradition in research design. It is, after all, only recently that the absolute professional judgment of physician or psychologist in matters of mental handicap has been questioned at all, and this is something that was not readily relinquished. Largely by default, through its general inaction, the broader academy reinforces the acceptability of obsolete arguments. The continued privileging of "fact" and of scientific method perpetuates the status quo.

This mindset is well illustrated by the controversy that took place in 1990 over a paper by J. Philippe Rushton that had appeared in the journal *Social Science and Medicine* (Rushton & Bogaert, 1989). Charles Leslie, the journal's anthropology editor, chose the occasion of a major conference to express his dissent from the editor-in chief's decision to publish the paper. His objections, later published (Leslie, 1990), cast Rushton's methods and assumptions firmly in the context of scientific racism. Another commentator (Wilson, 1990), dismissing Leslie's objections as "emotional," called instead for more objective scientific criticism of Rushton's paper. Rushton's own reply (Rushton, 1990) focused on the reliability of the data and the appropriateness of his psychometric analysis, claiming that Leslie denied the legitimacy of any evolutionary hypothesis and was willing to countenance only environmental explanations. Rushton's position was that the data themselves are "facts"; only their interpretation is controversial (Rushton, 1990, p. 908). The editor-in-chief defended his decision to publish by calling on the principle of freedom of expression and by extolling the efficacy of the peer review process (McEwan, 1990). The reviewers were evidently impressed by the design, method, and language of the paper, all of which conformed to their expectations for an acceptable manuscript. This despite the fact that, as another commentator (Lovejoy, 1990, p. 909) pointed out, "when translated into common parlance [the paper] is virtual nonsense."

When Rushton defended his work in a wide-circulation journal in 1993, however, he focused again on what he insisted were the "scientific facts": "In one study, 17,000 white 7-year-olds had larger head perimeters than their 19,000 black counterparts even though the black children were taller and heavier. In both groups, head perimeter predicted IQ scores" (Rushton, 1993, p. 8). One is reminded of the methods and opinions of countless anthropologists and others during the early years of this century, or even of Langdon Down himself writing 130 years ago. Their shared perspective is that intelligence is a measurable entity. Thus an old and venerated academic notion of a reified intelligence (one that has given social science some of its most widely used quantitative methods) is still very much alive. Rushton's crude correlations may be dismissed by some as the product of a fringe activity, unrepresentative of his field as a whole, but it is difficult to deny that inquiry into intelligence remains more generally in the grip of an unreflexive quantification. Its mantra is still the IQ and more sophisticated variants; its discourses remain grounded in notions of hierarchy and the normal distribution. The attempt to link intelligence with other characteristics—race, social class, ethnicity, sexuality—still rests substantially on an unremitting determinism. It represents not the celebration of difference but its construction. Inevitably, therefore, while modern science understands statistically derived definitions of subnormality, it remains uncomfortable with the notion of an intellectual disability imbued with subtleties, incongruities, and challenges.

Reaction to the appearance of *The Bell Curve* by Richard Herrnstein and Charles Murray in 1994 offers some hope of strengthening resolve in the academic community to expose the biases and limitations of such research. *The Bell Curve* arguments have a familiar ring: General intelligence is a single, measurable quantity that is genetically based and can be used to rank people in order of overall worth, revealing significant variations by race. The reaction was overwhelmingly negative. Several of the reviews published under the title of *The Bell Curve Debate* (Jacoby & Glauberman, 1995) agree that the arguments are old and the research flawed in many respects. Yet there is also concern that the very appearance of the work, and the necessity for rebuttal, fosters in the public mind a sense that the arguments must have some legitimacy.

Thus the academy presents to society an equivocal face, and fails to contribute greatly to removing the deep-rooted structures of exclusion as they apply to persons with an intellectual disability. Special education, which in the last 20 years has become a growth industry in many jurisdictions, should be an exception to this, but the large bureaucracies that have accompanied its expansion are as likely to perpetuate existing structures as to reform them. The university's research agenda does not exclude investigation of the integration experience in housing, workplace, and classroom, but the impact of such work on its ethos is limited.

CONCLUSION

The forces for social change in the area of intellectual disability continue to originate outside the university. They emanate overwhelmingly from the voluntary sector, from special organizations, from parents' groups, and from communities of self-advocates. It is only very recently that these groups have found anything in the academic world to guide their efforts, and they must still be highly selective. A superstructure of jargon and convention is used to devalue contributions that originate beyond sharply demarcated boundaries of academic and professional expertise. Ironically, it is often those academics possessing the most refined sense of ownership and professionalism whose work seems from the outside to be based on the most questionable assumptions.

Although it exists in the deinstitutionalizing era of the 1990s, the academy has yet to adopt a postasylum perspective on mental disability. Deinstitutionalization has inevitably weakened the longstanding dialectic between academy and asylum, but the characteristic stance of the former is indifference rather than reform. In the past, as we have seen, academic power was used in explicit ways to foster discrimination and to legitimate the custodial asylum. The motives went far beyond mere professional self-aggrandizement, reflecting a deep ideological commitment to a narrow interpretation of intelligence and a limited valuation of human worth. While this ideology persists today only on edges of the academic world, there are few signs of a total transformation within the mainstream. Sadly, the readiness of university researchers to endorse initiatives for integration and self-advocacy in our own day has so far failed to match the enthusiasm with which many of their predecessors earlier in the century supported the forces of exclusion.

NOTES

1. The term I prefer is "intellectual disability," but since this is unclear to many, I frequently settle for "mental disability." "Intellectually challenged" and "developmentally delayed" are both acceptable substitutes. In historical contexts the use of contemporary labels, however inappropriate, is often unavoidable.

2. In Britain the terms "idiot" and "imbecile" were used as in the United States,

but "feebleminded" was used to indicate perceived mild disability, and was therefore almost synonymous with the American "moron." Such differences in terminology caused much confusion, especially since each category was supposed to have a prescribed numerical range.

REFERENCES

Baumeister, A. A. (1970). The American residential institution: Its history and character. In A. A. Baumeister & E. Butterfield (Eds.), *Residential facilities for the mentally retarded* (pp. 1–28). Chicago: Aldine.

Chase, A. (1980). *The legacy of Malthus.* Urbana: University of Illinois Press.

Coren, M. (1992). *The invisible man: The life and liberties of H. G. Wells.* London: Random House.

Down, J. L. (1867). Observations on an ethnic classification of idiots. *Journal of Mental Science, 13,* 121–123.

Dugdale, R. (1910). *The Jukes: A study in crime, pauperism and heredity* (4th ed.). New York: Putnam.

Engel, A. (1983). The English universities and professional education. In K. H. Jarausch (Ed.), *The transformation of higher learning 1860–1930* (pp. 293–305). Chicago: University of Chicago Press.

Fancher, R. (1985). *The intelligence men: Makers of the IQ controversy.* New York: Norton.

Firey, W. (1978). *Man, mind, and land.* Westport, CT: Greenwood Publishing.

Foucault, M. (1979). *Discipline and punish.* New York: Vintage Books.

Galton, F. (1907). *Probability, the foundation of eugenics* (The Herbert Spencer Lecture). Oxford: The Clarendon Press.

Gelb, S. A. (1986). Henry H. Goddard and the immigrants, 1910–1917: The studies and their social context. *Journal of the History of the Behavioral Sciences, 22,* 324–332.

Gelb, S. A. (1987). Social deviance and the "discovery" of the moron. *Disability, Handicap and Society, 2,* 247–258.

Gelb, S. A. (1989). *"Mental deficients" fighting Fascism: The unplanned mainstreaming experiment of World War II.* Paper presented to the Cheiron Society.

Goddard, H. H. (1912). *The Kallikak family: A study in the heredity of feeblemindedness.* New York: Macmillan.

Goddard, H. H. (1914). *Feeble-mindedness: Its causes and consequences.* New York: Macmillan.

Goffman, E. (1961). *Asylums.* Garden City, NY: Doubleday.

Gould, S. J. (1980). *The panda's thumb.* London: Penguin Books.

Haller, M. H. (1963). *Eugenics.* New Brunswick, NJ: Rutgers University Press.

Hearnshaw, L. S. (1979). *Cyril Burt: Psychologist.* London: Hodder and Stoughton.

Herrnstein, R., & Murray, C. (1994). *The bell curve: Intelligence and class structure in American life.* New York: Free Press.

Horkheimer, M., & Adorno, T. W. (1969). *Dialectics of enlightenment.* New York: Seabury Press.

Jacoby, R., & Glauberman, N. (Eds.). (1995). *The bell curve debate.* New York: Times Books.

Kane, J. F., & Rojahn, J. (1981). Development of services for the mentally retarded in Germany: A survey of history, empirical research, and current trends. *Applied Research in Mental Retardation, 2,* 195-210.

Kevles, D. J. (1985). *In the name of eugenics: Genetics and the uses of human heredity.* Berkeley: University of California Press.

Leslie, C. (1990). Scientific racism: Reflections on peer review, science and ideology. *Social Science and Medicine, 31,* 891-905.

Lovejoy, C. O. (1990). Comment on Rushton. *Social Science and Medicine, 30,* 909-910.

Lowe, R. (1983). The expansion of higher education in England. In K. H. Jarausch (Ed.), *The transformation of higher learning 1860-1930* (pp. 37-56). Chicago: University of Chicago Press.

McClelland, C. E. (1983). Professionalization and higher education in Germany. In K. H. Jarausch (Ed.), *The transformation of higher learning 1860-1930* (pp. 180-197). Chicago: University of Chicago Press.

McEwan, P. J. M. (1990). Reply to Leslie. *Social Science and Medicine, 30,* 911-912.

McLaren, A. (1990). *Our own master race: Eugenics in Canada 1885-1945.* Toronto: McClelland and Stewart.

Mazumdar, P. M. H. (1992). *Eugenics, human genetics and human failings.* London: Routledge.

Miller, M. D. (1996). *Terminating the socially inadequate.* Commack, NY: Malamud-Rose.

Nirje, B. (1969). The normalization principle and its human management implications. In R. Kugel & W. Wolfensberger (Eds.), *Changing patterns in residential services for the mentally retarded* (pp. 179-195). Washington, DC: President's Committee on Mental Retardation.

Noble, D. F. (1997). *The religion of technology.* New York: Alfred A. Knopf.

Radford, J. P. (1991). Sterilization versus segregation: Control of the "feebleminded," 1900-1938. *Social Science and Medicine, 33,* 449-458.

Radford, J. P., & Tipper, A. (1988). *Starcross: Out of the mainstream.* Toronto: Roeher Institute.

Reilly, P. R. (1991). *The surgical solution: A history of involuntary sterilization in the United States.* Baltimore: Johns Hopkins University Press.

Robbins, T. W., & Cooper, P. J. (1988). *Psychology for medicine.* London: Edward Arnold.

Rushton, J. P. (1990). Comments. *Social Science and Medicine, 31,* 905-909.

Rushton, J. P. (1993, January 16-22). Letter. *The Economist,* p. 8.

Rushton, J. P., & Bogaert, A. F. (1989). Population differences in susceptibility to AIDS: An evolutionary analysis. *Social Science and Medicine, 28,* 1211-1220.

Ryan, J., & Thomas, F. (1980). *The politics of mental handicap.* London: Penguin Books.

Saul, J. R. (1992). *Voltaire's bastards: The dictatorship of reason in the West*. New York: Free Press.

Scheerenberger, R. C. (1983). *A history of mental retardation*. Baltimore: Brooks Publishing Co.

Scull, A. (1991). *The asylum as utopia: W. A. F. Browne and the mid-nineteenth century consolidation of psychiatry*. London: Rutledge.

Searle, G. R. (1976). *Eugenics and politics in Britain, 1900-1914*. Leydon, Scotland: Noordhoff International Publishing.

Seguin, E. (1866). *Idiocy and its treatment by the physiological method*. New York: William Wood.

Sidney, E. (1865). Idiot asylums. *Edinburgh Review*, 37-73.

Simmons, H. G. (1982). *From asylum to welfare*. Toronto: NIMR.

Smith, J. D. (1985). *Minds made feeble: The myth and legacy of the Kallikaks*. Rockville, MD: Aspen.

Snyderman, M., & Rothman, S. (1988). *The IQ controversy*. New Brunswick, NJ: Transaction.

Sternberg, R. J. (1985). *Beyond IQ: A triarchic theory of human intelligence*. Cambridge, MA: Cambridge University Press.

Thelin, J. R. (1982). *Higher education and its useful past*. Cambridge, MA: Schenkman.

Trombley, S. (1988). *The right to reproduce*. London: Weidenfield and Nicholson.

Wilson, E. O. (1998). Back from chaos. *Atlantic Monthly, 281*(3), 41-62.

Wilson, G. D. (1990). Comment on Rushton. *Social Science and Medicine, 30*, 910-911.

Wolfensberger, W. (1972). *The principle of normalization in human services*. Toronto: National Institute on Mental Retardation.

PART III

Prospects of
the University
in Late Capitalism

SEVEN

THE IVORY COMMONWEALTH
Higher Education Beyond Pure Commerce

MANFRED STANLEY

THIS CHAPTER presumes a story. It is about an institution, the university, embedded in a civilization that, in one sense or another, has long experimented with a primordially dangerous gamble. The gamble is entrusting to the conscience of humanity, a species it defines as suspended somewhere between animality and divinity, the responsibilities of reason and freedom. Obviously it cannot be our purpose here to recapitulate that drama (for relevant perspectives see Nelson, 1981). Let it suffice to illustrate the transcendental and eschatological significance of such a gamble through two mythic utterances by the Judeo-Christian Creator of the universe.

One is the well-known expulsion curse from Eden in response to Adam's sin of disobedience in eating of the fruit of knowledge (including self-knowledge). In Eden, God's reason was hidden from man, evident only in its opulent beauty. The other text is a kind of celebration of that sin, almost as if the Deity is accepting responsibility for creating the sort of being who would risk disobedience. These are the words of God speaking to Adam as imagined in 1487 by the Renaissance Christian humanist, mystic, and evangelist Pico della Mirandola:

> The nature of all other creatures is defined and restricted within laws which We have laid down; you, by contrast impeded by no such restrictions, may, by your own free will, to whose custody we have assigned you, trace for yourself the lineaments of your own nature. . . . It will be in your power to descend to the lower brutish forms of life; you will be able, through your own decision, to rise again to the superior orders whose life is divine. (1956, p. 7)

What has this to do with the Western university? A great deal. Although the university has undergone many changes since its inception in medieval Europe, it has always been affected by the uneasy relations between the sacred and the profane, between the ineffable and the literal, between reason and freedom. Sometimes these tensions took the form of revolt by advocates of philosophical speculation against guardians of theological literalism. At other moments, the university itself was condemned by mystics and monastics for the idolatrous worldliness of its own love for rationality and lust for social and political power. Over time, most articulated forms of reason and freedom found their way into the academy. Naturally, the university was not the only institution caught up in these conflicts. Arguably, however, it was among the most important because of its strategic significance for the definition of valid knowledge and its applications through professional practices. While originally under the discipline of the church, as church authority gradually waned with the Protestant Reformation and the growing secularization of European culture, the universities, along with the state, inherited some of the authority of the church. This should not be imagined as a linear process. The university's influence waxed and waned. In some places, such as North America, it did not enjoy much real power until the twentieth century.

This story of the university's role in Western civilization's search for balance between diverse forms of reason and freedom continues today. From the Protestant Reformation and the emergence of modern science to the rise of market capitalism and political democracy, simultaneous quests for the stable lawfulness of reason and the unfettered vertigo of freedom have characterized the project of modernity.

As I stand in the doorway of retirement after 36 years of service to higher education, I find myself among those who believe the university to be in a terminal stage of crisis. Naturally, this familiar correlate of "old codgerhood" has forced me into particularly intense introspection. One clue to the authenticity of my conviction may be that I cannot define an empirical moment in history when the university had achieved some golden age followed by decline, culminating in the total collapse of all hope morbidly coincidental with my retirement. What, then, is the problem?

The problem is not the literal end of the university as an organization or a site for some activities associated with the term (e.g., classrooms, laboratories, degrees, ceremonials). It is rather that the university has been colonized by a version of reason (and of freedom) that is inherently idolatrous, ideological, and destructive of any further unique role for the university in the political history of the human spirit. These are sharp words, and the remainder of the chapter will seek to clarify their meaning. Before moving on, it is reasonable to raise this important question: In the name of what ideal image of the university are the trends just cited to be labeled as corruptions? After all, has the university not always been ideologically subordinate to the dominant regimes of its times? When has the university ever played a morally unique role in any society? And from the perspective of later eras, do not the universities of earlier days come to be perceived as the servants of idols (dogmas, potentates, worldviews)?

These are fair questions, and I shall briefly try to acknowledge them. The argument developed in this chapter does not seem to require a highly specific institutional model of the university. What is necessary is a cultural ethos that regards the university as about serious things that transcend the immediate social distribution of interests, however much it may also be concerned with these. Such transcendent matters include religious salvation, the pursuit of truth, the development of human personality and character, the preservation of traditions, and the creation of a just polity. To be sure, other institutions have been concerned with such matters, too (churches, governments, arts). But at least the Western university has been singularly affected by a steady internal pressure toward critical autonomy. Even when most subservient to the powers, something we have come to honor with the label of "the liberal arts tradition" has stood aside from total submission to mere domination.[1]

Therefore, what I mean by a potentially terminal crisis of the university is the end of this tradition of critical autonomy, however it may be grounded. Lamenting this crisis does not require accepting exclusively any one doctrine of humanity, history, or eschatology. It implies only the right of humanity to examine its own collective and individual existence with at least a modest degree of freedom. As we see everywhere in the world, even this minimum commitment can appear radically controversial. Be that as it may, this is a commitment that crosses all ways of classifying universities: public versus private, parochial versus secular, graduate versus undergraduate. To deny the essential relevance of this commitment for the university is to foreclose its unique moral identity. But there is more to be said.

In the following sections, I seek to develop two arguments. First, the modern university has been domesticated into an ideological extension of late capitalism to a point of helplessness almost unprecedented in the modern history of free societies. Second, recovery by the university of a role unique to itself will require a reform movement designed to reimagine its character as that of a civil religious institution. I recognize the radically controversial nature of this claim and will therefore pay close attention to clarifying what meanings I do and do not wish to encourage. (A third argument that would have followed is that this proposal requires a major effort to invent a pedagogy for higher education appropriate to it. While there clearly is no space here to elaborate the details, I am preparing this analysis for presentation elsewhere.)

My defense of the university's critical autonomy celebrates more than that value alone. Being personally committed to the democratization of society and yet having myself been scarred by the events of this most radically evil of all centuries, my interest in the university is its capacity to help reconcile faith and resignation. The "theological" gravity of this demand requires a dramatic reconsideration of the university as an institution. This essay is best regarded as a conversation piece about what such a reconsideration might entail, with resources for ideas, policies, and research offered to those who share my hope for reform and my anxiety that it may already be too late.

LATE CAPITALISM AND THE SPECTER
OF EDUCATIONAL IRRELEVANCE

For approximately a hundred years dating from about the end of the Civil War, a period that witnessed the rise of the modern research university (Veysey, 1965), much of American society seemed able to accommodate myths of a historical direction. Although this was a period of considerable labor violence, major population shifts, and a general sense of radical transformation in the social order, it was also tempting to discern where all this was going. Progressivism offered a new vision of nationalism and collective pride, while social movements (unionism, settlement house activism, populism, civil service, public health) encouraged some reforms of alleged political dysfunctions and social injustice.

Theorizations of corporate civilization resulted in such ideological models as progressivism, welfare capitalism, and corporate liberalism (Lustig, 1981). After World War II, in the social sciences and especially sociology, the structural functionalists led by Talcott Parsons, with their model of modernization, provided a globally relevant intellectual resource for historical-evolutionary optimists. Both intellectual and social elites sought a postwar ideological balance between rationality (largely understood as the prerogatives of technical expertise) and freedom (imagined as entrepreneurship, a wide range of choice in employment opportunity, and expanding consumer sovereignty in a rapidly enlarging commodity market). One has but to glance at the advertising of the day to sense the almost breathless atmosphere of social mobility and material possibilities characterizing that time (Ewen, 1976). The impression spread that the era of warring ideologies might be over, the great world problems now amenable to technical solutions (see Stanley, 1981, for an explanation of this assumption).

Around the time of the Vietnam War in the 1960s and increasingly thereafter, things changed. Conflict theories began to displace functionalism in much of social science. And it seemed to many observers that a new stage of capitalism had arrived, different from what had preceded it. This newly emergent form affects the university in several ways. To see how, we need first to review some commonly noted features of this new capitalist stage: globalization; utopian efforts to integrate society and culture into the regime of market forces; and postmodernism (see Lash & Urry, 1988).

Globalization

One feature of late capitalism is globalization, envisioned as the increasingly unimpeded flow of information, capital, and labor. Thanks to computer technology, expanded competition from ex-colonies, and shifting strengths of global markets, late capitalism displays the vulnerability of large, rooted, bureaucratized corporations with fixed habits of production and social contract relationships with society. Postmodern organizations stress flexibility and fluidity of response to changes in their environments. Such responses have included not only new production styles (such as reliance upon loosely coupled, task-specific production teams), but also mass worker layoffs, outsourcing of functions, increasing use of part-time and temporary workers, cutting (or even eliminating) benefits, and funneling upward to a few the power to set life chance conditions for the many. In this new environment of deregulation, the declining significance of national borders, and the restratification of society into something approaching a two-tier system (rich and poor), all stable deals between the institutional sectors of big industry, labor, and government are off. Today the idea of corporate liberalism appears as a historical curiosity, born of postwar myths of eternal progress, and welfare capitalism sounds oxymoronic. Herbert Spencer's ghost roams the legislatures of the land.

Utopian Intensification of the Market Regime

The increasing hegemonic intensification of the market principle as the criterion of progress and the solution to all problems has been classically analyzed by Karl Polanyi (1944). Utopian, in this context, means that advocates of the self-regulating market idea took on such a burden of faith in its benign causal features as to blind whole generations to its limitations. But as Polanyi pointed out:

Such an institution could not exist for any length of time without annihilating the human and natural substance of society; it would have physically destroyed man and transformed his surroundings into a wilderness. Inevitably, society took measures to protect itself, but whatever measures it took impaired the self-regulating of the market, disorganized industrial life, and thus endangered society in yet another way. (1944, p. 3)

Postmodernism

Without presuming to tackle the web of concepts associated with this term, we may note that at least three broad arguments are implied by it. One regards postmodernism as a consequence of the end of organized capitalism (Lash & Urry, 1988, pp. 1–16). The emphasis here is on the byproducts of structural changes associated with the emergence of late capitalism, most specifically those arising from the undermining of stable structures (firms, governments, unions, communities) that provided the infrastructure of loyalty and obligation in civil society. These institutions, with their sense of place, are converted into what seem like flows (global labor shifts, investment, consumption, signals, information, decisions). Inevitably, so the argument goes, as "[s]pace is dissolved into flows, [places] become shadows that explode or disappear according to decisions that their dwellers will always ignore" (Castells, 1983, p. 314). In such a world, to retrieve Marx and Engels, "(a)ll that is solid melts into air, all that is holy is profaned" (Marx & Engels, 1959, p. 10). But this time around, in the era of disorganized capitalism, there is no confident assertion of "real conditions" or "real relations" because the meta-narrative these terms reflect also has melted away.

This abandonment of meta-narratives is a second alleged version of postmodernism. Some think this reflects mere shifts in the ideological surface of deeply structured features of late capitalism, such as the latter's disengagement from political-economic nationalism. Others condemn it as the nihilistic fruit of culturally unregulated philosophic skepticism. Still others celebrate it as the defeat of the tyranny of false reason over the playful freedom of the human spirit. Whatever the attitude, the alleged consequence of postmodernism, for good or ill, is the stripping of authority from all hegemonic myths among up-to-date intellectuals.

It is of some interest to note the ambiguity of the market principle in this regard. Is the market principle our civilization's current great meta-narrative, or does it refer merely to an amoral device for decisionmaking convenient in a society losing its faith in historical meaning altogether? My earlier reference to the utopian sense of the market required a meta-narrative perspective. Adam Smith, for instance, held an evolutionary view of commercial society's emergence, a view tied to claims about human nature.

Today, however, many people probably do not think in these terms, perhaps looking to the market somewhat like Winston Churchill thought of democracy: It's a terribly flawed system, but I just can't think of a better one. (Adam Smith felt a bit like this; he was no utopian.)

The third depiction of postmodernism is the radical, politically aggressive pluralism sometimes called multiculturalism. Perhaps the most challenging version of this view regards pluralism as the unintended product of Western imperialism and subsequent decolonization. Having colonized everything in sight for centuries, and then destroyed its credibility through two catastrophic world wars, by the mid-twentieth century the West suffered a world in revolt. From Tehran to the inner cities of America, from Malcolm X to Wounded Knee, movements arise bent on reappropriating the politics of naming.

IMPLICATIONS FOR THE UNIVERSITY

These developments have proven to be of enormous significance for the university, and the literature reflects this (for a mere sampling of the variety of studies and commentaries, see Bikson, 1996; Finkin, 1997; Gaff, 1997; Gamson, 1997; Gilliland, 1997; Lazerson, 1997; Newfield, 1997; Titelli, 1997). We shall restrict ourselves briefly here to four observations regarding the late capitalist university.

The Rise of Academic Capitalism

Conceptually and empirically elaborated by Slaughter and Leslie (1997), academic capitalism refers to the efforts of modern universities to make themselves as relevant as possible to the market regime for the sake of financial and reputational security. These efforts have profound effects upon the culture and social organization of universities. Cultural effects range from changes in notions of academic discovery, through perceptions of what a student is, to views about the relative worthwhileness of curricula. Social organizational effects include changes in the power and authority structure of the university and the academic division of labor (e.g., the ways in which academic capitalism sponsors the emergence of centers and institutes of applied research at the expense of departments). Also affected are relations between universities and the larger society.

> As centers and universities increase participation in the market, the contract between faculty and society, an implicit contract that grants faculty and universities a measure of autonomy in return for disinterested knowledge that serves

the public welfare, may be undermined. To some degree, academic capitalism undermines the *raison d'être* for special treatment for universities and faculty, increasing the likelihood that universities will be treated more like all other organizations and professionals more like all other intellectual workers. (Slaughter & Leslie, 1997, p. 222)

We must not assume that everyone considers this trend unfortunate. In some quarters the sheer utilitarianism of this trend is raised to the level of political philosophical celebration.

But the second step [beyond corporate universities] . . . when corporate universities and consulting firms become accredited is the establishment of an agency to function as a clearing house for individuals with the expertise who actually do the developing of creditworthy modules, who would then be able to sell directly to consuming individuals or organizations. This second step will, ultimately, *fully democratize the knowledge economy*. (Nirenberg, 1997, p. 10, emphasis added)

It should come as no surprise that these are the words of the Dean of Doctoral Studies at the University of Phoenix, the famous "virtual university." (For an account of this vision and of the campus as corporate accessory, see Matthews, 1997, pp. 238–242.)

Diffusion of Functions

Some of the accrediting and research functions of the university continue to be transferred to other institutions (corporations, government, libraries, foundations, think tanks, television, the Internet). Some corporate universities and think tanks now grant their own degrees.

Two other sorts of diffusion are occurring now as well. One has to do with distance learning, the other with lifelong learning, neither of which requires the university. These possibilities undermine the material basis of the university's autonomy as an institution located in time and space. Through a personal home computer, the world's databases are at one's fingertips. Learning at a distance uses satellites to make a classroom of the planet. And the increasing need for occupational renewal or transformation is reforming the image of the student into a lifelong consumer of education. It would be irrational for a person to return to his or her alma mater for every new educational episode. Thus we are encouraged to expect transferable student status, with a consequent perception of individual universities as mere way stations (or web sites) on a lifelong but highly individuated globe-spanning educational journey uninfluenced by traditions, loyalties, or memories associated with a specific place.

Still More Efficiency

Efficiency, of course, has always been a feature of capitalist society (see Haber, 1970; Noble, 1997b; Taylor, 1911/1967). But the rhetoric of reengineering, political accountability, cybernetic surveillance, corporate oversight, genetic assessment, and Total Quality Management implies new frontiers of technicist discipline whose self-conscious totalism transcends the simpler images of yesterday. In the universities, the idea of management has shifted from administration by persons who are also faculty members to management specialists trained for their particular, newly professionalized, roles. "From 1977 to 1989 [there was a rise in managerial professionals amounting to] nearly 100%, compared to 19% for faculty and 37% for executives/administrators" (Rhoades & Slaughter, 1997, p. 23). These types of professionals are productive in instructional technology, student services, assessment, curriculum design, grants, and contracts. In the eyes of administrators, compared with the new experts in such matters the faculty can be reduced to amateurs and therefore a lesser source of trouble, at least regarding authority over the university as an organized institution. It's very important to be precise about the dangers of such trends for the liberal arts tradition of the university. Two examples may suffice: the image of the student as consumer, and the imposition of assessment techniques.

A consumer is someone who comes onto the scene with wants and preferences he expects to have satisfied through commodity purchase. She would resent being required to entertain totally alternative ways of life, especially if such insights were to cause pain and destabilization of personal defenses. Yet the latter is exactly part of what we mean by becoming educated. A student totally converted to the image of consumer would probably feel that he or she has the right to sue the university for the discontent that can be provoked by a well-taught course in French existentialism.

Assessment requires the statement of course objectives and goals. This entails the "thingification" of educational content (see Miller, 1998). It collapses both teaching and learning into algorithms that preclude the adventures of quest and discovery and surprise (and their related emotions) for the sake of predictability and measurement. Appropriate for some sorts of courses, this is totally inappropriate for others (those usually connected with a humanities approach to education).

Just these two rhetorical trends, among others, constitute front lines in a war for the control of education and its meanings. They are also beachheads for the invasion of faculty prerogative by those in the grip of the most extreme ethos of capitalist standards of accountability.

The Postmodern University

With its ideological enemies and allies, postmodernism generates a broad front of campus culture wars that seem to subvert any specifiable vocation for the university as a singular moral institution. At the same time, however, postmodernism encourages methodological sensitivity to issues of objectivity, evidence, and, above all perhaps, to the ways of our encounter with others (both human and nonhuman). Thus postmodernism perhaps anticipates new expectations of what we might mean by justice, community, stewardship, and solidarity. Needless to say, no one has yet figured out how to reconcile such images of threat and promise. Much depends on that challenge being met.

Perhaps the most appropriate way to end this section and move on to the main task is to quote a thought by the vice president for public leadership of the Educational Testing Service. It stands in some contrast to the notion of democracy represented by the University of Phoenix cited earlier:

> The tightening vise of economic change can all too easily make us slaves to material necessity, eclipsing the educational needs of our culture and political system. *Liberal education needs to encourage us to question the basic purposes* of an economy, especially at a time when material necessity threatens other cultural and political values. Surely, we do not want to live in a society where access to all honors, love, leisure, standing, and public office are increasingly beholden to a wealth and income class. Money can buy anything in a society where there is no other currency. (Carnevale, 1996, p. 11, emphasis added)

IS THERE A UNIQUE CALLING FOR THE UNIVERSITY?

Is there anything the university is good for that cannot be provided by some other institution? Surely the time has come to pose that question, because if no answer is persuasive, perhaps this institution has no moral future unique to itself. I propose to argue that the American university is a civic religious institution. It's impossible to exaggerate the controversial character of this claim. While this designation once formally applied to most early liberal arts colleges and universities, it usually is not taken as applicable to contemporary secular universities. I shall argue that to some degree, it still is. This position should not be confused with the distinction between public (state-connected) and private universities, nor with the claim that the university is *only* a civil religious institution. It is many other things as well. Those other things, however, seem not of the essence. They are functions that could be expelled to other venues. With the elaboration of this argument, a process I can hope only to begin on this occasion, I shall try to develop a vision of the university that provides a lasting foundation for its own integrity

Civil Religion: Problems and Pitfalls of a Concept

I have tried to avoid the term *civil religion,* but found myself trapped between civic and civil religion. The term *civic* seemed too casual (the League of Women Voters), and civil religion too strong (a state religion). With the proper disclaimers, it seemed wiser to err on the side of the latter risk because it is more evocative of what I want to say. Making use of such a term will strike many, probably correctly, as foolhardy. The term has all but disappeared from American social science, and even those who use it agree that it corresponds to no stable or uniform empirical referent. Yet I do try to make use of "civil religion" because it helps me say something I think needs saying about the university in a secular democratic society.[2]

Civil religion is a public phenomenon, but not necessarily in the sense of one authorized by the state. Further, something can be of civil religious significance without being consciously so. An analogy may help clarify this last point. Consider the concept of the "individual person." Most Americans probably think of the individual as a supreme locus of the private (i.e., the natural bearer of rights, the site of subjectivity, the initiator of free action). It is not widely appreciated how much the private is itself a public concept. After all, it is through public institutions (e.g., common law, legislation, diplomacy, war, language itself) that private domains are carved out, so to speak. This applies to the notion of the individual person. Thanks to the sociology of Emile Durkheim (1958, 1984), we now understand the extent to which the individual person is not a fact of nature but a social institution that evolves out of the history of the societal division of labor. Individual personas emerge, says Durkheim, because as social roles become increasingly specialized and diverse, personal consciousness must adapt to ever more contingent circumstances. This greatly sharpens the self's sense of power, boundary, and responsibility. Eventually the conceits of individual-*ism* as ideology obscure society altogether and celebrate a market economy supposedly based on purely individual contractual rationality, in which it is forgotten that there must be a social consensus on the sanctity of all contracts that validates any single contract.

In the same way, civil religion (for Durkheim, all religion) is not merely a matter of subjective, freely chosen belief or faith. It is a profoundly social phenomenon that operates as much below the surface of awareness as above it. All religious experiences take the form of something experienced as sacred, separate from the profane. This process is mediated far more by ritual than intellectual belief, because it is ritual that raises social interaction to a "high" upon which members come to depend for the mobilization of their emotions. Since ritual is intimately connected with the forms of society, Durkheim concludes that religion is linked to social morphology. A religious (including civil religious) institution addresses itself to a group's transcendent sense of itself, to moral aspirations that lend mythic meaning to time and prevent the group's history from appearing as just "one damn thing after another."

This approach to religion has been considered classic in sociology and anthropology for some time. Given the enormous diversity of religious phenomena and their rough correlation with social forms, there is at least surface plausibility to the argument. Even with respect to civil religion, a notoriously elusive concept, one's skepticism hesitates before the raw power of nationalism around the world. Since the idea of civil religion will play a central role in my defense of the university, it may be helpful to review briefly why the concept has fallen on hard times so that my use of it can be properly located.

First, as with its larger parent—the idea of religion as a whole—it has been difficult to define civil religion. Does it consist in values, intentions, beliefs, functions, identification, subordination, perhaps even a type of method (as I shall argue later)? Is it primarily creed (e.g., codified affirmation), emotion (e.g., awe) or behavior (e.g., ritual or obedience to religious law)? Can it be a type of character structure as intended by the founders of the American character education movement (Yulish, 1980)? How "authentically" does it have to be felt, such that strategic motives count as a corruption? What about assumed qualities of consciousness (e.g., for civil religion to work, must its operations be unconscious or at least in some sense involuntary)?

Second, what is the empirical referent for civil religion? (Is it the whole of a society, a polity, specific groups, values, institutions, simulations, narratives, signs, and symbols?) Third, how does a referent affect the forms and dynamics of civil religion?[3] Here, briefly, are my assumptions on how civil religion ought to be conceptually constructed when applied to a democracy in general and to a university in particular. Please observe that this is a normative model reflecting my commitments to a certain understanding of democracy and of a university. I don't think these norms are merely fanciful, however. In the form of myth and to some extent in practice, they have some empirical resonance in American political culture even in the form of lip service among groups whose authoritarianism might seem to belie their sincerity.

First, the more complex a society, the more civil religion is a legitimately contested term. *The master referent for civil religion is one's "country"* (fatherland, motherland, soil, homeland, ranging from small to planetary in scope), but many other referents intervene to determine how one's country is experienced, defined, and understood. Thus, American social democrats and members of the Ku Klux Klan both work for their country, but obviously mean different things by it (Smith, 1997).

Second, civil religion must make its peace not only with democracy's pluralism but also with its privatization of the "sacred." Yet democratic civil religion also needs to pursue unity amidst this diversity. A democratic civil religion will celebrate procedural norms more than imposed utopian visions, a celebration that could be called a dramaturgy of the *quest*.

Third, the quest is guided by an *intention,* the development of a democratic personality capable of not reducing forms of reason and of freedom to the ideological reifications I shall later call idolatries. Of course, while most people claim to be balancing reason and freedom in this manner, there seems little evidence of consensus on what that means (see Berube's 1997 critique of Martha Nussbaum's effort to resolve this problem).

Further, this combination of a life of quest and resistance to idolatry implies a vision of civil religion as devotion to a *method.* That method has come variously to be called deliberation, discourse ethics, communicative competence, and forum. Locating such a concern for method at the center of one's perspective on civil religion implies commitment to a political philosophy of citizens as responsible social world-makers (see Barber, 1984; Stanley, 1981).

In addition, many practices and institutions produce side effects not necessarily enshrined in their purposes. Some of these latent functions (Merton, 1968, pp. 73–138) may provide an institution with civil religious significance that its members are not aware of and might not approve if they were. I shall argue shortly that this is true of the university.

Finally, given these points, the question of what is a civil religious *institution* inevitably arises. In a democracy, a civil religious institution is one whose functions (not necessarily its purposes) serve the alleged goods of all the citizens of a commonwealth. The nature of the goods is not a foregone conclusion. Therefore the institution must leave room for free but methodical inquiry that includes all members, not only in their capacities as specialized functionaries (important as these are), but also in their status of citizens concerned with the fate of the commonwealth at large.

Although this approach will now be applied to the university, it is relevant to all institutions of major influence. Not only government is included but the great "private" institutions as well, especially the large corporations. It goes without saying that virtually no institution today, including the university, conforms to this model. Perhaps applying it to the university will inspire people to raise their expectations of other associations as well.

Some Civil Religious Functions of the University

There is space here to consider only one aspect of the university's civil religious role, but it is an important one. I shall present five functions of the university. Because they are not usually thought of as its primary purposes (and indeed are often not thought of at all in these forms), they will be classed as latent functions.

Some cautions: Depicting latent functions imposes an epistemologically risky burden on the observer. It is justifiable only if the argument is empirically plausible and the stakes of the effort are high. I hope my examples will serve to suggest the plausibility of this model. As for the stakes, these are not just "any old" functions. Together they comprise an institutional calling for civic education and preparation for responsible citizenship unduplicated in any other large, bureaucratically organized institution. Further, this being a normative model, I am well aware that it is much honored in the breach. But many unsung people also attend to its observance. Finally, lest my argument be misunderstood, especially by those who would otherwise be friendly to it, I do not wish to say that the university should specialize in these functions. But if all universities do not begin consciously to reflect upon their common (though not uniform) duties to these functions, they will lose all hope of maintaining any stance of critical moral autonomy. What, then, are these functions that together comprise a civil religious model of the democratic university? (They are presented in no particular order of priority.)

First, the university *articulates moral order*. This is emphatically not to say that the university generates or creates moral order for the larger society, though it may contribute to that process. Although the university is beholden to other institutions and interests for conceptions of order, it is expected to evaluate, mediate, and reconcile these conceptions to some extent, or at least to baptize some of them with the holy water of certification. Consider, for example, how university curricula struggle with "theologies" of reality such as models of explanation (e.g., sociobiology and its significance for the ontology of human being, or the various meanings of scientific "evidence"); moral evaluation of institutional practices (e.g., the uses of cost-benefit analysis, or the conduct of science as reflected in rules for informed consent); and concepts of historical motion (e.g., "progress," social and economic "development," "modernization," and "Marxism").

Second, the university functions to *integrate the psyche with the social*. It does this in particular by helping to socialize people into society's division of labor. The most notable example, perhaps, is education for the professions including, as it is supposed to, induction into professional ethics. The significance of this function of the university comes into focus when one recalls that one of the major themes of classical social theory was the problem of how to reconcile subjectivity (the interior life) and objectivity (nature and society) under the new conditions of secular modernism. Rapid social change still generates anxieties and unpredictable destinies that people expect the university to help them interpret, be it through theories of justice, better social policies, or the sorts of spiritual scrutiny of life that are the province of the humanities.[4]

With the expansion of adult education programs, the university is becoming a sponsor of lifelong personal reflection on the relations between theory and practice in the world. In that sense, the ivory tower is taking on some of the features of a monastery—a temporary refuge from the immediate secular pressures of decision; a repository of moral resources such as books, teachers, and conversation; and thus also a potential retreat for contemplation and life review. (Lest this vision of adult education be unduly romanticized, however, it had best be kept in mind that most enrollees are still in pursuit of occupational upgrading, retraining, language instruction, and other such instrumental goals. But like motives for going to college generally, commitments tend to change over generations.)

Third, in a large complex society the university may be the only venue (except perhaps for the church) in which occasional serious efforts are made to *reconcile the general calling of citizenship with the particular callings of the labor market*. This topic generates almost instant cynicism. As Veysey remarks, "Talk about 'citizenship training' as a purpose of the university has become very cheap coin indeed, but in the nineteenth century such affirmations still possessed something of the power of innocence" (Veysey, 1965, p. 72).

Since these words were written, significant efforts have emerged throughout the country to experiment with some fresh, creative ways to educate for citizenship, though the innocence cited by Veysey is still somewhat in force. The innocence seems born of two assumptions. One is that citizenship is easy to define (such as voting, volunteering, etc.). The other is that the university can play such a role while yet dependent upon the authority and power of capitalist institutions, thus not being required to establish and maintain a rather strong stance of critical autonomy. Citizenship, of course, is not easy to define in purely mechanical terms, important as these are. But in recent years, the study of citizenship is ready to imbue civic education with an unprecedented degree of sophistication.[5]

Like citizenship training, the term *civic education* has all but lost credibility among those unacquainted with its more creative frontiers (for a summary, see Sirianni & Friedland, 1997). To the student benumbed by "civics" or the academician required to preach yet one more incoherent sermon on "good citizenship," the words evoke little passion. But civic education can be an institutionalized means for supporting students in their quest for the substance and limits of duty to their country. The vocabulary of interest groups has obscured the notion of citizenship as a general calling. It survives in the idea of national and community service, jury duty, charity, and volunteering. Civic education is best considered not as an intellectual object or isolated curriculum, but as a set of questions to be asked as an aspect of all our courses of study: How should anything (institutions, forms of education, occupations, forms of service, etc.) be understood in light of the state of our commonwealth? What must we do to make such assessments? How does anything (institutions, etc.) contribute to justice and other values and practices that make our commonwealth worth sharing as a legacy fit for our descendants?

The difficulty of sustaining such a civic educational enterprise can hardly be exaggerated. The debates over multiculturalism provide a potent reminder of the challenges confronting any effort to establish a general calling for citizens, or any stable conceptions of the "reason" and "freedom" that citizens of Western democracies are invited to balance in their pursuit of happiness. Decisions on moral and political questions such as multiculturalism, prayer in the schools, the obligations of government toward market regulation, budget priorities, and so forth, are the responsibility of citizens. Some simply wish to leave all this to the "market." Few knowledgeable people would deny the importance of markets. But given what we know about market failures, about relationships between markets, class, race, and power, and about the often engineered nature of "consumer sovereignty," using the market principle as a magical device for avoiding all other methods for thinking about public policy is as unacceptable as ignoring it. If civic education is successful, the student will discover that all education is partly political. Ideas and practices do not just hang in a Platonic space. They have origins and uses in the social world that generate problems of justice for which all people in their general calling as citizens are partly accountable. It is not just our delegates and experts but we all, as agents of the social life we create together, who comprise the forum of public conscience.

The fourth latent function to be considered here is the duty to focus society's attention upon the *problem of idolatry*. This obligation applies as much to the internal life of the university as to its environment. Idolatry is the ultimate technicism (Stanley, 1981). In Western religions, icons are considered an aid to worship, an aesthetic focus for contemplation and feeling. But as idols they are the mere technology of religious worship, the mark of impatience with the tasks of communion. Idols replace the work of imagination and interpretation. They may even be taken as gods themselves.

When weary of the rigors of critical marginality and the hermeneutic slipperiness of all thought, speech, and action, any institution (including the university) can be tempted by the captains and kings of society into the comforts of court prophecy. This is emphatically not to say that it is academic theories as such that are the idols. Nor are the idols the work of those who humbly attempt to apply theories to the work of the world. Idolatry is a form of seduction whereby some people allow themselves to be converted by theory into a sense of world coherence so strong as to inspire imperial conquest of all other ways of seeing the world. Idolatrous theorizing is dogmatism that makes itself known by its drive to achieve total conceptual and political dominion over anything pertaining to its field of vision, which can include the whole world.

To illustrate: Idolaters of society rule out all forms of explanation not reducible to social determinism. Idolaters of the market perceive commodity value, utility calculations, and self-aggrandizement in all aspects of motive and experience. The idolaters of corporatism believe there is nothing that cannot be defined and integrated by those prepared to use the managerial sciences of organization and administration. The ethos of applied science, often enforced through state auspices, is the idol of some professionals. The idolaters of classical politics seek to make all of life a test of virtue in the public arena according to standards of duty, consensus and sacrifice. Such outposts of idolatry sometimes appear to innovators as the dominant geography of the contemporary university.

The fifth function, weaving through the others like a wan shadow of once vital meta-narratives, is the university's efforts to *reconcile reason and freedom*. In this alleged postmodernist age, as noted earlier, there can be no confident definitions of what these terms mean. But that does not absolve the university from efforts to sort out their possibilities. Far too much is at stake: people's lives and the fates of societies. If the university cannot legislate the meanings of reason and freedom, it must at least educate. What are the forms of freedom people risk (interpretation, production, domination, experimentation, defiance, revolution in matters of language, society, morality, science, politics, and religion)? What barriers, imposed by nature or humanity, defy our will and thus appear to us as the majestic laws of reason? When do casualties of risk outweigh promises of liberation? If all

persons are now complicit in such decisions and their consequences, what
sorts of forums are appropriate for this terrifying democracy?
These, then, are some sacral functions of the modern university. They
justify a civil religious vision of that institution because university life is
the only venue where the student citizen encounters a generous range of
organized human knowledge in a unified place, with at least the presump-
tion that training is subordinate to broader educational goals. At the same
time, the university is a microcosm of the fragmentation of the larger society. Therefore, sentimental calls to unity will not suffice to generate much
beyond vague formulations of "roundedness" and sensitivity to "public service." The time may have come when many if not most individual universities can now probably be replaced by less expensive ways of doing many
of the things they have been doing. If there is a possibly unique role for
the university as a mediating institution between family and public life that
no other institution can fulfill, it must be more consciously renovated with
that purpose in mind. I hope what I have sketched out in this chapter is a
persuasive account of how to begin to think about that task.

ACKNOWLEDGMENT

I wish to acknowledge with thanks the efforts of Mary Stanley and Richard
Harvey Brown to help me get the ideas in this chapter straighter and more
lucidly expressed than they undoubtedly otherwise would have been.

NOTES

1. For a history of the liberal education idea, see Kimball, 1986; for a study of
attempted hegemonic domination of the American university by a newly forming
corporate capitalism, see Noble, 1997a, pp. 110–256.
2. In preparing to use it, I consulted helpful literature and thus cannot say I
wasn't warned (see Hughey, 1983; Mathisen, 1989).
3. For example, see Hughey's use of Thernstrom's study of Newburyport to
criticize Warner's uniform ahistorical functionalist interpretation of civil religion,
plus his analysis of modern utilitarian, bureaucratic society's effects upon it
(Hughey, 1983).
4. For evidence that these functions are in danger from student and university
decisions damaging to the liberal arts, see Engell and Dangerfield, 1998.
5. This richer understanding of citizenship has occurred under the influence
of historical sociology (Putnam, 1993; Somers, 1993); hermeneutics (see Alejandro,
1993); phenomenological studies (see Schutz, 1970); social constructivism (Berger & Luckmann, 1966); and deliberative notions of citizenship (Habermas, 1979,

especially pp. 1-69; Barber, 1984; Stanley, 1980); plus recently refined inquiry into models of democracy (Dahl, 1989; Gutman & Thompson, 1996; Held, 1987; Macpherson, 1966, 1977).

REFERENCES

Alejandro, R. (1993). *Hermeneutics, citizenship, and the public sphere.* Albany: State University of New York Press.

Barber, B. (1984). *Strong democracy: Participatory politics for a new age.* Berkeley: University of California Press.

Berger, P., & Luckmann, T. (1966). *The social construction of reality.* Garden City, NY: Doubleday Anchor.

Berube, M. (1997, September). Citizens of the world unite: Martha Nussbaum's campaign to cultivate humanity. *Lingua Franca, 7*(7), 78-81.

Bikson, T. E. (1996, Spring). Educating a globally prepared workforce: New research on college and corporate perspectives. *Liberal Education, 82*(2), 12-19.

Carnevale, A. P. (1996, Spring). Liberal education and the new economy. *Liberal Education, 82*(2), 4-11.

Castells, M. (1983). *The city and the grass roots.* Berkeley, CA: University of California Press.

Dahl, R. (1989). *Democracy and its critics.* New Haven, CT: Yale University Press.

della Mirandola, P. (1956). *Oration on the dignity of man.* Chicago: Regnery.

Durkheim, E. (1958). *Professional ethics and civic morals.* New York: Free Press.

Durkheim, E. (1984). *The division of labor in society.* New York: Free Press.

Engell, J., & Dangerfield, A. (1998, May/June). Forum: The market-model university. *Harvard Magazine, 100*(5), 64-67.

Ewen, S. (1976). *The captains of consciousness.* New York: McGraw-Hill.

Finkin, M. (1997, July/August). The assault on faculty independence. *Academe, 83*(4), 16-21.

Gaff, J. G. (1997, Summer). The changing roles of faculty and administrators. *Liberal Education, 83*(3), 12-17.

Gamson, Z. (1997, Summer). The stratification of the academy. *Social Text, 51*(2), 67-73.

Gilliland, M. (1997, May/June). Organizational change and tenure: We can learn from the corporate experience. *Change, 29*(3), 30-33.

Gutman, A., & Thompson, D. (1996). *Democracy and disagreement.* Cambridge, MA: Harvard University Press.

Haber, S. (1970). *Frederick Taylor: A study in personality and innovation.* Cambridge, MA: M.I.T. Press.

Habermas, J. (1979). *Communication and the evolution of society.* Boston: Beacon Press.

Held, D. (1987). *Models of democracy.* Palo Alto, CA: Stanford University Press.

Hughey, M. W. (1983). *Civil religion and moral order.* Westport, CT: Greenwood Press.

Kimball, B. A. (1986). *Orators and philosophers: A history of the idea of liberal education.* New York: Teachers College Press.

Lash, S., & Urry, J. (1988). *The end of organized capitalism.* Madison: University of Wisconsin Press.

Lazerson, M. (1997, March/April). Who owns higher education? The changing face of governance. *Change, 29*(2), 10–15.

Lustig, R. J. (1981). *Corporate liberalism: The origins of modern American political theory, 1890–1920.* Berkeley: University of California Press.

Macpherson, C. B. (1966). *The real world of democracy: The Massey lectures.* Oxford: Clarendon Press.

Macpherson, C. B. (1977). *The life and times of liberal democracy.* New York: Oxford University Press.

Marx, K., & Engels, F. (1959). *The communist manifesto in Marx and Engels: Basic writings.* (Lewis Feuer, Ed.). Garden City, NY: Anchor Books, Doubleday.

Mathisen, J. A. (1989). Twenty years after Bellah: Whatever happened to American civil religion? *Sociological Analysis, 50*(2), 129–146.

Matthews, A. (1997). *Bright college years: Inside the American campus today.* Chicago: University of Chicago Press.

Merton, R. (1968). *Social Theory and Social Structure.* New York: Free Press.

Miller, D. L. (1998, March). *Nothing to teach! No way to teach it! Together with the obligation to teach! Dilemmas in the rhetoric of accountability and assessment.* Keynote address at The Conference on Values in Higher Education, University of Tennessee, Knoxville.

Nelson, B. (1981). *On the roads to modernity.* Totowa, NJ: Rowman and Littlefield.

Newfield, C. (1997, Summer). Recapturing academic business. *Social Text, 51*(2), 39–66.

Nirenberg, J. (1997, Winter). Deconstructing higher education. *1997 Adult Assessment Forum,* pp. 11–12.

Noble, D. F. (1997a). *America by design: Science, technology, and the rise of corporate capitalism.* New York: Alfred Knopf.

Noble, D. F. (1997b, Winter). Education as a commodity: The virtual university and the cost of production. *Adult Assessment Forum,* pp. 7–10.

Polanyi, K. (1944). *The great transformation.* Boston, MA: Beacon.

Putnam, R. (1993). *Making democracy work: Civic traditions in modern Italy.* Princeton, NJ: Princeton University Press.

Rhoades, G., & Slaughter, S. (1997, Summer). Academic capitalism: managed professionals, and supply-side higher education. *Social Text, 51*(2), 9–38.

Schutz, A. (1970). *On phenomenology and social relations* (H. R. Wagner, Ed.). Chicago: University of Chicago Press.

Sirianni, C., & Friedland, L. (1997, January/February). Civic innovation and American democracy. *Change, 29*(1), 14–23.

Slaughter, L., & Leslie, L. (1997). *Academic capitalism: Politics, policies, and the entrepreneurial university.* Baltimore, MD: Johns Hopkins University Press.

Smith, R. (1997). *Civic ideals: Conflicting views of citizenship in U.S. history.* New Haven, CT: Yale University Press.

Somers, M. (1993, October). Citizenship and the place of the public sphere. *American Sociological Review, 58*(3), 588-603.

Stanley, M. (1980). *The public school and public policy.* New York: Pilgrim Press.

Stanley, M. (1981). *The technological conscience: Survival and dignity in an age of expertise.* Chicago: University of Chicago Press.

Stanley, M. (1990). The rhetoric of the commons. In Herbert Simons (Ed.), *The rhetorical turn.* Chicago: University of Chicago Press.

Taylor, F. (1967). *The principles of scientific management.* New York: Harper and Brothers. (Original work published 1911)

Titelli, V. (1997, Summer). Adjuncts and more adjuncts: Labor segmentation and the transformation of higher education. *Social Text, 51*(2), 75-91.

Veysey, L. A. (1965). *The emergence of the American university.* Chicago: University of Chicago Press.

Yulish, S. M. (1980). *The search for a civic religion: A history of the character education movement in America, 1895-1935.* Washington, DC: University Press of America.

EIGHT

TOWARD A RELEGITIMATION OF HIGHER EDUCATION
Reinvigorating the Humanities and Social Sciences

GRAHAME F. THOMPSON

IN A CLIMATE of review and reassessment, universities are increasingly being challenged to justify and account for themselves. Nowhere is this more so than in respect to the teaching of the humanities and social sciences. The period since the conservative turn in intellectual and policy matters has seen an unprecedented attack on the role of the university in respect to the disinterested pursuit of knowledge and as the embodiment of enlightened liberal values. A deep sense of unease has now fallen over many humanities and social science departments as they have become increasingly subject to internal performance assessments, funding retrenchments, public attacks upon their research outputs and teaching competencies, and even a questioning of the reason for their very existence in a time of severe economic austerity. As the commercialization of the university proceeds apace, the pressures to gather outside funding seem destined to overwhelm what shrinking time there still remains for the actual teaching of students and the conduct of research. Teaching time itself is under intense pressure, as a massive expansion in the numbers of students admitted to the universities has taken place without a commensurate increase in resources.

In fact, these processes are perhaps unwittingly part of a wider move that will result in the whole of the education system becoming a machine of mass mediocrity. Politicians and managers are relentlessly bureaucratizing all aspects of the production and distribution of knowledge in the pursuit of so-called academic "quality" and "accountability." A mind-numbing conformity to administrative procedures is what is called for, which is presented as the optimal good. The creative and innovative capacities of teachers are frowned upon, treated with suspicion and sometimes hostility. "Politicians may be satisfying a public demand for mass higher education, but without any conception of what this is supposed to accomplish other than to create a certificated mass workforce . . . a growth of hidebound specialisms has displaced broad intellectual curiosity . . . with narrow-mindedness and a narrowly-focused academic industry" (Hirst, 1993). What is required is an "organized mediocrity"—at best a conforming middlebrow cultural milieu that does not challenge the existing comfortable status quo.

But the general growth of managerial commercialism in universities and other teaching establishments is in danger of turning them from the remnants of cultural institutions into businesses. The implications of this can be seen clearly in the case of the United Kingdom's art schools and teacher training colleges, both of which are under threat as cultural institutions. The art schools are increasingly being used as mere conduits for a overtly commercialized and aesthetically dubious "hype." How far are pickled fish and the like an answer to the "crisis of modernism," rather than a prime indicator of its symptomatic implosion? The relentless attack on the credibility of teaching has so undermined confidence that the training colleges now face their worst-ever crisis of recruitment. And the schools themselves face an even more relentless drive to uniformity, mindless testing, and centralized managerial bureaucratic initiatives. Unfortunately, we see all these features manifesting in many other contemporary public and private arenas.

It is possible that these features and trends are part of a wider transformation in the nature of the social order in general. One way to characterize this is to name it a "kakistocratic social order." The concept of a kakistocracy is defined by the *Webster's Dictionary* as "government by the worst men," but it is preferably defined as *government by the least able*. The problem is that as the least able climb the ladder of "success" and become a critically important mass in positions of authority, it becomes extremely difficult to dislodge them. Those few genuine creative and innovative institutions that manage to survive in a kakistocratic order are themselves increasingly vulnerable, as they too are threatened with being overwhelmed by careerists who are increasingly attracted to their success and wish to firmly attach themselves to it.

This may all sound excessively pessimistic, and at one level it is. But a moment's reflection should bring home its essential truth. The trouble is that the kakistocrats are not only the least able, they are often also the most cunning and devious as well. This is not a contradiction—one of the pervasive features of a kakistocratic social order is the lack of intellectual ability of its leaders combined with their depressing ability to effectively maneuver into positions of authority and "success." Look, for instance, no further than those who now run the privatized utilities and corporations in the United Kingdom. Those who were previously the equivalent of managers of municipal water or gas works now present themselves as international businessmen and award themselves salaries accordingly. But in fact they operate in highly sheltered and almost risk-free commercial environments. Unfortunately, these attitudes also are being adopted in a wider range of organizations and institutions.

The issue pursued in the rest of this chapter is what might be an appropriate response to these trends. I confine myself here to the domain of higher education, and within this to the social sciences and humanities in particular. Four main responses to the predicament posed by the attack from the new right and its kakistocratic allies can be discerned, which, while distinct, are not unrelated to one another.

RESPONSES

I term the first response a "politics of despair." It is to deeply lament these developments and react to them with a resigned disaffection. It leads to a seemingly endless lament on the part of disillusioned academics, heard in senior common rooms, course or departmental meetings, and at almost every conference attended. What chance do we have to delay or divert these trends when faced with a determined and powerful opponent in the form of our political and funding masters and their internal managerial allies? None or very little is the standard response. Perhaps this is the most pervasive of the reactions. For instance, for all intents and purposes opposition from academics to internal and external "quality control" has collapsed in the United Kingdom as the language of this technology of governance has been accepted and embraced by all.

A second reaction is a variation on the first. This involves a "politics of exposure." It leads to detailed investigations and "revelations" of the moves being made by those opposed to a "liberal education"—broadly speaking, ultraconservative forces, whether these be in terms of some shadowy "national intelligence-gathering" regime or the more overt New Right think tanks and their allies. But as the embrace of the bureaucratic techniques referred to above widens within higher education, the politics of exposure might also expand to include our administrative masters as well as ultraconservative political forces. However, what is distinctive about this response is that exposure as such is somehow seen to constitutes the limit of an adequate defense.

The third reaction is one of the main positive responses. It is to offer a fight back, but a fight back in the name of the traditional values and roles ascribed to universities as part of an enlightened and universalistic liberal intellectual and governmental program. This I will term "the politics of nostalgia." Such a politics reasserts the value of a university education as part of a process of forming democratic subjects who are mobilized into a universal, enlightened, and emancipatory humanitarianism.

A final response, a variation on the third just outlined, is to invoke the "politics of relativism." The aim here is to defend an educational strategy based upon different perspectives on the same or similar problems. In this case, great care needs to be taken to invoke a defensible definition of relativism. This would be one that does not just duplicate the attacks of the opponents of the relativization of truth on their own ground by accepting that there is a genuinely real domain of Truth to begin with, against which different interpretations of it can be quite reasonably and legitimately measured. Such is the position adopted by philosophical realism, a strong element in the present configuration of forces arrayed along this oppositional dimension.

Now, while one would not necessarily wish to completely dismiss any of these positions, they do not seem to offer an adequate analysis of either the historical role of the university or a defense that can be mounted within the academy for a progressive interdisciplinary-based education in the humanities or social sciences. For the purposes of much of the rest of this chapter, I concentrate upon the latter two positive positions outlined above with which to conduct a critical engagement. To construct an adequate response to the challenges facing a progressive disciplinary and interdisciplinary education in the humanities and social sciences will require a reexamination of the ascribed role of the university and higher education more generally. This reexamination is designed to buttress the existing approaches with a set of telling arguments that relegitimize the position and future role of the university. Part of my aim here is to reconceptualize the economic arguments that are prevalent within both popular and professional discourses about the nature of the connection between the universities and the current concern with economic competitiveness.

UNIVERSITY EDUCATION AS PRODUCTION GOOD
OR CONSUMPTION GOOD?[1]

In policy planning and cost-benefit analyses, the output of the universities is usually considered, broadly speaking, a *production good*. Thus higher education is seen almost exclusively as one of the inputs that go into making a viable and productive economic structure. On a more general note, it is the production of knowledge that is considered the most important aspect of the whole process of knowledge-power relationships. This emphasis on the production side has served to obscure the utilization or consumption side of that process (which is elaborated below). In fact, however, one might argue that the conditions for the production of knowledge are less of a problem in a modern society than are the conditions for the effective utilization of that knowledge once produced. In one way or another, the production and distribution of knowledge remain a remarkably open process in Western societies, despite all manner of attempts (both commercial and governmental) to control it. Much less effective is the efficient utilization of that existing knowledge base once it is in "open circulation," so to speak. A striking proportion of it just goes to waste. This is where differential and particular institutional arrangements have an important impact on the way knowledge can be, and is, effectively utilized for the good. These arrangements are highly specific to particular nations in so far as their impact upon economic performance is concerned. The institutional arrangements of some countries are highly conducive to the utilization of knowledge for economic production, whereas the institutional arrangements for others remain unable to do this. More on this later.

Defenders of the argument that education is a production good generally connect the universities and the economy via the operation of the labor market. The labor market is structured around competencies and qualifications, and it is the educated outputs of the universities that play a major part in organizing this structure of inputs to the economy. Clearly, this is the site of a long and continuing debate focused on whether the higher education system actually provides the "right" set of input skills needed for the economy. By and large, employers have consistently complained that it does not. But if such employers are asked to be more specific (which they often are), they generally have little idea of exactly what educational skills they do require, other than as expressed in vague terms and in general notions. Thus whatever system of higher education were in place, complaints would invariably emerge, and it is probably wise to ignore these as far as possible. In the United Kingdom, for example, it has been the public authorities, the universities, but most importantly of all the public schools that have provided the impetus for any changes or initiatives in the development of educational competencies and skills, not commercial organizations. The latter have generally been the most conservative and backward in terms of their perception of what educational outputs are needed for an advanced industrial economy.

Increasingly, governments have jumped rather uncritically on the production good bandwagon, aided by university administrators, academics, and economists alike. A good many reports have been produced that try to point to the relationship between educational standards generally—and university qualifications more particularly—and economic performance. Now, it would be foolish to suggest that there is absolutely no relationship between the levels of educational competencies of a population and its level of well-being or economic development. The problems emerge, however, when the objective becomes to demonstrate a close or strong relationship between these two, and particularly between them when the outputs of various types of graduates are involved. Admittedly, some studies have shown some correlation between these two, particularly where science and technology graduates are concerned. But this has not settled the issues of whether such correlation implies a causation running from the number or type of graduates to the rates or levels of economic growth, and of the actual robustness of such correlations. By and large, a scrutiny of a large body of analysis and evidence, particularly country cross-sectional analysis, reveals that there is no consistent and robust causal relationship here.[2]

Indeed, this conclusion is bolstered by the difficulty of finding such strong causal relationships between a wider variety of specific economic inputs and national economic performance. Thus if one compares measures such as the amount of R&D expenditure, or other types of investment thought to be of particular importance in generating growth, or the numbers of patents taken out, or levels of technology, and the like, again little consistent relationship emerges. In fact, much more important for economic performance than these specific input categories are the more general institutionalized operation of the labor market in terms of outcomes over wage negotiations (centralized versus decentralized bargaining arrangements), the operation of the financial system in terms of how effectively and closely it links the raising of finance with a long-term investment strategy for industry, the forms of corporate governance, and the nature of the national political settlement between the dominant social interest groups or "partners" over negotiated outcomes to distributional disputes.

What, then, are we to conclude from this discussion about the dominant line of argument linking the universities to the economy? Contrary to the main thrust of this argument, it is suggested here that higher education be considered not so much as a production good but increasingly as a *consumption good*. Thus, just as they enjoy and demand fine cars and large houses, people also like and demand good-quality higher education, particularly in the case of the humanities and the social sciences. The benefits they perceive from such higher education may not be tied very closely to their supposed labor market effects in terms of enhanced opportunities in employment, but as a benefit in its own right, and as a way of understanding and engaging with an increasingly complex and interdependent world.

If I may speak for a moment from experience, I work in a nationally organized university of "the second chance" that has 200,000 undergraduate and other students, most of whom already have jobs. These students seem less interested in gaining their degrees for employment purposes (though they are by no means totally disinterested in this!) than in pursuing their study for its own sake. In the humanities and the social sciences in particular, the Open University seems to have tapped a market for good-quality, heavily interdisciplinary-based undergraduate education that is demanded as much for its benefit in explaining the nature of ideas and a complex world as for the enhanced employment prospects that a degree might offer. This leads me to believe that the output I am involved in producing has less to do with traditional notions of a production good as described above, but more to do with a consumption good that is demanded much on its own terms. What is more, I suspect this is a form of demand that will grow in the future.

Why is this? Largely because the kinds of demands for mass consumption in the post–World War II period are not necessarily those that will obtain into the future. Of course, I am not suggesting that such patterns of demand will change overnight or for all very quickly. The distribution of income and wealth is too uneven for that. But the problem with the post–World War II consumption patterns that have been based on a popular leisure culture is that they have been popular because they were, and are still, novel. But novelty itself is its own potential undoing. Shopping, mass-entertainment TV, mass travel, "drugs, sex, and rock 'n' roll," or what have you are all very well and will continue to have their place, but for how long will they maintain their hold over the imagination of a population rapidly increasing in information, intelligence, and education? This may sound fanciful, but my proposition is that as the plateau of educational competence and achievement rises, itself the result of the first-ever experiment in mass secondary education that was conducted in the post–World War II years (however unevenly and slowly this has spread), then the realm of ideas and understandings of a complex world will become an attractive pursuit, perhaps even more so than shopping or mass entertainment per se. The nature of what is considered pleasurable and even hedonistic is thus likely to change.

If this admittedly rather speculative argument has any merit, it is to suggest that a new case for higher education needs to be made. Even if students continue to take a hard instrumental attitude toward their own studies and pursue particular subjects because they think these will enhance their prospects in the labor market, there would be no justification on the part of the university authorities to directly link this to arguments for increased national competitiveness. Uncomfortable though it might be, this nettle should be grasped.

Let us begin with what might seem to be the most disturbing implications of the issues outlined so far. If fine cars and large houses are paid for directly in the marketplace, why should not the same conditions of distribution now apply to higher education? This is a process that is, in fact, increasingly the case in many countries. But the point about the term *consumption good* as used above is that it is not necessarily to imply that it means a total commodification of higher education in the humanities and the social sciences. Contrary to an argument directly by analogy, just because fine cars and large houses are bought and paid for in a market does not necessarily mean that the same must apply to good-quality education. Note that the emphasis here is on the notion of no *necessary* implication. It may well be, therefore, that the question of paying directly for higher education is raised anew by the consumption-good argument considered here. But to reiterate, there is no necessary implication for how it is to be provided. There are good arguments from economics about education being a collective good of some kind, that is, a so-called "public good" or "merit good." These are goods that meet the criterion of nonexcludability and nondivisibility in their consumption; the consumption benefits derived from these goods can be made available to all consumers at no extra cost if they are to be supplied to any single consumer, and such consumption benefits cannot be divided in any sensible way between those consumers.

These are arguments justifying the public provision of education and should be no less compelling when applied to the idea of consumption goods used here. Examples of this already exist: publicly maintained parks, beaches, and museums. In a moment I explore an explicit argument for education as consumption good. To do this, however, requires us first to examine afresh the historical and contemporary nature of the university.

THE UNIVERSITY: WHAT IS IT?

As mentioned at the outset, one defensive way to conceive of the university is as a bastion of enlightened and universalistic values, the quintessential institution of the liberal emancipatory project. No doubt there is at least some residual truth in this conception. But I would like to pose the nature of the university in a different manner to highlight some of its rather less enlightened characteristics and other neglected aspects of its operation and significance.

The problem is that for much (perhaps most) of its history, the university has been a bastion of conservatism and reaction rather than of liberalism and the Enlightenment. How can we make sense of this if we insist on conceiving it in the manner of the politics of nostalgia, discussed briefly above? This point is not necessarily to decry the project of the Enlightenment as conducted within the university, but to recognize that it has been pursued (of necessity in some instances), and continues to be pursued, in many other arenas at the same time. Thus for much of its history the Enlightenment project has been conducted in the publishing house, through the medium of the pamphlet, in independent institutions like the Royal Society of Arts and the Royal Academy in Britain, within the institutions of the legal profession in terms of judgments and case histories, within the hospitals and nonuniversity educational establishments, even within the penal system and political parties. In the United States, public Congressional hearings have offered another site where this project has been at least in part pursued, and this is duplicated in the case of the Royal Commissions in the United Kingdom and other parliamentary procedures of scrutiny and accountability. A good many of these alternative arenas were set up precisely because of the indifference or open hostility on the part of the university to their intended investigations and work. Thus we should neither exaggerate the universities' own commitment to enlightened values nor underestimate the importance of other arenas in fostering them. One problem in the contemporary period, however, is that many of these other sites for the pursuit of the Enlightenment project (or any other similar project, for that matter) are themselves increasingly in disarray. Substitute sites for a civic education and critical thought, like the political parties, the media, parliamentary commissions, and so on, are also in decline.

In addition, it is important to recall why the great universities of Europe were founded in the thirteenth and fourteenth centuries. They were designed to fulfill quite utilitarian tasks of the time, namely to train men of medicine, the law, and religion. In many cases this continued to constitute the main rationale for university education in the humanities and the social sciences well into the nineteenth century (such that these distinctions were operative in that period). It was only then that, in British universities for instance, education in the humanities and social sciences was first comprehensively overhauled. But this was not done in the name of some belated Enlightenment project. Again, it was for very instrumental reasons; now to train home, and particularly colonial, administrators rather than doctors, lawyers, or ecclesiastics.[3]

When one recognizes these features of intellectual life, one is of necessity forced to reconceptualize the nature of the university. One way to do this is to conceive of it as a mechanism of governance and as an institution, in Foucault's sense, of "governmentality" (Foucault, 1991). As a mechanism of governance, the university—like any other institution of governance—is characterized by multiple objectives, often conflicting, and diverse forms of calculation designed to meet those objectives. These are always historically and socially contingent. As an arena of governmentality, the university can be linked to all those diverse strategies and technologies that serve to produce a certain type of selfhood: the construction of the self-referential subject able to mediate the mentalities of conduct, types of vocational training, and the forms of self-discipline commensurate with the wider technologies of governance and power circulating at any time.

These ways of re-posing the nature of the university move away from conceiving of it as a unitary entity with a single (almost transhistorical) purpose—the construction of an enlightened and humanitarian being. They also enable us to make another argument for the humanities and the social sciences without feeling that this would compromise a general principle. Thus, accepting the instrumentality and utilitarian features of the university of the past provides the basis for arguing that a large section of the contemporary working population required to make a modern society function— such as administrators, teachers, professionals, those in the arts, managerial personnel, civil servants, and so forth—find their natural training home within these kinds of departments. This vocational aspect of the university is one that needs a more robust defense. The competencies of this large group of the working population, who fulfill a vital and unavoidable set of tasks and functions, are for the most part the products of the humanities and social sciences departments, and they can be justified as products of the university in perfectly good faith. Nor need this argument be linked to the increasingly discredited one about the direct economic utility of such a training task now fulfilled by the university. Social science and humanities departments may not be producing critically rounded and enlightened subjects but rather a set of prosaic administrative and critically informed functionaries, who are of vital importance nevertheless.

This reconceptualization of the role of the university provides yet another defense of the social sciences and humanities. This is to invoke a rather old fashioned civic virtue argument about the reason for the existence of universities. This argument is related to that made for the traditional university in terms of the Enlightenment project, but it is not made in terms of a universal subject, and it does respond closely to the arguments of the contemporary New Right.

The universities still play a major role in the construction of civic personhood, and indeed of the civilized person in terms of conducts, manners, and the virtue of toleration.[4] There are great social benefits (not just private benefits) to be had from the efficient fulfillment of this task, especially those associated with the proper conduct of civic duties. These include competence in assessing competing social, economic, and political programs, civic and administrative initiatives, aesthetic and moral issues and the like that emerge from within the public domain or that are pressed into it. If there remains a commitment to political and democratic pluralism (even if only a residual commitment), there must be a mechanism that guarantees a range of informed voices available to debate the merits, consequences, and implications of such social initiatives and projects. What the humanities and social sciences do in some large part is to create lay expertise and informed opinion in the general public that enable the scrutiny and assessment of these matters. Both the New Right and the Old Left speak of empowerment and devolution of governmental functions to local communities, and are keen for there to be a more active citizenry in respect to many social welfare and administrative functions. But the expertise to conduct these functions does not just drop out of thin air. It must be taught, and it should be remembered that it is already taught in the context of humanities and social sciences education.

Another positive argument for higher education arises quite naturally from this point about civic competence: that a university education can be a mechanism for enhancing political equality. That is, the university can open opportunities for those without a voice in civic matters to gain one. It can act to draw in those from different socioeconomic strata, refreshing their competencies in the skills needed to fulfill a range of necessary civic duties and responsibilities, and thereby to have a greater stake in the system. Thus the importance of a training for citizenship can be stressed as against the neglect fostered by either paternalism or the belief that these skills are simply innate.

Here we also need to stress the importance of a diverse and multilayered higher education system for the generation of a plurality of voices. Suppose we were all members of one large university institution. Under these circumstances, the conditions for sensible and robust debate would be stifled. It is notoriously difficult for members of the same institution to publicly disagree with one another. Thus, to generate an effective debate requires a range of institutions, differentially placed within the social milieu, that can generate a variety of positions in debate. The reduction of the universities to a homogeneous dull uniformity undermines this objective.

In sum, it is vital that we link the consumption good model of higher education elaborated earlier to these arguments for training in civic virtue and competence. Part of the reason for a strong interest in the interdisciplinary study provided by the humanities and the social sciences is precisely to gain the intellectual skills and confidence to engage, initiate, and partake in debates and discussions about the major social and political issues of the day. This constitutes a strong reason for its demand. Such a training for citizenship remains a major and absolutely necessary and legitimate public responsibility that needs to be strongly reasserted under present conditions, where there is a renewed public emphasis on personal accountability and citizen responsibility from almost all political quarters. The humanities and the social sciences are the chief mechanisms for this training for citizenship through the construction of civic selves and of civilized persons.

THE NEED FOR A STRONGER MODEL?

This may all sound reasonable and even feasible, set as it is within the existing contours of the contemporary university. But the implications of a kakistocratic social order referred to above could easily be its undoing. Perhaps we need a new and different conception of the university to reenergize its project and role for late capitalism?

The key question here is whether the university, as an institution of culture and ideas, can coexist with a trend toward potential mass mediocrity and managerial commercialism. Any society that refuses the implications of a leadership through ideas and a cosmopolitan cultural milieu based upon competence, honesty, and the promotion of ability of the best is destined for marginalization and decline. Thus the only way out may be to promote a "new elitism" based upon these principles. To say this, however, is to risk the approbation of the intellectual equalizers and the perspectivizers, as well as to be highly controversial politically. But perhaps it should be said nevertheless. The issue is not to in any way promote a new social elitism based upon birth, social position, or contacts. Rather, it is to promote an intellectual elitism, where those with ideas, with intellectual creativity, and with capacities for cultural innovativeness are given a space to think and encouraged to offer advice and find solutions to the pressing politico-economic problems of the day. These ideas can neither be imposed upon citizens nor used to patronizingly talk down to them. On the other hand, there would seem to be the necessity for an intellectual elite; not all citizens either have the ability, the time, or the inclination to generate such ideas. It is just foolishly utopian to think otherwise. One possible metaphor for such reinvigoration of the university might be the ideal of craft production, somewhat akin to Alisdair MacIntyre's (1981) notion of "practices." Craft, in its widest connotations, embraces skill, dexterity, and excellence. Its ethical principles—which were so integral to its production principles—involved honor, integrity in performance, honesty, grace, and competence. It also implies regulation by intrinsic standards of excellence. The craft form of organization—which has its contemporary equivalence in the modern-day networking form of social coordination—offers a way of recouping the best from a diverse institutional resource that characterizes the present sorry intellectual state of the university sector.[5]

CONCLUSION

This chapter did not set out to address the enormous political obstacles and difficulties facing the continued teaching of a critically informed and interdisciplinary-based humanities and social sciences. Indeed, the problem is to find ways—many different ways—to circumvent these obstacles, or at least to partially undermine them. In this respect, one of those strategies must be to provide good arguments. But although there has been much discussion of the political obstacles facing the humanities and social sciences in the university, there has been relatively little imaginative thinking about how to defend them through realistic but honest argument. Here I have tried to redress that imbalance. A lot of this might sound naive and fanciful, but until it is intellectually explored, we will never know. It is time the academic community went on the offensive with some clear, positive, and forward-looking arguments for its existence.

But in addition I set another objective for the chapter. This was to highlight a possible significant shift in the contours of the contemporary social order, one characterized as being the development of what was termed a kakistocracy. This unwelcome event is having profound effects upon the nature of the university (and on the social order more widely), which prompted a discussion of a very different model for the university involving a radical change in its purpose and function. As far as can be judged, the jury remains out on this issue, but its controversial implications need much further thought and investigation.[6]

NOTES

1. In this section I declare a personal note that might help clarify the nature of the argument being made. As an economist, I approach the question posed by this heading in that capacity.
2. See Edgerton (1996) for a discussion of this literature in the context of the relative demise of the economic performance of the British economy.
3. See Hunter et al. (1991) for an elaboration of these ideas.
4. I owe much of the following discussion to Minson (1993).
5. For the genesis of these none too systematic remarks about craft produc-

tion, a "guild constitution," and networking, see: Black, 1984, 1992; Franklin, 1971; Hirst, 1993, 1994; Nicholls, 1990; and finally Thompson, 1993.

6. This is an issue I intend to explore, among other things, in Thompson, 1999.

REFERENCES

Black, A. (1984). *Guilds and civil society in European political thought from the twelfth century to the present.* London: Methuen.

Black, A. (1992). *Political thought in Europe, 1250-1450.* Cambridge: Cambridge University Press.

Edgerton, D. (1996). *Science, technology and the British industrial "decline," 1870-1970.* Cambridge: Cambridge University Press.

Foucault, M. (1991). Governmentality. In G. Burchell et al. (Eds.), *The Foucault effect.* Hemel Hempstead, UK: Harvester Wheatsheaf.

Franklin, J. H. (1971). Sovereignty and the mixed constitution. In J. H. Burns (Ed.), *The Cambridge history of political thought, 1450-1700.* Cambridge: Cambridge University Press.

Hirst, P. Q. (1993). *Is the university the enemy of ideas?* London: AA Files.

Hirst, P. Q. (1994). *Associative democracy.* Cambridge: Polity Press.

Hunter, I. (Ed.). (1991). *Accounting for the humanities: The language of culture and the logic of government.* Brisbane, AU: Institute for Cultural Policy Studies, Griffith University.

MacIntyre, A. (1981). *After virtue: A study in moral theory.* Notre Dame, IN: Notre Dame University Press.

Minson, J. P. (1993). *Questions of conduct.* Basingstoke, UK: Macmillan.

Nicholls, D. (1990). *The pluralist state.* Basingstoke, UK: Macmillan.

Thompson, G. F. (1993). Network coordination. In R. Maidment & G. F. Thompson (Eds.), *Managing the United Kingdom: An introduction to its political economy and public policy.* London: Sage.

Thompson, G. F. (1999). *Between markets and hierarchies: The history and significance of network coordination.* Oxford: Oxford University Press.

NINE

OBJECTIVITY, RELATIVISM, AND THE PUBLIC AUTHORITY OF THE SCHOLAR

DAVID R. SHUMWAY

ONE OF THE ironies of the right's recent attack on the new humanities has been its claims that these fields both encourage relativism and thereby a disregard of truth, on the one hand, and, on the other, that they have established a "New McCarthyism" in which views not meeting rigid standards of political correctness are censored. Such standards presumably entail the assumption of their own truth. I've never heard anyone on the right remark on the relation of these positions, so that it's not clear whether consistency or inconsistency is implied. The right treats these two charges as separate because they are designed to perform different functions. Of course, political correctness is the more powerful charge. Its purpose is to discredit the moral authority of the cultural left by charging it with Stalinism. The charge of relativism is designed to discredit the intellectual authority of the right's opponents by showing them to be unable to appeal to any truth or method in support of their positions. The charge that the left politicizes teaching and research combines both the moral and intellectual challenges. To politicize is both to relativize and to restrict. These charges are serious because they put into question the professional authority of left academics by making them seem to deviate from the ideals of objectivity and disinterest upon which professional expertise is held to rest.

My point will be to oppose a conception that identifies all knowledge with limited and parochial interests. That knowledge is inevitably interested does not imply that knowledge and interest are identical, nor that the production of knowledge is the same as the production of propaganda. To make knowledge production significant, it must be assumed that there are things we do not already know, rather than that there are merely interested positions or beliefs of which others must be persuaded.

In a moment I will argue that whatever critiques of professionalism we might make, professional authority is something we cannot afford to give up. I want to look first, however, at the history of the charge of politicization in literary studies. The terms of the academic right's position emerged in their current form in the early days of the Cold War. Actually, these terms first were brought into use even earlier, during the late 1930s, by the anti-Stalinist literary critics of the *Partisan Review*. Prior to this time, one counted on literary criticism—and literature itself—to be political. Even the genteel critics of the turn of the century assumed that part of their role was to discuss the political content and significance of literature, and to oppose literature that was politically pernicious. The political became more important in the criticism of the early 1930s, especially in the work of Marxist critics. The effort of the *Partisan Review* critics to define literature against politics emerged out of this earlier, highly politicized criticism, and by the late 1940s, it was largely successful. To assert that literature was political was to commit Stalinism, because it seemed to permit the control of the literary by nonliterary considerations. The New York intellectuals' position on this coincided with the New Critics' opposition to "extrinsic" approaches. Though the New Yorkers continued to assert connections between literature and culture, they held that great literature did not intervene politically. Rather, it portrayed the ambiguity or complexity of the social situation or human condition. It did not take sides. By the 1950s, literature in this sense became identified with freedom and democracy, while didactic literature was associated with communism. Lionel Trilling was now able to go so far as to treat literature as almost the antithesis of politics (Trilling, 1965). But this claim masked the politics that literature was being made to serve. Neither anticommunism nor American cultural nationalism were understood as political positions. Literature and criticism were now permitted to serve only those interests that were not recognized as political, which is to say, as interests.

This story of American literary criticism took place mainly outside of the university. Prior to World War II, criticism was not the normal practice of literary scholars. English professors were mainly literary historians who regarded themselves as disinterested compilers of facts. It is not a coincidence that criticism became a standard academic practice at the very moment when New York intellectual anti-Stalinism and New Critical formalism claimed to divorce criticism from politics and thus to make it disinterested. The ideology of the research university was positivist, and academic literary studies shared this ideology. Thus the introduction of criticism into the university represented a massive epistemological shift, but it occurred

largely without proclaiming itself as such. In their different ways, both the
New Critics and the New York intellectuals claimed objectivity, even as
they made interpretation the principle activity of criticism. The new hermeneutic foundation for English in practice rendered the meaning of texts
indeterminate, while the texts themselves and interpretations of them were
understood as undetermined by social or political conditions or any other
extrinsic factors. Authors and critics were both understood to disinterestedly serve only art.

At the same time that disinterested criticism was being institutionalized, the attack on the left that we call McCarthyism was all but ignored
by literary critics, especially by the New York intellectuals, newly converted
apologists for American culture. McCarthyism was not at first recognized
as a threat to freedom because only those opposed to freedom were its
targets. By the time McCarthy was exposed, his excesses had become
widely understood as a threat to democracy. It is important to remember,
however, that the bulk of McCarthyist activities were not the work of the
senator, but of the American internal security apparatus and other government bodies, including state and local ones (Schrecker, 1989, p. viii). Many
academics lost their jobs for actual or reputed Communist activities or sym-
pathies (see Schrecker, 1986; Holmes, 1989). Such McCarthyist activities
slowly declined, but they were not in general repudiated. However, McCarthyism came in time to represent—especially in the minds of academics
and other intellectuals—the threat to freedom that it had been. The right,
in calling political correctness the New McCarthyism, is using a more culturally powerful term to once again accuse their opponents of Stalinism. Thus
in the political correctness smear, the right has portrayed itself as defending
freedom of speech and academic freedom (for a demonstration that political
correctness was in fact a right-wing smear campaign see Wilson, 1995). But
the goal of the right's effort should not be misunderstood: it is to delegitim-
ize, and thereby silence, the speech of its opponents.

It is in this move, however, that we recognize that the antiprofessional-
ism of the right is itself a part of the system of professions. According to
Andrew Abbott, professions are best defined historically as groups that compete for control of work, and he notes that interprofessional competition
is a fundamental fact of professional life: "Control of knowledge and its
application means dominating outsiders who attack that control. Control
without competition is trivial" (1989, p. 2). Abbott thus rejects the notion
of an essential professional form toward which professionalization invariably leads. Nevertheless, professions need certain characteristics to be able
to successfully control jurisdiction of the work they perform. "The tasks of
professions are human problems amenable to expert service" (p. 35). Insofar as they engage the particular problems of their clients, professions typi-

cally perform diagnosis, make inferences, and prescribe treatment. But behind such work there must exist a body of academic knowledge together
with a different body of workers whose job is not to solve particular problems but to develop abstract formal systems. A body of abstract knowledge
is necessary for a profession to be able to maintain its claims to cognitive
exclusivity. A field that cannot assert the necessity of abstract knowledge
will have a jurisdiction too easily invaded by the self-taught:

> The ability of a profession to sustain its jurisdiction lies partly in the power
> and prestige of its academic knowledge. This prestige reflects the public's mis-
> taken belief that abstract knowledge is continuous with practical professional
> knowledge. . . . In fact, the true use of academic knowledge for professional
> work is less practical than symbolic. Academic knowledge legitimizes profes-
> sional work by clarifying its foundations and tracing them to major cultural
> values. In most modern professions, these have been the values of rationality,
> logic, and science. (pp. 53–54)

This is a somewhat different argument than the one Zygmunt Bauman
makes in *Legislators and Interpreters* (1987), where he notes the tendency
during the twentieth century for intellectuals to move from being outsiders
who offer social and political commentary to becoming insiders with the
power to make or influence policy. Those who produce the academic
knowledge Abbott discusses may or may not be intellectuals in Bauman's
sense, that is, those who seek to have a political voice. They are more like
Foucault's "specific intellectuals," whose power and influence is restricted
to their sphere of expertise (1980, pp. 127–129). Indeed, there is a sense
in which the professional is the antithesis of the intellectual in the sense
that the former typically claims to stand above or beyond politics, while
the latter is defined by his political stance.

The values of rationality, logic, and science are connected in the public
mind with disinterest, and disinterest is at the heart of our dilemma. Our
abstract knowledge holds that disinterest is impossible, but the public continues to value disinterest, to believe that there is knowledge above politics.
In our critique of science, of rationality, of logic, and even of aesthetic taste,
we open ourselves to delegitimation because as professionals our authority
rests in these values. Those left populists who expand the critique to include all expert knowledge leave no ground to be defended. Since we are
willy-nilly a part of the system of professions, this amounts to conceding
authority to our opponents, who have no qualms about asserting their own
expertise in spite of their antiprofessional gestures. Perhaps it is obvious
that the solution lies in asserting other values to replace those we reject or
at least believe to be overvalued, but we have not been very effective at
making a case for a set of new values, other than critique itself. Critique is

a necessary value, but it is insufficient. Others, such as equity and diversity, need to be more effectively promoted, but they will not by themselves support our claims to authority.

We have largely failed to establish our authority, especially in the public sphere, and this failure owes at least something to the way in which we have insisted on a certain version of relativism. An unfortunately telling example comes from an organizational meeting of Teachers for a Democratic Culture held several years ago. One member of the audience rejected a claim in one of the group's publications questioning the accuracy of the right's attacks and urging that the truth be made known. The word "truth," the audience member said should be avoided, since to use it was epistemologically illegitimate. Doubtless she believed that if we cannot know truth, then to claim it is a mere exercise of power. A little later, someone said he felt uncomfortable maintaining that our views were "better" than their views. What these examples show is that our relativism has a debilitating effect on our own discourse. It functions as a kind of self-censorship. Although it allows anything to be said, it permits nothing to be affirmed. You can see where these scruples must lead. If we refuse to assert that our position is in some way or another to be preferred to opposing positions, then we will surely lose the rhetorical battle to those whose epistemology does not demand such restraint. Invoking the postmodernist objection to closure, that is, to the idea that serious philosophical questions can be answered definitively, does not solve the problem, for even if one resists closure, one must in the meantime still advance one's arguments as if they were better than opposing arguments, some of which, at least, one must continue to believe are not merely different, but in error.

Regardless, it is a premise of my remarks that relativism as an epistemological position must be accepted. I say this not only from the perspective of the theoretical arguments that support that position, but also from the perspective of how business is conducted in most academic disciplines today. In that realm, relativism is not merely influential, but hegemonic. To make sense of this claim, you must understand a broad, theoretically imprecise definition of the term, and one purged of many of the radical implications that often are asserted by antirelativists and relativists alike. My point is simple: The only forms of knowledge in our society that remain absolutist are religious or old-humanist, which explains the otherwise inexplicable alliances of the religious right with secular humanists such as Alan Bloom. It is unnecessary to provide an extended argument for the hegemony of relativism here, but a few familiar examples are worthy of mention: the revolution in physics in the early twentieth century that shifted the most prestigious of sciences from problems of mechanistic determinism to problems of indeterminacy; the shift in Anglo-American philosophy from logical positivism to analytic philosophy, illustrated in the difference between Wittgenstein's *Tractatus* and his later *Logical Investigations*; and the shift in literary studies from positivist literary historical studies to hermeneutic literary criticism.

There is one more example that I want to explore at some length, however, because I think it reveals the dominance of relativism in ways that examples from innumerable academic disciplines could not. I am referring to the work of William Perry, the counselor of Harvard undergraduates who used his work with these students to develop a model of cognitive and ethical development. Perry's model describes individuals beginning in adolescence as having the potential to progress through nine stages. At stage one, dualism, individuals believe that there are right and wrong answers to all important questions, and that authorities know those answers. This faith is progressively qualified in stages two and three without being overturned, but in stage four, called multiplicity, an individual adopts a position exactly contrary to stage one: that there are no answers to important questions that anyone can say are right or wrong. Individuals who grow out of this stage develop toward what Perry calls stage nine, committed relativism, a condition in which one understands that choices can and must be made in the absence of certainty or absolute authority (1968). Perry believed that most Harvard freshmen fell somewhere below stage four, and subsequent researchers who have devised tests to measure development on Perry's scale assert that the typical class of beginning college students has not progressed as far as those whom Perry studied. Such tests also have revealed a correlation between other measures of academic success and the level of development on Perry's scale. In other words, those students who have come to assume relativism tend to be the most successful academically.

It is obvious, I think, that what Perry did was to write a history of Western epistemology, projected into the developing heads of the students he discusses. Thus I make no claims for the universality of Perry's developmental scheme. On the contrary, it is its cultural specificity that interests me, for it suggests just how fundamental relativism is to our dominant knowledges. Nevertheless, it must be admitted that what Perry means by relativism is not the cognitive and ethical anarchy that a D'Sousa or a Bloom believe it to be. Relativism for Perry assumes a diversity of opinion, values, and judgment, but predicated upon coherent sources, evidence, logics, systems, and patterns, and subjected to analysis and comparison. As Perry describes it, relativism is characteristic of most forms of contemporary academic knowledge. In fact, what this description suggests is that the assumption of relativism makes possible the practice of most disciplines. If diversity of opinion, values, and judgment were not the norm, there would

be far less need for academic work. We might suggest a symbiotic relationship between the growth of academic disciplines and of relativist assumptions.

One lesson that the hegemony of relativism teaches is the irrelevance
of explicit epistemology in most disciplines. The development of a hermeneutic practice in literary studies took place under the guise of a rhetoric
of objectivity, even as the practice itself failed to produce results that were
perceived as objective. On the other hand, the new physics proclaimed its
various forms of relativity without giving up the assumption of its objectivity. Doubtless most of Perry's students didn't know that they had a theory
of knowledge. The irrelevance of epistemology suggests that we may be
fighting the wrong battle in attacking notions of truth or objectivity. Let me
make it clear that I am far from denying the oppressive, socially pernicious
character of much academic knowledge. I am asserting that faulty epistemology is at best a minor contributor to this character. I hasten to add that
the critique of Truth continues to have a role. As Jack Amariglio (1992) has
observed, many more people have died at the hands of regimes of truth
than regimes of indeterminacy. Epistemological relativism does function in
this context as a safeguard against the desire to eliminate untruth by mur-
dering its messengers. It is not the regulation of disciplinary practice that
epistemology mainly serves, but rather the rhetorical dissemination of the
knowledge that academic disciplines produce. To refer again to literary
studies and physics, both disciplines have continued to rely on assumptions
or claims of truth even while the practice of each called into question non-
relative forms of such claims.

We need to remember that relativism—except as imagined by its opponents—is not multiplicity. It does assume *relative* judgments and discrimi-
nations about the truth or value of statements or discourses. All speakers,
all writers seek to establish their own authority, to be, in Foucault's phrase,
within the true. Even Derrida, who may be the theorist least dependent on
traditional strategies of authorization, still produces authoritative texts. One
traditional strategy he does use is knowledge of the canon, which remains
authoritative even as Derrida deconstructs it. But more important for Derrida's authority is his astonishing virtuosity as a reader. It is this which makes
Derrida so appealing to literary critics who have long accorded great authority to the sheer performance of the critic. Great skill will always carry rhetorical weight, but its impact is necessarily limited to those who have cultivated an appreciation for such performance. In other words, skillful
performance will not by itself do much to secure the authority of the cultural left in the public sphere.

Deconstruction is not the most important legacy, however, of the rise
of what in America is usually called "literary theory." More significant is a

position, derived from Marxism but supplemented by Foucault and other poststructuralists, that identifies knowledge with interests. Marx and Engels say that in each age the ruling ideas are the ideas of the ruling class. Thus each dominant group is now understood to have produced ruling ideas appropriate to its interests. We now recognize that knowledge in its dominant form is not only bourgeois, but male, European, and heterosexual. In the face of this discovery, new forms of knowledge have arisen to represent the interests of subordinate groups. Women's Studies, Afro-American Studies, and Gay Studies are examples. The *raison d'être* for such movements is disputed. One claim, which is most often made to administrators and to the public at large, is that such movements are necessary to make up for the neglect of subject matter by the dominant knowledge producers. But there is another rationale, which is that each of these groups has a unique perspective or standpoint from which to view the world, and thus is capable of producing a knowledge that no other group could produce. The theory behind this is also derived from Marxism—specifically from Georg Lukács—but has recently received its most thorough debate within the feminist context. I cannot enter into that debate here, but I do wish to identify my own position with Sandra Harding's elaboration of standpoint theory. Harding argues that the standpoints of different oppressed or marginalized groups do give them "distinctive resources" with which to understand the world. She does not assume that such limited or isolated standpoints are sufficient, but argues that they allow "Others" to make unique contributions to objective knowledge (1990). In this move, Harding seeks to reclaim objectivity from the positivists, a project that I see as vital.

Let me make it clear, then, that I am not writing in opposition to the new academic formations I have just mentioned, but in opposition to the identification of knowledge and interest. Increasingly, knowledge has come to be conceived as if it were merely a body of propaganda for this or that group. Such a conception both devalues knowledge in general while at the same time rendering the particular knowledges in question rhetorically hobbled. Such knowledges are at risk of becoming identity ghettos. Moreover, since there are no natural limits to the construction of new identities, identity politics can continue to fragment ad infinitum. Imagine, for example, the sort of knowledge formations that might emerge out of the conflicting national, class, and religious groups in what used to be Yugoslavia. Closer to home, imagine the plethora of knowledges that identity politics might foster in the United States. I do not make epistemological objection to such a conception of knowledge, but I do wish to make a rhetorical objection. Such knowledges are unlikely to serve the political interests they claim to represent. A Bosnian Studies might well serve the interests of a future Bosnian state because it would help legitimize that state to its own

people. Similarly, parochial knowledge can serve the interests of group solidarity or the interests of those who seek power within the group. But if
the group is to influence those outside of it, its knowledge cannot be merely
parochial. It must seek to reach beyond the group.

The history of Marxist theory can help us to understand both the appeal and the limitations of parochial knowledges, for Marxism has historically not supported such a conception of knowledge. For Marx, the interested knowledge of the bourgeoisie was distorted knowledge, and he
appealed to science as an antidote to this ideology. As a result, Marxism
was able to derive rhetorical power from its claims to having uncovered
the laws of history. This is not to deny that Marxism was also identified
with the working class, but to point out the special status that that class
has in Marxist theory. The proletariat for Marx and Marxism is not merely
one among several competing social elements. It is the historically appointed representative of humanity. To a certain extent, the importance of
the proletariat can be understood by reference to their relative strength of
numbers within England and perhaps other European countries. But it was
not their numbers, but their historical function that made their interests
synonymous with those of everyone except the bourgeoisie. The theory of
interested knowledge has a radically different meaning if the interests of a
class and the interests of all can be seen as identical.

I need not repeat the elaborate critique of Marxist humanism and of
Marxist totalizing that poststructuralism has offered. It is rather more effective to simply note the historical failure of the industrial proletariat to play
its appointed role and the meaninglessness of the term "working class" in
the current political context. The argument I am making is not that the
majority of us are no longer being exploited—having the surplus value we
produce expropriated by those who own the means of production—but
rather that we do not identify ourselves as a class on that basis. As a result,
neither Marxism nor any other theory of interested knowledge is able to
present a convincing argument for the priority of one group's interests over
another. Knowledge produced under the interest theory thus can only continue to fracture, and thus continue to lose power.

The usual solution in current left rhetoric to the dilemma of fractured
knowledges is to form alliances, which do work very well for specific projects. For example, an alliance among various groups within a university or
another organization may help to win concessions on certain issues of interest to one or more of them. But it is not clear how knowledge can be
forged on the basis of alliance, unless alliance means allowing the different
forms of knowledge each group produces to be modified by the others. If
that happens, however, then the knowledges lose their dependence on a
single standpoint. In Harding's terms, they would be moving toward objec-

tivity by incorporating the standpoints of others. Were this to happen, it would be all to the good, but it would still be insufficient for producing rhetorically powerful knowledge. That requires that we actively claim objectivity as a goal. We do not need to return to positivism, but we do need to be able to credibly claim that what we assert is not merely propaganda for a few. We need to be willing and able to make evaluative judgments about different sorts of knowledges. We have the cultural authority, for example, to oppose racism, sexism, and, increasingly, homophobia. We can claim that such values are not interested, but disinterested, because they reflect not the special interests of any group but the common interest in just and fair treatment for all. We must be willing to make such claims if our views are to prevail.

REFERENCES

Abbott, A. (1989). *The system of the professions*. Chicago: University of Chicago Press.

Amariglio, J. (1992, November). Plenary session of the Rethinking Marxism Conference, Amherst, MA.

Bauman, Z. (1987). *Legislators and interpreters: On modernity, post-modernity, and intellectuals*. Ithaca, NY: Cornell University Press.

Foucault, M. (1980). *Power/knowledge: Selected interviews and other writings 1972-1977* (C. Gordon, Ed.). New York: Pantheon.

Harding, S. (1990, Fall/Winter). Starting from women's lives: Eight resources for maximizing objectivity. *Journal of Social Philosophy, 21,* 422-443.

Holmes, D. (1989). *Stalking the academic communist: Intellectual freedom and the firing of Alex Novikoff*. Hanover, NH: University Press of New England.

Perry, W. (1968). *Forms of intellectual and ethical development in the college years*. New York: Holt, Rinehart and Winston.

Schrecker, E. W. (1986). *No ivory tower: McCarthyism and the universities*. New York: Oxford University Press.

Schrecker, E. W. (1989). Foreword. In David Holmes, *Stalking the academic communist: Intellectual freedom and the firing of Alex Novikoff* (pp. vii-x). Hanover, NH: University Press of New England.

Trilling, L. (1965). *Beyond culture: Essays on literature and learning*. New York: Viking.

Wilson, J. K. (1995). *The myth of political correctness: The conservative attack on higher education*. Durham, NC: Duke University Press.

TEN

THE EROTICS OF
ACADEMIC CONVERSATION
Love, Ethics, and Reason
in Scholarly and Civic Discourse[1]

RICHARD HARVEY BROWN

*It is only through . . . conversation . . . that ideas come into existence. Two
human beings are as necessary for the generation of the human mind as
they are for the generation of the human body.*
—Feuerbach, 1972

*She applied for his reasons. Now though he has none, as we have seen,
that he could offer, yet he has armed himself so well at this point, fore-
warned by the study that he had made of his catspaw mind, that he was
able to pelt her there and then with the best diligent enquiry could provide: Greek and Roman reasons, Sturm und Drang reasons, reasons metaphysical, aesthetic, erotic, anterotic and chemical, Empedocles of Agrigen-
tum and John of the Cross reasons, in short all but the true reasons,
which did not exist, at least not for purposes of conversation.*
—Beckett, 1972

IT IS A TRUISM for critical thinkers that discourse shapes reality. But we
often fail to ask what kind of realities we create with our own forms of
speech, particularly our critical academic discourse. Critique is the main
kind of talk of scholars concerned with civic life, at least since the Enlightenment and perhaps since Plato. Perhaps this is encouraged by epistemological absolutism: If one grasps a Truth external to discourse (in forms, in
God's word, in nature), then all contrary expressions are mere shadows on
the walls of the cave, to be erased by the light of Wisdom, Revelation,
Reason, or—in its contemporary form—Critique. Such speech is oppositional, unmasking, demythologizing, subversive, or deconstructive. For criti-

cal theorists or postmodernists, as examples, enlightenment and modernist thinking is always deeply flawed. Its foundationalism is unfounded, its universalism is partial, its instrumentalism is hegemonic. Conservatives oppose political or textual leftists, but they also define and resist their enemies with critique. They fight to restore traditional ideas and values by demolishing through critique the Marxists, critical theorists, feminists, or postmodernists. Both leftists and rightists partake of the same narrative that rewrites violence in discourse as part of the ethical struggle for a better world (Bannet, 1996; Sabato, 1993).

The metaphors of this meta-narrative are of struggle, battle, and war. "Sir, may there not be very good conversation without a contest for superiority?" asks Boswell. "No animated conversation," responds Johnson, "for it cannot be but one or the other will come off superior." And for this reason Johnson urges that students be excluded from dining with the fellows at the Colleges at Oxford, for then "there can be no real conversation" because the losers in these battles would be "lessened in the eyes of the growing men" (Boswell, 1980, p. 278). In the same spirit, Marx observed "that philosophical consciousness has been drawn into . . . the ruthless criticism of all that exists." Similarly, John Stuart Mill justified "negative criticism" as the means and the mark of a noble end. For Mill, public debate is a "collision of opinions" and "violent conflict," and truth is "the fruit of conquest" between "enemies in the field" (1962, pp. 170–171). Michel Foucault also writes of discourse—as done with scalpels, Molotov cocktails, or minefields. Mitroff (1974) describes moon scientists as filled with egocentric self-esteem and scornful of everyone else, always pushing their own ideas, rejecting criticism, and disinterested in other people's research. Moulton (in Harding & Hintikka, 1983) reports on "The Adversary Method in Philosophy"; Levine describes it in psychology (1974); Rescher, in philosophy: "Theory confronts theory, school rivals school in implacable opposition. Paul Feyerabend calls other philosophers of science incompetent (1978a) and devoid of ideas (1981), superficial readers, illiterates, and propagandists (1978b, chap. 7); or irrelevant (1970)" (Diesing, 1991, p. 323). And any of us might say, "That's right on target," "He shot down my argument," or "That position is indefensible," thereby construing scholarly conversation as war (Brockriede, 1972; Lakoff & Johnson, 1980; Richardson, 1990).

The clash of ideas is essential to creative inquiry (Bourdieu, 1976; Brown, 1997), but an acrimonious style of discourse is not. Instead it silences many and weakens the bonds of comity and solidarity that are necessary for academics (or citizens) to protect their arenas of open competition from those who would close them. In seeking to represent Truth or to attack untruth, adversaries forget that in discourse we also are representatives *of* truth. That is, we forget the affective, human presentness of the speakers and the existential and political worlds that we create in speaking. Thus in our talk about a better society we betray our purpose if we do not bear witness to those ideals in our own discursive practice.

My purpose in this chapter is not critique, however, but invention and persuasion—to imagine forth an alternative to the attack discourse and politics that currently dominate academic and civic life. Such an alternate discourse would be erotic in the sense that it desires the joining with (rather than the abolition of) the other. Like loving relations generally, it also ideally is informed by prudent judgment, a practical fusion of ethics and reason. Just as we need to reconfigure reason, we also need to reinvent love, especially in relation to public language.[2] As Julia Kristeva (1987, p. 6) said, "Today . . . we lack a code of love; no stable mirrors for the loves of a period, group, or class. The analyst's couch is the only place where the social contract explicitly authorizes a search for love—albeit a private one." As scholars and as citizens, we need to do better than that.

ETHICS AND REASON IN EROTIC CONVERSATION

A number of parallels between love and conversation can be drawn from our own experience. One is that desire for the other, like desire for truth, does not wish ultimately to be satisfied.[3] Someone who is loving, and not just lusting, does not want to be sated, does not want to stop desiring, does not want the loving to end. This is because what is desired is the other, or unity with the other, or to *be* the other and to have the other absorb and become the I. But this of course is impossible, or is a transference that we would call regressive. Thus, what is shared, and what *can* be *shared* because there is not total fusion, is the mutual desire for unity and completion. The mutuality of desire, its mutual arousal and mutual sustainment, is what is created and shared, and when desire is sated, if it can be, that sharing is less intense.

Conversation is similar. Unlike mere talk and like love, conversation is a mutual engenderment, a creation of a world between the sharers. It is also driven by desire, the desire to create understanding, the desire for pleasure, truth, and common welfare. Like unity of the self with the other, the identity of consciousness with truth is impossible. Consciousness and truth, like two lovers, can achieve total unity only in the mind of God. And so the conversants continue their conversation and so sustain their desire for truth, truth that becomes elusive as it is elaborated in conversation, truth that can less be given a single name the more that it is discussed. Thus, like love, which seeks to sustain the desire for the other rather than to capture that other and thereby end the mutuality of desire, so conversation seeks to sustain the desire for truth rather than to capture it and so end the conversation. When persuasion succeeds, as Kenneth Burke said, it dies. "If union is complete, what incentive can there be for appeal? Rhetorically, there can be courtship only insofar as there is division. Hence, only through interference could one court continually, thereby perpetuating genuine 'freedom of rhetoric'" (Burke, 1969, p. 271).

To be truly in love and conversation, love and conversation also must have attention. We often say that we do not have enough time for this or that. But much more scarce than time is attention. Even when we do have time for another person or idea, we rarely bring to them an openness of awareness, a receptiveness of them on their own terms, a willingness to listen with respect and closely, a readiness-for-the-moment to suspend categories and prejudgments, to see things, as Verlaine said, without their names. Such attention gives value to the other and, in conversation as in love, thereby authorizes their speech not only with the mind but also from the heart.

Attention may come from curiosity and interest in what the other will say. But more important is that such listening offers power to the other to establish his or her own presence as a source of meaning and authority. Thus, listening is not merely a passive aspect of conversation. By extending focused silence to the other, the listener/lover defines their space as a fully common one awaiting the other's co-presence. Such a listener accepts the speaker as always to an extent unknown, unexpected, and thus requiring an ear that respects distance and strangeness. Such a listener not only *com*prehends the other by understanding their utterance, but also *app*rehends the other as a being that creates meaning. "Listening, thus, is not merely the act of understanding what is said, but also an act of recognition" (Gurevitch, 1988).

What Roland Barthes (1987, p. 84) said of reading a text applies also to listening in conversation: "No one knows anything of the sense that reading gives the work [or that attention gives the speaker. Perhaps that is] because this sense, being desire, establishes itself beyond the code of language. Only reading loves the work, maintains with it a rapport of desire. To read is to desire the work, is to want to be the work."

This desire is not for absorption into the other, nor is it a reproduction of the program implicit in the other's speech (the way, for example, that some of Goethe's readers imitated Werther's suicide). Instead, erotic attention to the other opens oneself to the world. The erotic pleasure of reading or listening occurs whenever the other's speech "transmigrates into our life" and "succeeds in writing fragments of our own daily lives, in short, whenever co-existence occurs" (Barthes, 1975, pp. 7–8). Attention thus requires both closeness and farness—being in contact and in understanding, and being at a distance and postponing understanding by letting the other define himself.[4]

Such authentic attention should be distinguished from mere ritualistic performance. Usually we are able to smooth the rapid transitions from speaking to listening without really stopping our own speech internally. We perform "listening" while preparing our next sentences. Beyond this simulacrum, however, the lover's or listener's obligation of attention involves something more: to create a shared space into which the other can fully enter.

Love and conversation also require sincerity, that we be as we wish to seem. What we are is not so much the nexus of our various qualities as that unique person who could regularly act the way we do. Consistency of action around some moral locus is a definition of self and, hence, the basis of character and sincerity. To be sincere is to present oneself to the lover or conversant as the moral person that one regularly is, to give this true self to the other. Thus, in love and in conversation, truth has an existential as well as propositional meaning. It involves more than telling or reporting the truth. It also requires that we be in truth, that we bear witness with the other to the truth of our own existence. This is perhaps why true love and true conversation are so difficult and so rare. They demand much of us and of our partners: Because when a lover or a speaker is sincere with us, we are asked to also be sincere, to be truthful to them and to ourselves in an existential sense. This requires moral courage, which is another virtue that both love and conversation depend on and elicit. In these ways, love and conversation are not only an exchange. They also create and transform. This indeed is the desire of love and conversation—not so much to possess the other as to create a world of meaning *with* the other that transforms both participants.

This formulation also implies a recasting of the Christian separation of *eros* from *agape*—instrumental desire versus disinterested altruism. For our purpose, this dichotomy is misleading and harmful (see Osborne, 1995). First, it polarizes self and other, which instead are mutually engendered. Second, the opposition of *eros* and *agape* also puts desire and disinterest in opposition (Osborne, 1995). In our view, however, love and conversation both ideally fuse instrumental desire with disinterested altruism to fulfill themselves. This is a paradox. But it is a paradox that should be deployed rather than destroyed. Perhaps the example of a *breach* of love or conversation will illuminate this. The crisis of a sexual or conversational friendship comes when the other acts in such a way that we can no longer consider them part of the moral universe that we thought we both inhabited and, more precisely, the moral universe that we had built together. What then can we do? Aristotle advises us to lower our expectations for the future and keep kind memories of the past. Contemporary therapists might advise us to tell the other of our feelings and renegotiate the contract. But Allen Scult, my teacher in these matters, reminds us that only rarely can we effectively both judge and instruct others at once. That is, in order to change the other, we first must accept them as they are. Reflexively, to accept the other as he or she is requires us to accept ourselves as we fully are. This perhaps is the hardest part of love, where we go beyond moral judgments in order to keep ourselves open to the other for love or conversation. Such charity, or forgiveness, or loving kindness, is akin to *agape*. But it also is akin to *eros,* for it aims at allowing us again to *desire* union or truth with the other, in union and truth *with* the other. Thus desire and disinterest, sexuality and spirituality, *eros* and *agape both* are as essential in love as in conversation.[5]

Of course, our idea of eros also could be seen as instrumental insofar as it views lovers or conversants as engaging each other for the purpose of producing what is larger than what either of them could realize alone—the creation of a community of discourses that allows each to stand and speak with the other nakedly, that is, without artifice, deceit, or will to domination. As Biener, following Aristotle, put it, "What friends hold in common is a common view of [and joint desire to pursue] what is just, and it is to this extent that friendship is a form of community" (1983, p. 80).

Eros loves not only *what* the beloved is, but more, *that* the beloved is. This involves a suspension of judgment, an attentive acceptance of the other even while preserving his or her otherness. Erasmus advocates this with lighthearted seriousness at the end of the *Ciceronianus* (Erasmus, 1643, pp. 446–447), where he invokes Ovid's *Amores* (2.4) to plead for greater acceptance and charity toward persons with views that differ from our own, and particularly the pagan philosophers who had been condemned by earlier Christian writers (e.g., St. Augustine [Green, 1995]). The traditional Christian argument went something like this: If you employ artificial and flashy coloring out of fear that your natural (Christian) coloring will not be pleasing, you reveal your own displeasure, you teach your "lover" to love another, a pagan, and are thus responsible for your lover's adultery and your own injury (Woods, 1989). But Erasmus answers Augustine thus:

> . . . let us, in reading our authors [pagan as well as Christian], display in all seriousness the attitude of mind which Ovid jestingly tells us he found himself displaying in his various affairs with girls. He found a tall girl attractive because she was easy to handle; youthful bloom commended a young one, experience one who was a bit older, the naiveté of an uneducated girl was delightful, in an educated one the attraction was wit, in a fairskinned girl he adored the

> loveliness of her colouring, in a dusky one he imagined I know not what lurk-
> ing charm. If we show the same generosity of spirit [*candore*] and extract
> from each writer whatever deserves commendation, we shall disdain none of
> them, but channel off something from each to give a flavor to our own speech.
> (pp. 446–447)

Thus Erasmus hints at St. Augustine's lack of good faith, and implies that
Christian *caritas,* like pagan *eros,* should be brought to our encounters with
other texts, peoples, and ideas.

This necessary distance in eros has a moral dimension beyond humanistic tolerance, for without distance we would be more inclined to sacrifice
our own integrity for the loved one or to make unreasonable demands on
him or her. Plato spoke of a love of truth as central in a noble love for the
other. A practical dimension of such a love is the distance in what Hans-
Georg Gadamer called "genuine conversation"—that discourse that engen-
ders compassion and good judgment. Crucial to genuine conversation is
sufficient separateness to understand the other *individual* but also to understand what the other individual *says*; we must attend not only the *person* but also the *topic* of our interaction (Gadamer, 1975, p. 347; see Scult,
1989, p. 11). Distance preserves a communal space, a space for communion, for co-union, so that the conversation is "conducted by" their joint
desire to share and know a topic and not only by their respective desires
to have or to please the other.

Thus it would seem that love and conversation both require us to recognize the otherness of the other. Z. D. Gurevitch, upon whom I depend
greatly in this section, puts this well:

> Without an element of distance between self and other there is hardly any
> point in the connection. For [love and] conversation, we are asked to over-
> come our usual tendency to appropriate the other into the controlled world
> of the self, to own the other. This also involves relinquishment of our wish to
> use the other and our fear of the other's essential strangeness from which we
> recoil into our own (strange) otherness. (Gurevitch, 1988, p. 1182)

Instead, the other must be invited into the world of the self and yet also
be endowed with the right to remain other. The self, in turn, is called upon
to take a part in that otherness. Tedlock recommends such a dialogue for
anthropologists because it:

> creates a world, or an understanding of the *difference between* two worlds,
> that exists between two persons who were indeterminately far apart, in all
> sorts of different ways, when they started out on their conversation. This *be-*

tweenness of the world of the dialogue is something I want to keep before us, or between us, all the way through. (1983, p. 323)

Hannah Arendt (1959) expressed a similar ideal for civic conversations: "Human plurality, the basic condition of both action and speech, has the twofold character of equality and distinction" (pp. 151-156). Without equality, we would be unable to understand one another, much less create a public space. Without distinction, human beings "would need neither speech nor action to make themselves understood; signs and sounds to communicate immediate, identical needs and wants would be enough" (p. 158). Thus, our simultaneous sameness and differences is a "paradoxical plurality of unique beings" (p. 218), a plurality among equals that is actualized in communication that "respects the other person from the distance that the space of the world puts between us" (p. 218; see Dallmayr, 1984, p. 101).[6]

Such interpersonal reflexivity defines *eros* and conversation and their ethics as the giving, and the claiming of, the right of moral presence. The right to remain other even while entering into the other's I is expressed practically in the constant adjusting of distance in speech, gestures, and physical space. This ethical distance takes linguistic forms in the way one addresses the other (Brown, 1989), tacit interactional forms such as face-saving (Goffman, 1955), and physical forms such as respecting the other's personal space (Sommer, 1969). When these ethics of love or conversation are violated, we may find ourselves not on speaking terms with the other. Then a power game ensues. Who will be most distant, who will first call whom? Who will invite the other first into presence and so first be present themself? Our anguish when we are faced with such questions shows both our power and our vulnerability. Through speech we can commit the other to be present, but in so doing we also reveal our own need for presence with them.

EROTIC CONVERSATION, PUBLIC KNOWLEDGE, AND THE RHETORIC OF CIVIC FRIENDSHIP

If we have established a liaison between *eros,* ethics, and conversation, we now may ask how such conversation might relate to public knowledge and civic life. Responses of course will vary with assumptions about what persons can know and how they come to know it. This has been a central question in the agonistic histories of both philosophy and rhetoric. For example, Plato denigrated rhetoric as dependent upon verbal seduction and vulgar opinions. Thus, Plato viewed the erotic nature of the human soul as a source of hope for philosophic insight but not for democratic life. *Eros* meant that one can become a lover of wisdom, which is not available to ordinary persons (Plato, 1956, 1961).[7]

Following Plato, Richard Weaver argues that the noble speaker and the evil or base speaker each has a characteristic attitude toward their audience: "The noble speaker exalts the intrinsic worth of the audience and reflects such attitudes as respect, concern, selflessness, involvement, and genuine desire to help the audience actualize its ideal potentials. The evil or base speaker reflects attitudes of exploitation, domination, possessiveness, selfishness, superiority, deception, and defensiveness" (Weaver, 1970, p. 22; see Johanneson, 1966). By this reasoning, noble sophistry or public argument depends on expertise in erotics (*ta erótika*), as Socrates claimed for himself. Noble sophistry not only is a critical art that removes obstacles to comprehensive knowledge by subverting dogmatism and dissolving attachment to unfounded opinions. It also is a loving art that helps the other (the audience) realize its own best nature. This erotic aspect of noble sophistry—its desire to elicit reason and goodness in its publics—redeems the cleverness that also is required of rhetorical effectiveness.

Plato's rejection of rhetoric as intrinsically deceptive was itself rejected by his pupil Aristotle, who defended rhetoric as the appropriate form of reasoning on matters where certainty is not possible:

> And if it be objected that one who uses such power of speech unjustly might do great harm, that is a charge which may be made in common against all good things except virtue, and above all against the things that are most useful, as strength, health, wealth, or generalship. (1991, pp. 3-7)

Aristotle's idea of civic friendship shifts and extends Plato's conception of *eros* and its relation to knowledge and discourse. He does this in two ways: By relocating knowledge from philosophic forms to shared understandings, and by shifting *eros* from a love of philosophy to civic friendship, from *philia sophia* to *philia politike*. Aristotle posited a body of common knowledge as a natural corollary to his conceptions of human nature, reason, and public decisionmaking. Such common social knowledge rests upon an ideal consensus. That is, a consensus is attributed to an audience that might not in fact share it. The assumption of consensual knowledge may even be counterfactual—some persons may disagree with what is attributed to them. Yet it is this assumed understanding of agreement, virtual rather than factual, that makes rhetorical argument possible (Farrell, 1976, p. 2; see Singer, 1994, pp. 93-95).

Such an attribution of shared understandings is important for Aristotle's concept of civic friendship. In the *Nicomachean Ethics,* Aristotle describes three types of friendship—instrumental, hedonistic, and moral—the last of which embraces and subsumes the other two:

> It is only between those who are good and resemble one another in their goodness that friendship is perfect. Such friends are both good in themselves and, by the same token, desire the good of one another. But it is those who desire the good of friends for their friends' sake who are most completely friends, since each loves the other for what the other is in himself and not for something extrinsic which he need not have. (1983, book 5, chap. 3, p. 123)

Friends, unlike allies, will not abandon us when loyalty is no longer in their interest, because friends love the rational good that they bring forth in each other independent of external expediencies. This can be highlighted by comparing the exchange of commodities between traders with the exchange of meanings between friends. In a commodity exchange, the focus is on things that exist outside the relationship of the traders, whose connection is only a means for each to get some thing. But in discussion between friends, the focus is on realizing the moral meanings that they can create or affirm together. The utterances serve no external purpose except to build the civic world of which both friends are part. Through conversation, civic friends redeem themselves from their thingness; each comes forward as a moral self, a co-creator of that civic world through which each in turn can realize their human nature. Each validates the other as a source of the real from which meaning is issued and understanding produced outside the self in a larger political community (Gurevitch, 1988). Thus, civic friendship is moved by desire not merely for the other or for some external thing, but for the other as scholar or citizen, as co-seeker of truth, ethics, and prudent judgments in civic life.

For this reason, civic friendship must be based on shared ideals, "on a recognition of moral goodness" in another person, which is expressed in a "mutual well-wishing and well-doing out of concern for one another" (Cooper, 1980, p. 302). It is in the political arena that such friendship assumes its quintessential moral function—a function basic to leading the good life, which also must be a life of civic engagement. Civic friendship is not merely for companionship, says Aristotle; instead it "exists for the sake of noble actions" (Ross, 1927, p. 306; see Scult, 1989). Such friendship can provide a context for good judgment because it is based on the desire to realize shared moral ideas. "What friends hold in common is a common view of what is just, and it is to this extent that friendship is a form of community" (Beiner, 1983, p. 80). "We need friends to make our judgments *with*—to help us make the sorts of decisions that are essential to living out our lives as moral beings" (Scult, 1989). The *eros* of civic friends is the committed desire to raise their relationship to the highest moral level through conversation that leads to prudent judgments and noble actions. It is this eros that leads friends to uncover and deploy the tacit moral knowledge that they share. Aristotle gives the name *homonoia,* "thinking in harmony," to the friendship among citizens that makes political community possible (Beiner, 1983, p. 80; see Kingwell, 1995).

In Aristotle's time it was still possible to at least imagine a political community of citizens who knew each other, shared a common moral telos, and regularly engaged in face-to-face civic conversations. Indeed, rhetoric was invented as a discipline at this time precisely to understand and create links between reason, ethics, and conversation for decisionmaking publics. But how can these ancient conceptions make sense in an age in which rhetoric has lost much of its philosophical and moral significance and been reduced to mere technique? Technicism is the dominant public discourse in modern societies, and the result is that we are much less able to discuss questions involving moral or political values in an intellectually responsible way. Without a prudential rhetorical discourse, the only kinds of value talk available become voluntarism (what I want), emotivism (what I feel), or utilitarianism (what is efficient). The result, whether already upon us or only a potential, is that human knowing and doing are reduced to the amoralities of will, emotion, or calculation, and political discourse and action become power politics legitimated by arational moralism.

The tradition of rhetoric that I have drawn on in this chapter perhaps provides an alternative to the dominant technicist discourse. Unlike science as usually understood, rhetoric—that is, public conversation—is inherently moral. This is because rhetoric stresses the practical over the theoretical, the primacy of prudent judgment (*phronesis*) over abstract universal laws. Moreover, in addition to technical competence in the issues at hand (e.g., that sulphur is a cause of acid rain), the public rhetor also is an interpreter of moral traditions. That is, she casts technical knowledge within a narrative of the ethical *census communis* of her public. To do this effectively requires "good will," a desire for sympathy and understanding with the other. For a conversation to succeed—that is, for it to produce understanding, agreement, or "truth"—the interlocutors must *desire* to come together. "Both partners must have the good will to try to understand one another" (Gadamer, 1989, p. 33). "When good will is lacking, the conversation will fail; either . . . it will not generate real, effective understanding at all, or . . . the understanding that it does generate will simply be a misunderstanding, the mere projection of one's own prejudices onto the other" (Madison, 1989b, p. 270). Such goodwill is of course a hallmark of civic friendship.[8] Nietzsche gives this idea a dialectical twist with his concept of the "spiritualization of enmity," an agonistic care and forbearance that emerges as arguers realize they are bonded together through awareness of the essential contestability of the respective positions that each brings to the other. This is a goodwill that we also owe to ourselves, a *caritas* to "'the enemy within': there too we have spiritualized enmity, there too we have grasped its *value*" (Nietzsche, 1968, pp. 43–44; see Connelly, 1993, pp. 382–383; Alford, 1989).

In the context of the ideal of the university, colleagues are those friends in knowledge who concert their relations in terms of their need and desire for each other in the pursuit of knowledge. They thereby affirm a shared commitment to academic practices erotically rather than scholastically, commercially, or confrontationally. The environment created through such commitment and practice, motivated by desire, provides for the integration of pleasure and work. Such an environment should induce not only productivity but also, and more basically, pleasure. By contrast, when desire is anxious yearning or nostalgic longing for extrinsic or solitary objectives, it is experienced as a lack, rather than as a fulfillment. Imagine, for example, a fate lived out among a sullen, loveless "body of students ('A' students?), straight as arrows, without supple compassion, receptivity, or play? And a faculty, desultory and productive, joylessly committed to the privatization of 'my work' and the professionalization of 'my career' or worse, beside us in . . . the hallways, or at every faculty meeting? Could this hell not picture a modern university of bored, vulgar, and humourless souls, its demographic *multis*?" (Blum, 1991, p. 32). This is the Sartrean *No Exit* that appears as our fate when we abandon *eros* in the face of the very real difficulties of its actualization.

Our description of academic and civic friendship so far might suggest a preference for parochial bonds and familiar settings that runs counter to the global interpenetration of cultures that characterizes our age. This impression is strengthened if we rigidly distinguish friends from enemies. However, such an interpretation forgets that in civic friendship we are obliged to respect the otherness of our friend, to preserve an unfamiliarity that we do not wish to invade or transgress. This view is congruent with Heidegger's notion of man as a "creature of distance," or rather as a creature whose farness emerges precisely under conditions of nearness or close proximity.

> Thus, attention to proximate surroundings and local settings is able and likely to generate also a taste for the unfamiliar or for what Eichendorff called "beautiful strangeness" (*schöne Fremde*), and consequently for those distant lands and cultures which internationalists today rightly pit against . . . ethnocentrism. On the other hand, the stress on familiarity is in one sense not entirely misguided. Only by participating in local and regional affairs . . . do we learn, and

become proficient in, political practice . . . while the reverse procedure invariably ends in speculative abstractions. From this perspective, local and regional politics emerges as the training ground for global interactions, and the small-scale polis as the laboratory for cosmopolis." (Dallmayr, 1984, p. 10)

The rhetoric needed to perform civic friendship in both local and more global settings is much more open than the logical, deductive "attack" discourse so common among scholars. Unlike the one-step argumentation of facts and reasons that aims at demonstration, civic discourse aims at wise concerted actions. This requires a two-step argumentation practice.[9] The first step is to establish a common ground with the other, to make it known that their self is appreciated and their interests respected. Only then are they likely to be receptive to whatever reasons and evidence we may have to offer. Once this common ground has been prepared, my or your views may now be criticized without either of us feeling that our status as an equal party to the dialogue is being maligned. "Ideally, this two-step strategy works a Hegelian miracle—the mutual cancellation of the Sophist's manipulative tendencies and Socrates' intellectually coercive ones. For persuasion arises in preparation of an open encounter (and so no spurious agreement results), while criticism arises only after the way has been paved for it to be taken seriously (and so no fruitless resistance is generated)" (Fuller, 1993, pp. 57-58).

Most scholars, however, are surprisingly unpracticed in the art of changing minds and motivating action. We teach to docile, captive students and read papers to indifferent colleagues. This breeds an insensitivity to the ways in which we communicate and a narrowing of our rhetorical skills. Indeed, instead of accepting a responsibility to motivate and persuade our publics, we typically blame them for any lack of comprehension or enthusiasm for what we have said. Consequently, we regularly overlook the first steps in rhetorical persuasion, the *ethos* and *pathos* of honestly taking the view of the other as a valid starting point of our own reasoning. And thus we are often unable to convey in our speech and writing the commitment and motivation to action, not only to policymakers but also to our colleagues and comrades.

REPRISE

Our reflections suggest an erotic mode of conversation as a normative ideal for discourse between friends, colleagues, and citizens. This ideal differs from the dominant Western tradition of conflict in argument that forgets the preconditions and goals of overcoming conflicts, which include comity and peace. Our formulation also departs from theories of conversation whose chief norm is reason. Instead, an erotics of conversation emphasizes desire, the desire to find union with the other, to seek and create truth together. This pursuit also involves ethics and reasons, but mainly as these derive from and serve to further the erotic ideal.

This chapter is only a sketch, of course, but if we were to take seriously the ideal it proposes, we would have to ask what changes this would require of us. I think that first of all we would have to examine ourselves, to listen to our own speech and note how much of it is vain or self-serving, how much of it is directed toward our own agendas and not toward what we can create with others. Probably we would also wish to become better listeners, to pay closer attention, to take the other's point of view more fully into account, to seek to create truth together rather than merely to win the argument.

Many would probably agree that this is a serviceable ideal for lovers, couples, or good friends. I have tried to extend this ideal to include the scholarly and political discourse of citizens, particularly scholar-citizens who presume to articulate values and images for the polity as a whole. This implies a further obligation: to help create those practical political and institutional conditions that most foster erotic discourse. Unless those wishing to create a more humane and radically democratic society can be more generous with each other, unless we learn to affirm what brings us together as a community, unless we subordinate particular grievances to larger conceptions of the common good, until then we will have little chance of articulating a cogent message to which we ourselves bear witness, and of building a significant movement for cultural and political change.

NOTES

1. This chapter is largely an inscription of various conversations that I have shared with friends and colleagues since 1992. My role is mainly that of scribe. In some cases, as with the writings of Eve Tabor Bannet, Fred Dallmayr, Steve Fuller, Z. D. Gurevitch, G. B. Madison, and Allen Scult, I have interwoven their thought and words into this text in paraphrases and adaptations far beyond the direct quotations and specific textual acknowledgments. Lois Braverman, Linda Kauffman, Julie Klein, Darlene Ann Lancer, Miles Orvell, Daniel Schubert, and Herbert Simons also were part of these conversations. This chapter is also theirs, though of course its limits are mine alone.

2. Many popular American writings portray love as an affliction that must be cured. Books such as *Abused No More* (Ackerman & Pickering, 1989), *Christian Men Who Hate Women* (Rinck, 1990), and *Women Who Love Too Much* (Norwood, 1985) all construct women as sick with love and love as a dysfunction or addiction.

Such books are written by and for females, are relentlessly heterosexual, and convey images of woman as victim, love junkie, or masochist (Kauffman, 1995). In addition to such popular reproductions of femininity for mass consumption, many scholarly writings warn us of poststructuralists who love too much (Kauffman, 1995). For example, such critics as Nina Auerbach, Mary Belensky, Elaine Showalter, and Jane Tompkins advocate a return to personal criticism and advise their readers to resist the seductions of poststructuralist thought. Likewise, Tompkins (1985) defines theory as male, and warns that "theory is one of the patriarchal gestures women ought to avoid." As an antidote to male reason, Tompkins valorizes Sentimental Power and exhorts her readers to get in touch with their feelings (see also Gilligan, 1982; Keller, 1982, 1985; List's [1985] as well as Jansen's [1990] analytic summary of feminist epistemologies; and critiques by Kauffman, 1995, and Hesse, 1994).

For our purposes, the idea of critique as mannish destruction and the conception of sentiment as antirational and female are both inimical to an erotics of conversation that is radically intersubjective and androgynous. Instead, we need to unsettle the dichotomies between public/private, erudition/eros, and male/female, and to rewrite the social contract by shifting the exploration of love from the analyst's couch to the social arena (Kauffman, 1995).

Work in these directions, which eschews constructs such as "male theory" or "women's way of knowing," is found in other feminist writings, as well as in the other schools of thought such as phenomenology, dialogical anthropology, hermeneutics, and critical and rhetorical theory. For example, Sandra Harding and Eve Tabor Bannet respectively seek to develop "a feminist logic of both/and" (Bannet, 1992); queer theorists (e.g., Morton, 1993, p. 121) urge us to develop "an erotics of the social"; phenomenologists and hermeneuticists such as Alfred Schutz (1970), Hans Georg Gadamer (1975, 1983, 1989), and Z. D. Gurevitch (1988, 1990a, b, 1997) articulate the radical intersubjectivity of human experience from the silent embrace to scientific knowledge; Dennis Tedlock describes a "dialogical anthropology" (1983, chap. 6); communication theorists speak of "arguers as lovers" and "rhetoric as seduction" (Brockriede, 1972; Kelly, 1973); literary critics such as Linda Kauffman (1995), Jacques Derrida (1980), and Roland Barthes (1978) describe a "lovers' discourse"; and political thinkers from Plato and Aristotle to Hannah Arendt have discussed eros and friendship in relation to knowledge and political life (e.g., Arendt, 1959, pp. 35-65, 217-219; 1968, pp. 12-14, 30-31; Beiner, 1983, pp. 119-125; Nussbaum, 1986, pp. 354-372). Scholarship on the dialogue model of communication also is important—see Martin Buber's *I and Thou* (1970), as well as John Stewart (1978), Richard L. Johanneson (1971), and Hans Georg Gadamer's *Truth and Method* (1975), where he shows how two persons engaged in genuine dialogue are transformed in the process of trying to understand each other. See also Kathryn Carter and Mick Presnell (1994).

3. Bataille (1986, p. 127) and Derrida (see Dillon, 1994, chap. 6) make a similar point, though with meanings and reasons different from my own. Brockriede (1972) ingeniously elaborates sexual metaphors of arguers into three main types. For him, attack discourse is akin to rape, and an ignoble or manipulative rhetoric is akin to

seduction: "Whereas the rapist conquers by force of argument, the seducer operates through charm or deceit" (1972, p. 4). By contrast, arguers as lovers seek a collaborative relationship with co-arguers:

> Whereas the rapist and seducer argue against an adversary or an opponent, the lover argues with his peer and is willing to risk his very self in his attempt to establish a bilateral relationship. Put another way, the lover-arguer cares enough about what he is arguing about to feel the tensions of risking his self, but he cares enough about his coarguers to avoid the fanaticism that might induce him to commit rape or seduction. (1972, p. 5)

As in our text, rhetoric of attack, war, or ultimatums are examples of rape, and diplomatic or commercial talk usually is akin to seduction. A dialogical rhetoric of love might be that of a scientist presenting research and gratefully seeking unflinching suggestions for improvement, friends who listen and learn with each other, partners who resolve differences in an open and caring fashion.

Fred Alford, discussing *Melanie Klein and Critical Social Theory* (1989), makes a similar distinction between instrumental reason and reparative reason:

> Love lets its love be. In doing so the lover may learn to know other aspects of his or her beloved, aspects that become apparent only when the beloved is valued in his or her own right, not just as a satisfier of needs. This is as true of epistemological relations as it is of personal ones. Whereas the paranoid-schizoid (instrumental) reason sees its objects in terms of the categories of prediction, manipulation, and control, reparative reason experiences its objects as they are mediated by a richer, more creative set of phantasies, phantasies concerned with precisely what Adorno wished art to concern itself with: assisting the object to become itself. (p. 152; see also Benjamin, 1988)

4. Kristeva (1987, p. 15) describes a similar nearness/farness in psychoanalytic terms by distinguishing fusion love from the healing love of transference and countertransference. Transference love is optimum "because it avoids the chaotic hyper-connectedness of fusion love as well as the death-dealing stabilization of love's absence, by allowing the salvaging of accidents on a higher level of symbolic organization: the I/other relationship is reworked into the relationship of the I with the Other."

5. Here our formulation also differs from that of the Christian existentialist Søren Kierkegaard, who elevates *agape* above all other forms of love. His example, tellingly, is love of the dead, to whom love must be given nonreciprocally, without hope of repayment. "Remember one dead and learn in just this way to love the living disinterestedly, free, faithfully" (Kierkegaard, 1962, p. 32). Kierkegaard limits *eros* and *philia* to the domain of exchange, and thereby idealizes love (for him, *agape*) as transcendent and unsullied by any actual finite relationships (e.g., Kierkegaard, 1962, p. 319).

6. A central theme of Arendt's work is the problem of political community in the modern era. Arendt notes that *eros* has been reduced to intimacy, which displaces *philia politike* and leaves the social sphere dominated by instrumental reason.

7. The eros of Socratic conversation is directed toward an ideal that only the intellect can apprehend and only the soul can love. The knowledge that it desires emerges in public conversation and is different from mere opinion. The idea that the communicator/rhetor/advocate might take a nonlover (i.e., neutral, dispassionate, disinterested) stance toward the partner in a communication relationship is discussed in Plato's Phaedrus (1961) (Socrates finds the nonlover relationship an offense against the god of love). It had an important place in late nineteenth- and twentieth-century thinking about the relations of the scientist to his or her audience. More recently, postmodern critics have questioned whether human beings, including scientists, may engage in dispassionate relationships. See Kenneth Burke's Rhetoric of Motives (1969) and Michael Polanyi's Personal Knowledge: Towards a Post-Critical Philosophy.

8. As Schrag (1986, p. 199) put it, "Rhetoric as the directedness of discourse to the other, soliciting a response, is destined to slide into ethics." "Good rhetoric aims at good results, at producing a consensus, an understanding or agreement, which will be as general and as lasting as possible. And this itself is possible only if the rhetor operates with good will and with respect for the opinions of his interlocutor or audience, only if, that is, he commits himself wholeheartedly to the give-and-take of genuine dialogue (risking his own beliefs in the process), for only in this way will the agreement reached" rest on free and mutual conviction and will thus tend to be genuine and lasting (Madison, 1989b, p. 271). While propaganda serves merely to prolong for a while the power of the tyrant, rhetoric, as Cicero emphasized, generates the solid moral authority which is the necessary basis for any enduring community of free men. It was perhaps considerations such as these that led people like Cicero to insist that the rhetorical and the ethical are inseparable and that the good rhetor must be a good person. Cato the Elder defined the orator as vir bonus dicendi peritus, a good man, skilled at speaking. And Quintilian insisted that "[t]he perfect orator cannot exist unless he is above all a good man" (Quintilian, 1965; quoted in Madison, 1989b, p. 272).

9. As Steve Fuller (1993, pp. 305–306) noted

A rhetorically adept speaker typically enables an audience to see her viewpoint as an extension of theirs. This strategy certainly smooths the passage between intellectual assent and motivated action. A truly democratic rhetoric, one comprehensive enough to cover academic discourse, requires that change of mind not be the product of what may be called the belligerent syllogism:

> One of us must move.
> I won't.
> Therefore, you will.

Instead, change of mind must result from the facilitative syllogism.

> We're already trying to move in the same direction.
> There is an obstacle in your way.
> Therefore, let me help you remove it.

The form of the facilitative syllogism reminds us that the task of changing minds begins only once the speaker already detects a common core of intellectual agreement with her audience, but the audience has yet to see that agreement as a basis for action.

REFERENCES

Ackerman, R., & Pickering, S. E. (1989). *Abused no more.* Blue Ridge Summit, PA: Human Services Institute/TAB Books.

Alford, C. F. (1989). *Melanie Klein and critical social theory: An account of politics, art, and reason based on her psychoanalytic theory.* New Haven, CT: Yale University Press.

Arendt, H. (1959). *The human condition.* Garden City, NY: Anchor.

Arendt, H. (1968). *Men in dark times.* New York: Harcourt, Brace, and World.

Aristotle. (1983). *The Nicomachean ethics* (D. Ross, Trans.). Oxford: Oxford University Press

Aristotle. (1991). *Rhetoric* (G. Kennedy, Trans.). New York: Oxford University Press.

Bannet, E. T. (1992). The feminist logic of both/and. *Genders, 15*(Winter), 1-20.

Bannet, E. T. (1996). The end of critique in a democratic society. In R. H. Brown (Ed.), *From critique to affirmation: New roles for rhetoric in creating civic life* (Chap. 2) [Special number]. *Argumentation, 1*(3).

Barthes, R. (1975). *The pleasures of the text* (R. Miller, Trans). New York: Hill and Wang.

Barthes, R. (1978). *A lover's discourse: Fragments* (R. Howard, Trans.). New York: Hill and Wang.

Barthes, R. (1987). *Criticism and truth.* Minneapolis: University of Minnesota Press.

Bataille, G. (1986). *Eroticism: Death and sensuality* (M. Dalwood, Trans.). San Francisco: City Lights Books.

Beckett, S. (1972). *More pricks than kicks.* New York: Grove Press. (Original work published 1934)

Beiner, R. (1983). *Political judgement.* Chicago: University of Chicago Press.

Benjamin, J. (1988). *The bonds of love: Psychoanalysis, feminism, and the problem of knowledge.* New York: Pantheon.

Blum, A. (1991, Spring). The melancholy life world of the university. *Dianoia*, 16-42.

Boswell, J. (1980). *Life of Johnson.* Oxford: Oxford University Press.

Bourdieu, P. (1976). Le Champ Scientifique. *Actes* (2eme année) 2-3 juin, 88-104 [The Specificity of the Scientific Field and the Social Conditions of the Progress of Reason]. *SSI, 14*(6), 1976, 19-47.

Brockriede, W. (1972, Winter). Arguers as lovers. *Philosophy and Rhetoric, 5*(1), 1-11.

Brown, R. H. (1989). *A poetic for sociology: Toward a logic of discovery for the human sciences.* Chicago: University of Chicago Press.

Brown, R. H. (1997). *Toward a democratic science: Scientific narration and civic communication.* New Haven, CT: Yale University Press.

Buber, M. (1970). *I and thou* (W. Kaufmann, Trans.). New York: Scribner.

Burke, K. (1969). *A rhetoric of motives.* Berkeley: University of California Press.

Carter, K., & Presnell, M. (Eds.). (1994). *Interpretive approaches to interpersonal communication.* New York: State University of New York Press.

Connelly, W. E. (1993). Beyond good and evil: The ethical sensibility of Michel Foucault. *Political Theory, 21*(3), 365-389.

Cooper, J. M. (1980). Aristotle on friendship. In Amelie Rorty (Ed.), *Essays on Aristotle's ethics* (pp. 301-340). Berkeley: University of California Press.

Dallmayr, F. R. (1984). *Polis and praxis: Exercises in contemporary political theory.* Cambridge, MA: MIT Press.

Derrida, J. (1980). *The post card: From Socrates to Freud and Beyond* (Alan Bass, Trans.). Chicago: University of Chicago Press.

Diesing, P. (1991). *How does social science work? Reflections on practice.* Pittsburgh: University of Pittsburgh Press.

Dillon, M. C. (1994). *Aletheia, poiesis, and eros: Truth and untruth in the poetic construction of love.* Unpublished manuscript, Department of Philosophy, State University of New York at Binghamton.

Erasmus, D. (1643). *Dialogus Ciceronianus.* Lugduni Batavorum rare books collection, University of Maryland, College Park.

Farrell, T. B. (1976). Knowledge, consensus, and rhetorical theory. *Quarterly Journal of Speech, 62*(1), 1-14.

Feuerbach, L. (1972). *The fiery brook: Selected writings* (Z. Harfi, Trans.). Garden City, NY: Anchor.

Feyerabend, P. (1970). Philosophy of science: A subject with a great past. In R. Steuwer (Ed.), *Minnesota studies in the philosophy of science, Vol. 5* (pp. 172-181). Minneapolis: University of Minnesota Press.

Feyerabend, P. (1978a). From incompetent professionalism to professionalized incompetence. *Philosophy of Social Science, 8,* 37-54.

Feyerabend, P. (1978b). *Science in a free society.* London: New Left Books.

Feyerabend, P. (1981). More clothes from the emperor's bargain basement. *British Journal of Philosophy of Science, 32,* 57-94.

Fuller, S. (1993). *Philosophy, rhetoric, and the end of knowledge: The coming of science and technology studies.* Madison: University of Wisconsin Press.

Gadamer, H. G. (1975). *Truth and method* (J. C. B. Mohr, Trans.). New York: Continuum.

Gadamer, H. G. (1983). *Reason in the age of science.* Boston: MIT Press.

Gadamer, H. G. (1989). Text and interpretation. In E. M. Felder & R. Palmer (Eds.), *Dialogue and deconstruction: The Gadamer-Derrida encounter.* Albany: State University of New York Press.

Gilligan, C. (1982). *In a different voice.* Cambridge, MA: Harvard University Press.

Goffman, E. (1955). On face work: An analysis of ritual elements in social interaction. *Psychiatry, 18,* 213-231.

Green, R. P. H. (Ed.). (1995). *Augustine de doctrina Christiana.* New York: Clarendon Press.

Gurevitch, Z. D. (1988). The other side of dialogue: On making the other strange and the experience of otherness. *American Journal of Sociology, 93*(5) (March), 1179-1199.

Gurevitch, Z. D. (1990a). The dialogic connection and the ethics of dialogue. *British Journal of Sociology, 41*(2), 181-196.

Gurevitch, Z. D. (1990b). The embrace: On the element of non-distance in human relations. *Sociological Quarterly, 31*, 2.

Gurevitch, Z. D. (1997). *Symposium: Culture as daimonic conversation.* Unpublished manuscript, Department of Sociology, Hebrew University of Jerusalem.

Harding, S., & Hintikka, M. (Eds.). (1983). *Discovering reality: Feminist perspectives on epistemology, metaphysics, methodology, and philosophy of science.* Dordrecht, The Netherlands: Reidel.

Hesse, M. (1994). How to be postmodern without being a feminist. *Monist, 7*(4), 445-452.

Jansen, S. C. (1990). Is science a man? New feminist epistemologies and reconstructions of knowledge. *Theory and Society, 19*, 235-246.

Johanneson, R. L. (1966, Fall). "Richard M. Weaver on standards for ethical rhetoric." *Southern Communication Journal*, 133-145.

Johanneson, R. L. (1971). The emerging concept of communication as dialogue. *Quarterly Journal of Speech, 57*, 373-382.

Kauffman, L. S. (1995). Dangerous liaisons: The reproduction of woman in Roland Barthes' *A Lover's Discourse* and Jacques Derrida's *The Post Card.* In R. H. Brown (Ed.), *Postmodern representations: Truth, power, and mimesis in the human sciences and public culture* (pp. 168-196). Urbana: University of Illinois Press.

Keller, E. F. (1982). Feminism and science. *Signs, 7*, 589-602.

Keller, E. F. (1985). *Reflections on gender and science.* New Haven, CT: Yale University Press.

Kelly, W. G. (1973). Rhetoric as seduction. *Philosophy and Rhetoric, 6*(2), 194-222.

Kierkegaard, S. (1962). *Works of love* (H. Hong & E. Hong, Trans.). New York: Harper & Row.

Kingwell, M. (1995). *A civil tongue: Justice, dialogue, and the politics of pluralism.* University Park: Pennsylvania State University Press.

Kristeva, J. (1987). *Tales of love* (L. S. Roudiez, Trans.). New York: Columbia University Press.

Lakoff, G., & Johnson, M. (1980). *Metaphors we live by.* Chicago: University of Chicago Press.

Levine, M. (1974). Scientific method and the adversarial model. *American Psychologist, 29*, 661-667.

List, E. (1985). Die Mannliche Stimme der Vernunft. *Osterreichische Zeitschrift für Zeitschrift für Politikwissenschaft*, 185-196.

Madison, G. B. (1989a). Gadamer/Derrida: The hermeneutics of irony and power. In M. Felder & R. Palmer (Eds.), *Dialogue and deconstruction: The Gadamer-Derrida encounter* (pp. 122-146). Albany: State University of New York Press.

Madison, G. B. (1989b). The new philosophy of rhetoric. *Texte: Revue de Critique et de Théorie Litéraire, 8/9*.

Mill, J. S. (1962). *Utilitarianism, On liberty, Essays on Bertham*. London: Fontana.
Mitroff, I. (1974). *The subjective side of science*. New York: Elsevier.
Morton, D. (1993, Fall). The politics of queer theory in the (post)modern moment. *Genders, 17,* 121-149.
Nietzsche, F. (1968). *Twilight of the idols* (R. Hollingsdale, Trans.). New York: Penguin.
Nussbaum, M. (1986). *The fragility of goodness: Luck and ethics in Greek tragedy and philosophy*. Cambridge: Cambridge University Press.
Norwood, R. (1985). *Women who love too much: When you keep wishing and hoping he'll change*. Los Angeles: J. P. Tarcher.
Osborne, C. (1995). *Eros unveiled: Plato and god of love*. New York: Oxford University Press.
Plato. (1956). *Great dialogues of Plate* (W. Rouse, Trans.). New York: Mentor.
Plato. (1961). *Plato: The collected dialogues* (R. Hackforth, Trans.). Princeton, NJ: Princeton University Press.
Polanyi, M. (1958). *Personal knowledge: Toward a post-critical philosophy*. Chicago: University of Chicago Press.
Quintilian. (1965). *On the early education of the citizen-orator [Instituto Oratoria]*. Indianapolis: Bobbs-Merrill.
Rescher, N. (1977). *Dialectics: A controversy-oriented approach to the theory of knowledge*. Albany: State University of New York Press.
Richardson, L. (1990, April). Narrative and sociology. *Journal of Contemporary Ethnography, 20*(1), 33-56.
Rinck, M. J. (1990). *Christian men who hate women: Healing hurting relationships*. Grand Rapids, MI: Pyranee Books.
Ross, W. D. (Ed.). (1927). *Aristotle selections*. New York: Scribner.
Sabato, L. J. (1993). *Feeding frenzy: How attack journalism has transformed American politics*. New York: Free Press.
Schrag, C. O. (1986). *Communicative praxis and the space of subjectivity*. Bloomington: Indiana University Press.
Schutz, A. (1970). *On phenomenology and social relations* (H.R. Wagner, Ed.). Chicago: University of Chicago Press.
Scult, A. (1989). What is friendship?: A hermeneutical quibble. In James A. Anderson (Ed.), *Communication Yearbook 12* (pp. 203-212). Newbury Park, CA: Sage.
Singer, I. (1994). *The pursuit of love*. Baltimore: Johns Hopkins University Press.
Sommer, R. (1969). *Personal space*. Englewood Cliffs, NJ: Prentice-Hall.
Stewart, J. (1978, April). Foundations of dialogic communication. *Quarterly Journal of Speech, 64,* 183-201.
Tedlock, D. (1983). *The spoken word and the work of interpretation*. Philadelphia: University of Pennsylvania Press.
Tompkins, J. (1985). *Sensational designs: The cultural work of American fiction, 1790-1860*. Oxford: Oxford University Press.
Weaver, R. M. (1970). Relativism and the use of language. In R. L. Johannesen, R. Strickland, & R. T. Eubanks (Eds.), *Language is sermonic: Richard M. Weaver on the nature of rhetoric*. Baton Rouge: Louisiana State University Press.
Woods, E. (1989). *Problems in the history of rhetoric*. Unpublished manuscript, Program in Comparative Literature, University of Maryland, College Park.

ABOUT THE CONTRIBUTORS

Richard Harvey Brown is professor of sociology at the University of Maryland in College Park. He has written widely on the social and linguistic construction of scientific knowledge in such books as *A Poetic for Sociology, Society as Text,* and *Social Science as Civic Discourse* (all with the University of Chicago Press). His most recent book is *Science as Narration* (Yale University Press). Professor Brown is also involved in the study of relationships between liberal capitalism, postmodern culture, and the public space, and is the president of the Washington Institute for Social Research.

J. Daniel Schubert is assistant professor of sociology at Dickinson College in Carlisle, Pennsylvania. His research interests include critical theory and cultural studies. Recent publications include studies of Bourdieu, Foucault, Marx, and Durkheim.

Karl-Michael Brunner is Assistant Professor of Sociology, Vienna University of Economics and Business Administration, Austria. He is interested in social theory, environmental sociology, the sociology of food, migration, and qualitative methods. He is co-author of *Soziologische Theorien* (1994) and *Manager und ie* (1994), and has written primarily on environmental sociology and migration.

Remi Clignet has been professor of sociology at the University of Illinois-Evanston and the University of Maryland. He has written many books on the sociology of culture, development, and education. He currently is a research scholar at the Centre Nationale de Récherche Scientifique. His next volume, with Richard Harvey Brown, *America in Transit: Postmodern Culture, Capitalism, and Democracy,* will appear next year from Yale University Press.

Steven Fuller is professor of sociology at the University of Durham, UK. Originally trained in the history and philosophy of science, his research program, social epistemology, has been developed in a journal (founded 1987) and six books, most recently *The Governance of Science: Ideology and the Future of the Open Society* (Open University Press, 1999) and *Thomas Kuhn: A Philosophical History for Our Times* (University of Chicago Press, 1999).

Johanna Hofbauer studied social sciences in Innsbruck, Austria, and was a postgraduate student and researcher at the Institute for Advanced Studies in Vienna. Since 1991 she has been a University Assistant at the Institute of Sociology at the University of Economics, Vienna. Her research, publications, and teaching focus on the areas of organization studies, industrial sociology, and women's studies.

Hans Mommaas is associate professor of leisure studies at Tilburg University, the Netherlands. His teaching and research interests concentrate around themes of leisure, culture and urban developments, and leisure and modernity. He is the coordinator of an international M.A. in European Urban Cultures (POLIS). Among others, he has published *Moderniteit, vrijetijd en de stad* (*Modernity, Leisure and the City*, 1993), *Het Vraagstuk van den Vrijen Tijd* (*The Question of Free Time*, 1991, together with Th. Beckers), and *Leisure Research in Europe* (1996, with P. Bramham, I. Henry, and H. van der Poel).

Gerald Prabitz studied business administration, political science, and philosophy in Innsbruck, Austria, and was a postgraduate student at the Institute for Advanced Studies in Vienna. He is a lecturer at the Institute of Sociology at the University of Economics in Vienna. His research, publications, and teaching focus on the areas of media studies and organization theory.

John P. Radford is an associate professor in the Faculty of Arts at York University, Toronto. He has written widely on the structure of nineteenth-century American cities. He is also the author of a number of papers on historical constructions of intellectual disability in journals such as *Social Science and Medicine* and *Journal of Historical Sociology*. His most recent paper, "From the Case Files: Reconstructing a History of Involuntary Sterilization," co-authored with Deborah Park, appeared in *Disability and Society* in 1998.

David R. Shumway is professor in the Department of English at Carnegie-Mellon University in Pittsburgh, Pennsylvania. He is the author and editor of numerous books, including *Creating American Civilization* (University of Minnesota Press) and *Michel Foucault* (University Press of Virginia).

Manfred Stanley is professor emeritus at the Maxwell School of Public Administration at Syracuse University in Syracuse, New York. He is the author of numerous books and articles on education, technology, and public space, including *The Public School and Public Policy* and *The Technological Conscience*.

Grahame F. Thompson is professor of International Political Economy in the Faculty of Social Sciences, The Open University, Milton Keynes, England. For several years he has been working on issues of international economic integration, particularly on the concept and process of globalization. In 1996 he published *Globalization in Question: The International Economy and the Possibilities of Governance* (with Paul Hirst), a new edition of which is due to appear in 1999.

INDEX